P9-CFM-180

*O*rchid
of the *B*ayou

WALLINGFORD PUBLIC LIBRARY.
20⎯ ⎯⎯⎯ STREET
WALLINGFORD, ⎯⎯⎯ 06492
WITHDRAWN

WITHDRAWN

Orchid of the Bayou

A Deaf Woman

Faces Blindness

Cathryn Carroll

and

Catherine Hoffpauir Fischer

Gallaudet University Press
Washington, D.C.

WALLINGFORD PUBLIC LIBRARY
200 NO. MAIN STREET
WALLINGFORD, CT 06492

B
FISHER
CA

Orchid of the Bayou: A Deaf Woman Faces Blindness

Gallaudet University Press

Washington, DC 20002

© 2001 by Cathryn Carroll and Catherine Hoffpauir Fischer

All rights reserved. Published 2001

Printed in Canada

Library of Congress Cataloging-in-Publication Data

Carroll, Cathryn.
     Orchid of the Bayou : a deaf woman faces blindness / Cathryn
Carroll and Catherine Hoffpauir Fisher.
          p. cm.
     ISBN 1-56368-104-8 (alk. paper)
       1. Fisher, Catherine Hoffpauir. 2. Usher's syndrome—Patients—
Biography. 3. Usher's syndrome—Popular works. I. Fisher, Catherine
Hoffpauir. II. Title.
RF292.8.C372001
362.4'1'092—dc21
[8]   00-050410

Interior design by Nancy Singer Olaguera

Composition by Peng and Nancy Olaguera

Cover design by Dorothy Wachtenheim

The cover photo shows a Dactylorhiza orchid and appears courtesy of
© copyright judywhite/GardenPhotos.com

♾ The paper used in this publication meets the minimum requirements
of American National Standard for Information Sciences—Permanence
of Paper for Printed Library Materials, ANSI Z39.48-1984.

$\mathcal{C}$ontents

Acknowledgments   vii

Introduction   ix

1   Devil Child   1

2   A School for Kitty   12

3   "I Don't Think She's Retarded"   22

4   A Seasoned Student   30

5   Home and School: Ever the Twain   48

6   Mama   66

7   Life After Mama   78

8   Two Revolutions: My School, My Soul   88

9   At Home At School   102

10   Jeanette and David   114

11   "You Should Be Proud"   127

12   Gallaudet: McDonald's In Thailand   141

13   The Race to Who We Are   154

14   Summer of '67   165

15   An End to All That   180

Contents

16 The Reentry of a Coed   192

17 Kitty and Lance: An Item   204

18 Why Me?   217

19 "Yes, I have Usher Syndrome"   228

20 Catherine: Acadian and Cajun   234

21 On with the Party   245

$\mathscr{A}$cknowledgments

We need to thank so many people for helping us get this material together. Thanks to Luther B. Prickett for allowing overnight visits to the Louisiana School for the Deaf, Diane Stuckey for making the visits so pleasant, and Mary Smith and Sylvia Bradford for their enormous help with the Louisiana School's archives. Thanks to Elise Broussard for the time she spent trying to help us find our way around southwestern Louisiana. Thanks also to Harry Lang, McCay Vernon, Charles Hoffpauir, Jeanette Breaux Zerangue, and the people involved with the Hoffpauir Web site and E-mail list. Thanks to the helpful people at the St. Martinsville visitor's center, Louisiana State University Archives, Gallaudet University Archives, and the state archives of Louisiana and Maryland. Thanks also to Geraldine Armstrong, Carl Brasseaux, Plumie Gainey, Ernest Hairston, Muriel Kaiser, Ruth Phillips, Joy Redman, Edward Scouten, and Linda Thomas—their review of certain portions of the manuscript is very deeply appreciated.

And thanks to our colleagues and coworkers Mary Ellen Carew, Anita Gilbert, Susan Flanigan, Thomas Kluwin, Shawn Mahshie, William Marshall, William McCrone, Marteal Pitts, Jill Schultz, Catherine Valcourt, Oluyinka Williams, and Carolyn Williamson for their help and support. Thanks also to John Vickrey Van Cleve,

Acknowledgments

Ivey Pittle Wallace, Christina Findlay, and Rainey MacArthur Ratchford at Gallaudet University Press for their guidance and encouragement throughout the development, writing, and editing of this material. And thanks to our parents, Nola and Alexander Hoffpauir and Hazel and Charles Carroll; our husbands, Lance Fischer and Barry Strassler; our children, especially Rachel and Jason Fischer and Rachael and Angela McCrone; and new arrivals Jordyn McCrone and Kiley Gagin.

Finally we want to express deep gratitude and appreciation to the people in this book: Geraldine Armstrong, MJ Bienvenu, Helen Carbo, Plumie Gainey, Victor Galloway, Anna Gremillion, James Guidry, Ernest Hairston, Lenora Heinen, Jim Hynes, Grady Istre, David and Jeanette Oglethorpe, Carolyn McCaskill, Kathy Jones, Ruth Phillips, Ronald Nomeland, Max Ray, Mrs. Clet Richard, Art Roehrig, Thelma Scanlan Covello, Ed and Eleanor Scouten, Rachel Stone, Pat and Bobby Trosclair, Sarah Stiffler Val, Madan Vasishta, and Rose White Barbin. It is an honor and pleasure to share their stories.

Cathryn Carroll and Catherine Hoffpauir Fischer

*I*ntroduction

SO WHAT DOES IT FEEL LIKE TO BE A HALF CENTURY?
I watched over Lance's shoulder as the letters formed one at a time on our TTY screen. My brother was teasing my husband about his fiftieth birthday. Out in California, he talked into the phone, while a TTY relay operator transferred his voice into successive TTY beeps, and the printed version of what he said was spelled out on our home TTY in Maryland.

I couldn't quite make the letters out, and Lance turned and signed them to me before he typed back his answer. He didn't mind the teasing. My husband accepted being fifty better than I had.

YOU SHOULD KNOW, he typed. Grady had had his fiftieth birthday several years before.

I was nervous, afraid that Grady would say something about the party. Perhaps he hadn't noticed that the invitation specified it was a secret. Perhaps he had forgotten it. Perhaps he didn't think it was important. Now he was out in the hills of Ventura, talking blithely into the telephone, putting all my plans in jeopardy.

I should have known better. Men, when they can talk at all, don't say very much, and Lance was too restless to sit long at the TTY anyway. After a few more pleasantries, he turned the conversation over to me.

I eased into position and squinted at the screen. It was unusual to communicate on a TTY these days—we almost always used E-mail rather than the slow TTY, because despite discounts by states and phone companies, the TTY costs much more in long-distance charges. A quick hello would do. I could see the type clearly now, even read the little paper printout that recorded our conversation.

HI BROTHER, I typed, adding GA, the old teletype language for "It's your turn, go ahead."

HI CATHERINE, he responded. The relay operator affixed the GA for him.

Catherine and Brother—just like when we were little kids.

HOW ARE YOUR EYES? he asked.

It was the first time he had mentioned my eyes.

OKAY, I said. SURGERY WEDNESDAY THEN NO MORE CATARACT.

I didn't want to explain more than that. For one thing, the lousy interpreter at the hospital had left Lance and me guessing what we were being told, and I wasn't sure of more than that. For another, I hated the details of it. Either the operation would work or it wouldn't. Even if it worked and the remorseless cloudiness that kept the brightest days dim disappeared and the new plastic lens admitted light like the natural lens of my youth, I was still out most of my peripheral vision. And I would continue to lose more of it.

And I would be blind. Sooner or later. That was just how it was.

Grady didn't press me for details. At almost sixty, he had his own physical problems. We would show each other the respect of asking about and then gracefully ignoring each other's debilities. Conversation came a trifle awkwardly to us anyway. Growing up we weren't so close. Grady couldn't sign and I couldn't hear or speak. We had communicated through our little sister, Nana, whom we both loved. She could sign and speak—and she did both all the time.

Nana was the one who told me most everything. She told me about Mama and she told me about Daddy, and she told me about Brother (whom I now try to call Grady) and the entire town of Rayne, Louisiana, where we all grew up. She told me about myself, too, how I was lucky to be deaf and go away to school, and not end up like her. The only person Nana didn't tell me about was herself. But I wouldn't realize that until later.

Rayne is in the heart of what the Louisiana tourist bureau calls Acadiana, or Cajun country. Richard Leaky, anthropologist and South African politician, defined *culture* as "the human adaptation," and the culture of Rayne and the surrounding bayou was deep Cajun. Instead of webbed feet or sharp eyes, I had my parents and Cajunness during my earliest years to keep me alive on the planet. Cajun is cool now, but when I was growing up, it was a culture disdained; I didn't even see the word until I was an adult. The language of the Cajun people is French, but my mama and daddy spoke only English to us. They were determined that we would be better—that we would not become like them.

Of course, we did become like them. Grady may live in California, and I may live way up north near Washington, D.C., and our dear Nana may be dead, but in the end we are all our parents' children, and I am as proud to be Cajun as any of them—maybe more proud. If there's one thing Cajuns have more of than hot sauce, it's pride. And family. We always had each other. I loved them and they loved me. They were prepared to take care of me as long as any of them were standing. Just as I would take care of them.

Still the disconnect between me and my family was profound. My deafness closed off my relationship to the culture that was my birthright. In some ways, I was no more connected to my parents than to the furniture. I can never understand how deaf people shown on television and in the movies understand so much of what goes on around them. For me, and for most of my deaf friends, everyday communication with my family was a struggle. Our language wasn't quite English, wasn't quite sign language, but a combination that used everything we could think of to convey our meaning. Sometimes, we just gave up. Having a conversation across such a monumental language barrier proved nearly impossible—especially for talking about things like my family's history, or all the family skeletons that only get talked about in whispers and innuendo. So it was only as an adult that I could explore what being

Cajun meant. Then instead of breathing it and becoming it, like Nana and Grady did, I found my cultural place through books and reading and translated tales.

We've tried to show this disconnect, the great divide that ensues when people do not share a language, by using italics for conversations to which I did not have full access. I hope the italics will help show just how much work it is for two people—even mother and daughter—to communicate when they don't share the same linguistic base.

Still, while deafness closed up one culture, it opened another. This was the culture of deaf people. I met other deaf children for the first time as a child at the Louisiana School for the Deaf. I met other educated deaf people and became one myself at Gallaudet University. School was a godsend. It was where I found my friends and where I learned what it really meant to be deaf. It was where Mama and Daddy found out that, contrary to what the doctor had told them, I wasn't mentally retarded.

I wasn't "just deaf" either. No one knew it then, but I have Usher syndrome, which caused me to be born deaf and will cause me to become blind. Actually, I am almost blind now, at least by legal definition. Of the 180-degree field of vision that most people enjoy, I see a 14-degree sliver with my left eye and another 17-degree sliver with my right eye, for a visual field of 31 degrees. It's a tiny circle of precious light under the best conditions, and the doctors say it is steadily closing.

Lance's birthday, and the party I'm giving him, comes in the midst of so much else. There were bar mitzvahs and weddings this year. Not our friends, anymore, but their children. So much travel and purchasing of presents. Then having my position eliminated at work. And the finishing of this story. I am determined to finish this story.

It's true that I distrust these contracted flashes of memory that I am about to share. I am not sure of what I experienced and what Nana said I experienced. I've had to reconstruct these conversations from my own memories and those of Nana. Still, I'm not sure what I remember and what she said I should remember. Perhaps I saw something. Perhaps I imagined it. Perhaps I misunderstood. Grady says some of this is flat-out wrong—and Grady should know. But the flashes are there. I can't deny them.

We, the alumni of Louisiana School for the Deaf, call it the Louisiana School, with a sign for Louisiana and a sign for residential schools. The school has changed its name several times throughout its history, but here I just call it the Louisiana School. A few names are changed, but most are as real as the people who bear them. Many of them took a look at this text, by the way. So did Grady. Not for me to present the lives of my family and friends through a prism of memory without asking. To speak is to lie, says the mystic, and to write—well, that is worse than lying.

Aunt Happy, Daddy's family, and Brother always called me Catherine. Mama called me Kitty, and Nana called me Little Kitty. Most deaf people have name signs by which other deaf people refer to them in sign language. Today my sign is a *K* handshape that moves in a swift repeated motion against the lip, miming the stroke of an imaginary cat's whisker. This stands for KITTY. That's what most folks call me now.

And this is my story.

Orchid of the Bayou

1

Devil Child

Into the strenuous briefness . . . I charge laughing.

—E. E. CUMMINGS, "POST IMPRESSIONS, IV"

Brother chased Skeet around the yard while Skeet held the gun high in the air, shooting at the bushes. It wasn't a real gun, of course, just one of those tiny toys that were so popular back in the fifties. My brother didn't have a gun. He aimed and shot with his forefinger. I watched from the doorway. Skeet and Brother didn't play with girls—and I was five and they were already twelve.

Brother turned and tackled Skeet, and they wrestled and fell to the ground. The gun went up and down, silver in the sunlight. Brother struggled to his feet. The gun was in his hands now. He turned and aimed at Skeet, but Skeet was faster. Skeet held up his finger and fired. A direct hit. Brother keeled over and fell to the ground. He writhed about on his stomach, then flopped over onto his back, and writhed some more. His arms spread out wide. His eyes were all squinched tight. He didn't see me even though I got very close.

In front of me, the gun lay on the ground, shining in the dirt. I had to use both hands to pick it up. I raised it carefully and held it

1

an instant against the sky. Then Skeet was leaping at me, his mouth and nostrils open wide. Brother stopped dying real quick. He jumped up and pushed Skeet away. While they tussled, I twisted free.

It was my turn. I swung the gun up to take aim.

Whack!

The gun caught Skeet just above the eyes. Blood sprang from his hair and splattered across his face and into the air. His hands went up and over his head, and he collapsed right in front of me. He didn't roll around like Brother. Skeet lay very still, an arm over his bloody head. Brother picked me up with one hand. With the other hand, he released the gun from my grip as if I had no strength at all.

I was astonished at his face. Brother was crying.

Mama swept through the doorway, her eyes brought together in a frown. I cried then, too, and struggled against my brother's arms. I cried while Mama put her arms around Skeet and helped him get back on his feet. It was easy to cry because Brother kept thrashing me back and forth, his mouth moving fast the whole time, and his face all wet with water from his eyes.

Mama took off her apron and Skeet pressed it to his face. A thin red line showed against the white swell above his eye. Mama turned to me and Brother, and her mouth worked. Her eyes flashed at Brother. All this was Brother's fault, Mama's eyes said. When she looked at me, her eyes turned gentle.

By this time she knew I was "not right." She knew the real words for "not right," too, though she never said those words. I was deaf and dumb. Brother knew it, too. He was supposed to take care of me. It was his job. He was never to allow anything like this to happen.

Mama held out her arms, and Brother gave one last shake and yielded me to her. Up and over her shoulder I went. Her closeness was a comfort. I could smell the old hen she had killed that morning.

Pauvre petite, she said. At lease I think she said that. My parents used French on really important occasions and, with blood still fresh in the dirt, this surely qualified.

2

I knew I was innocent, though. I was always innocent. Against my back, I felt the soothing pressure of her hand.

Behind us Skeet and Brother huddled together as if they had surmounted a great pestilence. Brother's arm was across Skeet's back when they both glanced over at me. At the eye contact, I stopped crying for a moment and stuck out my tongue. I grinned, too. Their faces darkened, and I returned to my tears.

Back inside, my mother tried to set me in a chair, but I wouldn't let her. I stood and cried. I was shut out again. I was shut out from everything, all the time—except when I misbehaved.

In despair, Mama walked over to check on Nana, my baby sister. Nana slept peacefully on the sofa. She didn't know about Skeet, or the gun, or the blood. Nana could sleep through anything, eat through it too. Mama's face went all soft when she looked at Nana. Then she turned back to the hen, hanging half skinned over a cauldron of boiling water. I stopped crying and sat on the floor, lip out and angry. Mama tugged off one feather after another. The neck was almost naked when sunlight and air flooded the room.

It was Brother exploding through the doorway. He was alone.

He didn't say anything, just stormed into the back room. Behind him the door closed fast and the house shook. The temperature cooled. Mama glanced again at Nana. My sister's eyes squeezed tight and her mouth stretched open. She was waving her hands. I followed Mama over to the sofa, forgetting to cry. I loved sweet Nana. Mama picked Nana up and tucked her under her shirt.

Through the window, Mama's apron was forgotten in the grass. I darted out and picked it up. Back inside, I tried to return it. Mama didn't look at me. Her hands were all tangled up with Nana, and her eyes were on the door to the back room. I shook the apron, and dust and grass fluttered loose across the floor. But Skeet's blood, brown as dust, stayed no matter how hard I shook. Mama accepted her apron finally, tucking it against her side with her elbow. She still didn't look at me.

I didn't know it but Skeet ran home after I hit him. Brother begged him not to go, but he went anyway.

"Please stay," Brother said.

"Your sister's too mean," Skeet said.

Everyone called me mean. Not just Skeet. Not just Brother. Everyone. I was mean because I hit Brother's friends.

"Hit her back," Daddy told Edward Lee Richard. Edward Lee and his big brother Darryl were our neighbors and some of Brother's favorite playmates. Brother would sneak over to the Richards' house when I wasn't looking. But I always knew he was there.

I came upon the three of them playing in a clump underneath the Richards' house. They were lining up little sticks around a landmark box in the cool, shaded dirt. I didn't have to duck to get under the house like they did. I just slithered between the wooden posts that held up the house.

They looked up, saw me, and looked away real quick. I picked up a stick or two and they ignored me, like I wasn't even there. So I whacked Edward Lee. He was the smallest, but he was still bigger than I was.

Edward Lee didn't run from me like he usually did. He pushed at my hands and kept at his play. I escalated the attack. First I hit his arms, then I went for his stomach. I didn't know about my daddy telling him to hit back.

Edward Lee turned on me suddenly. Using all his strength, he half hit and half pushed. I went spinning, lost my balance, and fell into the dirt. Shock turned to fury. I opened my mouth and hollered as strong as I could.

Brother was right there. He stood right beside me. His mouth moved real hard and ugly as he faced Edward Lee.

"Whad'a ya doin'?!" he screamed.

"She hit first!" cried Edward Lee.

"Why'd ya hit her like that?" Brother was beside himself.

"Your daddy told me to do it! She hit first! She hit first!" Edward Lee cried again.

"She can't hear and she can't talk!" Brother said.

"Maybe she can't hear or talk, but she sure can hit," Edward Lee sobbed.

We left in a huff, me and Brother, side by side. I kept up crying. It was a little hard to cry because I felt so happy. Next to Brother was the best place in the whole world.

Poor Brother. He says I drove off all his friends.

I was almost certainly born deaf, although my parents didn't know it at first. Everything about my birth was normal, even joyous, according to Brother. First the doctor pulled up to our house in his car. That right there was a big deal. Brother had never seen a doctor in our house before. But he didn't have time to puzzle about it because Aunt Happy suggested that they go outside. A fabulous idea, Brother thought. At seven, he wasn't too excited to hang out in the house with grown-ups anyway.

Brother remembers countless fireflies flickered in the September dusk and Aunt Happy wondering if he could catch any of them. Of course he could. Brother was an expert at catching fireflies. He caught one and then another, and then a whole bunch. Aunt Happy caught some too. And they laughed and chased the flashing bugs until the sun went down.

When they finally got back inside, it was completely dark, and there I was, Catherine Patricia Hoffpauir, his little sister. I was lying in Mama's bed right next to her, all six pounds or so of me, nestled in the flickering light of the gas lamp. Brother was incredulous. He was old enough to know that babies didn't hop out of the bedcovers like that.

"What, you didn't notice?" Aunt Happy asked him incredulously. "You didn't see the stork?"

Brother swore to God. He had seen no stork.

By this time, my daddy was there.

Brother had been too busy catching fireflies, my daddy said. Otherwise, he'd have seen the stork for sure.

My cousin said that my mother's mother frowned when she saw me. Some of the older folks know when something's not right, he said, and my grandma looked down at me at the very beginning, and she just knew.

There's something not right about that baby, she said. She didn't say that to my mama though. If she had said that to my mama, my daddy would have killed her.

My grandma kept quiet until I was nine months old. Then she couldn't keep quiet anymore. She was living in a little house a step or two behind our own. She took me outside to feed the chickens, and set me down in the yard to play. I smacked at the dirt, and maybe tried to eat a little, too. My grandmother didn't like the eating part. She scolded me, but I ignored her. This didn't upset her, too much. But the rooster did.

The rooster was old and mean, and he thought he owned the yard. When my mother waved her hands, all the chickens would scatter, but not that old rooster. He would just stare from his perch and dare her to come near. He held adults at a standoff and he petrified children. I refused to go anywhere near him.

Still, I had to see him to be scared, and that day he came up behind me. He was crowing and flapping and asserting his prerogative to parade right through the spot where I was sitting. We were almost the same size, but he was on his feet, stretched high and ready for war, so his head was a few inches further from the ground than my own. Busy with the bits of grass and dirt, I didn't see him. Loud bleats and shaken feathers and still I remained oblivious. He might have taken a piece of me right there, except for my grandmother. She'd turned at the screeching and watched the whole thing. She ran over, reached down, grabbed me, and shooed him away. Only then did I see him in his wicked glory and begin to cry and cling.

That night she told my mother what happened, in French, for she knew no English.

"*Catherine n'entende pas,*" she said. Catherine doesn't hear.

My mother didn't believe it and neither did my father. Their baby daughter deaf? Impossible.

Other reasons were offered for my indifference to the rooster. I was just too immersed in whatever I was doing, they decided. They had noticed my powers of concentration before. Once I was engrossed in something, I ignored everything else. It was a sign that

I was smart, said Mama. As for not moving when Grandma yelled? Well, I was stubborn. They had noticed that before, too.

The evidence continued to accumulate.

We were still in our old three-room house in Rayne, Louisiana. Now, more than 8,000 people make their home in Rayne. But before the interstate highway and the yearly frog festival, which as its boosters say, gave the town "a lot to croak about," Rayne was mostly a series of tiny streets with a ribbon of homes along the sides of each one. The town also had a rice mill, where my daddy worked, a Dairy Queen at the intersection, a gas station, two churches, and a school, all of it barely interrupting the surrounding countryside.

My father's parents lived several streets away from us, where the houses tapered off into farmland. One day, we all piled in Aunt Happy's car to drive over to their home. A train track cut through the middle of town. On the other side of the track lived Rayne's black families—our tiny town was as hopelessly split as any town in the South. The quickest way to my grandparents' was across the railroad track and through the black section.

Mama was at the wheel and Daddy beside her. I slept between them. Brother was in the backseat. As our car rolled to the track, a train approached, and Mama pulled to a stop. Just before it roared past us, its whistle blasted. The sound was so close and so loud that the adults and Brother jumped.

I slept on.

As the train pulled away, they looked at me in consternation. Even Brother was surprised. He told me so long afterward. When I didn't react to the whistle, he knew I was deaf.

My mother must have known, too. Surely she stiffened next to me, remembering her mother's words. My world was as big as everything I could see, but no one ever saw a sound, not even a sound as big as a train's whistle. It meant nothing to me.

The testing began when we returned home. Mama put me on the bed, got two old pots from the kitchen, and banged them behind me. Mama and her mother shouted my name from behind me. Hearing the noise, Daddy ran into the room, alarmed. I was contentedly gurgling at the window, and my mother was in tears.

"Our little girl can't hear," she sobbed.

Daddy didn't even pause. He grabbed one of the pots and whacked hard. I turned around, probably in response to the breeze created by his movement. My mother circled around behind me and repeated the demonstration. It continued off and on for hours—out-of-sight pandemonium. Every so often I turned and caught them. I'd grin and lurch toward them, happy to play a new game. When I did this, they immediately questioned their previous findings and recommenced the cacophony.

But if I turned at the right moment, it was just chance. I heard nothing.

Finally they began to understand. By the end of the day, they didn't question it anymore. I was deaf. Deaf and dumb.

But they still had hope. Not my Uncle Frank, a folk healer—Mama hardly trusted him with a cold sore. She turned to Ethel, a healer and her own best friend. Mama did some healing, too, but she was nowhere near as successful as Ethel. *Traiteuse* the neighbors called Ethel: Healer. She carried herbs in her hands and incantations in her head, and she was ever ready to help. Ethel had already blessed me. Now she took my head into her hands and rocked back and forth. She came almost every day. She rocked until she was exhausted, but I was as deaf as when she'd started.

Still they wouldn't give up hope. Someone told them about a doctor down in Lafayette, a specialist. Mama insisted that I be taken to him. There was a time and a place for healing and a time and a place for doctoring. Mama never went beyond the third grade herself, but she knew about degrees and she knew about education. She was explicit. I was to see the doctor down in Lafayette—a real doctor with a stethoscope, white coat, degrees on the wall, and traffic outside his office.

Still, she was so afraid of the doctor's verdict that she couldn't bring herself to do it, and Daddy was busy working at the rice mill during the day and taking a carpentry course at night. Aunt Happy would take me.

Aunt Happy was my favorite aunt. She was the prettiest of my mother's five sisters. The nicest, too. Her real name was Elodie, but everyone called her Happy from the time she was a little girl. As I grew older, I liked the name. It was easy to see on the lips.

Aunt Happy drove over to pick me up and bundled me into her car. We sped past the small streets of Rayne and made our way through the Louisiana countryside to see the doctor who met Mama's requirements.

Today, doctors can test reactions in a newborn's brain stem and determine with near certainty whether or not the infant has a hearing problem, or at least if more tests should be done. In the fifties, audiology was nowhere near as advanced. The Lafayette specialist—with his degrees and stethoscope and traffic—peered and poked, then commenced his own version of banging pots and pans.

The verdict was definitive: My deafness was complete and absolute. There was no treatment; there was no cure. The doctor didn't even recommend hearing aids. They would do no good, he said.

"Her cry's fine," Aunt Happy said, when she brought home the news to my parents. She didn't go into detail. Mama and Daddy didn't want details. Unpleasantness could be born, but there was no point in wallowing in it—and details were a form of wallowing.

I heard the story of my examination and diagnosis from Nana. She told me that the doctor also said I was mentally retarded. By the time she told me this, she was fluent in sign language and we communicated easily. Nana was explicit, signing *M* and *R* at her temple, meaning "mentally retarded."

After Mama and Daddy died, I asked other members of my family, and most said Nana was wrong. They never thought I was mentally retarded, they said.

But a few said that it was true. "Something else was wrong," explained one relative darkly, unwilling to explore what it possibly could have been.

Perhaps Nana or Aunt Happy put their own interpretation into the doctor's words? I don't think so. I think Nana was right about this like she was right about so much. I think the doctor told my Aunt Happy that I was deaf, dumb, and mentally retarded. That's certainly what my parents believed, at least at first. Even in the

1970s, when I worked at a deaf school in Washington, D.C., I met city kids with nothing amiss but their hearing who had received that diagnosis.

Of course, my parents and their friends didn't couple the words *deaf* and *dumb* just by happenstance. In those days, "deaf and dumb" slid out automatically, three undulating syllables, as natural as "horse and carriage." Sometimes "dumb" triumphed over "deaf" entirely.

This was increasingly ironic. In some places in America, deaf people had been active and working in communities, especially since World War II. They were mostly printers, factory workers, and assembly line employees, but there were also a few deaf teachers, at least one diplomat, and one deaf African American preacher who was getting ready to go to Africa to establish schools for the deaf children over there.

Still the civil rights advancement of the sixties and seventies was far away. Sign language, used every day by deaf people in schools and communities, was ignored by educators and misunderstood by linguists. And a psychologist up North (who never even talked with deaf people because he refused to use sign language, even though his own brother was deaf) was formulating theories about deaf personalities, and graduate students were being taught the mighty theory that people who were born deaf could not think abstractly.

Clearly, my parents and I were in way over our heads. Still, Mama and Daddy responded like the good Cajun people they were. Not understanding my difference, my parents accepted it anyway. They compensated. They took care of the little idiot growing in their midst, and they protected me. When the adults weren't around, Brother and Nana protected me, too. Through no fault of my own I was adrift, and others were expected to accommodate me. The rest of the world would simply make way. My mother, grieving, angry, and blaming herself, indulged me even more than she indulged my sister. She simply refused to allow me to be disciplined.

Some people go their whole lives and never meet a deaf person, but both my parents knew deaf people. Tons of deaf people lived in the Bayou. My daddy had grown up right near a family that had a whole slew of deaf children. It was a bad family, Daddy said. The family members fought with each other, and they fought with their neighbors. They stole, too. When I was little I understood that the family's misdeeds centered completely on its deaf members. Only later did I learn that within the family was a hearing father who killed a hearing neighbor for stealing away with his daughter. Growing up, I thought it was the deaf family members who caused all the ruckus.

"They're animals," Daddy said. That's what he called them—animals. I thought he meant only the deaf people.

2

❦

$\mathcal{A}$ School for Kitty

The aim was song . . . The wind could see.

—ROBERT FROST, "THE AIM WAS SONG"

I was five when I attacked Nana's mouth. I had wiggled loose a few of my own baby teeth—a side tooth first and later one of my big front teeth. In both instances, a little blood and pain turned quickly into a stroke of good fortune. First, I would have my own tooth in the palm of my hand, an event in itself. Then I would take the tooth to Brother who would take it to Mama. Mama would wash it up and put it under the old pillow in the bed we shared, and the next morning it would be gone—replaced by a shiny coin.

I saw the cause and effect clearly, though I had no name for either. A tooth tucked underneath a pillow overnight became a coin. The understanding was deep as instinct. Unfortunately, try as I might, the rest of my teeth were holding firm. Despite my efforts to free them, they wouldn't budge.

Thus it was that I approached Nana. She was two years old with a few sparkly teeth of her own. I looked at them and realized what magic each could perform under my pillow. First, of course, they would have to be removed. Forcing her jaws apart, I put my hand inside my sister's mouth. Nana cried and tried to get away. But I held her tightly and tested each tooth. Like mine, each held fast. Carefully, I tried to loosen one of the large ones. As I wiggled and pulled, my nail caught on Nana's gums. A little blood came and her chest heaved hard. Perhaps after the coin came, I would split it with her.

I climbed on top of her to hold her still, then picked a tooth and pulled.

Never far away, Mama swooped to the rescue. I withdrew my hand, red and wet and utterly bereft of booty. Mama picked up Nana. From Mama's arms, Nana hurled her face toward the ceiling, her mouth wide open, her face wet with tears, and her teeth still sparkling gleefully.

Mama's eyes found me. I was good at reading the variety of expressions that light the human face. Mama's face said something was very wrong. However, worried faces work well for expressing simple things, but they are utterly inadequate when trying to explain about tooth fairies, property rights, or bodily integrity. I had not a clue why Mama looked so troubled. Further, I was incensed. Mama was unreasonable! Why was she still holding Nana? Nana stopped crying almost immediately. And why was she so mad at me? I followed Mama and Nana about the room, scolding and crying. But Mama still wouldn't let go of Nana. Her fingers stroked at Nana's curls. I cried and screamed and stomped about. Brother came to see the ruckus and shook his head at me. So did Mama, though she didn't stay angry long.

At a loss as to how to entertain me, Mama thought of a little girl who lived across the street. This little girl was also "not right." She could hear though, which I suppose put her a notch above me. She had shoulder-length brown hair, an awkward way of moving, and vacant hazel eyes. Two not-quite-right little girls who were also neighbors seemed to be natural playmates for each other, and our mothers regularly undertook to get us together. Shunned by everyone else, they figured we could play together. Thus it was that I was dragged again and again to this child's house or she was dragged to mine.

Poor little girl. There was no way I was going to play with her. I ignored her, sometimes elaborately. Instead, I played with her younger sister. The two of us would set up dominoes in a winding line, then one of us would flick the first one and watch them all fall down. This caused us untold delight. We would laugh and laugh. I remember seeing a larger child in the unclear background scowling at us from a distance. Occasionally, she would approach and we would rebuff her mercilessly. She would retreat again, her face a study of confusion and hurt.

Our mothers were confused, too. But I wasn't. I might have been a child bereft of human communication beyond that of prods and points and the codes of the face, still I knew what I wasn't. And I wasn't meant to be a playmate for this poor little girl. It was a colossal mismatch.

We struggled along, my family and I. I continued to be outrageous. They continued to make way. Maybe one of the worst things I did was pee on Brother. This began, I think, when I was still a toddler—before my parents moved our house to their own lot, and built a place that included a real inside bathroom. Brother and I shared a room, and slept side by side in the same bed. A three-year-old doesn't take up much room and neither does a skinny ten-year-old. That was the year Nana arrived, which meant that there was no room in my parents' bed.

I think it was fear of the dark that started it. Too scared to get out of bed, I simply lay there, trying to ignore the insistent pressure and hoping for morning. I didn't have to go outside to relieve myself; I just had to walk across the hall to use what I think was a slop jar, which would be emptied in the morning by my mother. Still, sliding out of bed is like stepping into another country when one is three and trying to peer through the dark. I could have called out for Mama, I suppose. I knew by then that a rattle in my throat would bring adults running and the heftier the rattle, the faster they would come. But I didn't do that either.

When you wet the bed, first it is warm and then it gets cold. I've read this, and I can verify that it is indeed the case. Brother says I reaffirmed it night after night. I think he is right. Somehow in those days before I knew how to communicate or even knew what real communication is, I made a series of pertinent discoveries. Here's the deductive process at work:

1. If a sister positions herself carefully on top of a sleeping brother, he doesn't wake up.

2. A sister can empty her bladder completely while the brother still sleeps.

3. When he wakes up, the brother appraises the situation swiftly.

4. The brother removes himself from the bed.

5. He bolts as far and as fast as possible, taking most of the pee, by now cold and offending, along with him.

6. Sometimes he administers a thump to the slightly abashed sister.

7. The thump doesn't hurt much.

8. The sister avoids a walk in the dark.

QED: It became a system.

Brother shed a lot of angry tears, and Mama changed a lot of sheets. And I was never punished.

As I look back, I think I was a monster. Nana was at my mercy. I dragged her about wherever I went. When I was bored with her, I chased after Brother, always ready to charge into whatever game he was playing and whomp a few of his smaller friends. Most nights I wet on him, too. I was jealous and misunderstood, even within the family that loved me. I was frustrated, too, and angry—always, always angry.

When I was four, we moved—the whole house. An aunt and uncle had bequeathed us a larger plot of land several lots away. The neighbors got together, unfastened our house from its foundations, picked it up like a gigantic Lego model, pushed it onto the back of someone's pickup, and carted it down the street. Our house was pressed into its new foundations, four posts that held it above the Louisiana dirt. My father began adding rooms to the back so

Brother could have his own bedroom. I now shared my bed with Nana, who was almost three and old enough to move out of my parents' room. We had a bathroom inside, too, right in the center of everything. No more slop jar for us, but Nana was now my unlucky bedmate, because I was still afraid to go to the bathroom at night.

❦

One day when I was five, my Aunt Happy arrived at our house all speed and purpose. Aunt Happy lived down near Baton Rouge so my Uncle Speedy would be near the oil company where he worked. Her car came up real fast, and her feet were quick on the pavement. The mouth stuff began even before she was inside the house.

"Topsy!" she called as she came striding through the yard. That's what everyone called my mother. Her real name was Nola, but no one ever called her that. Aunt Happy bounded up the steps, barely even looking at me. Instead of catching the door and closing it gently behind her like she usually did, she swept it aside like a curtain and walked on through. I watched it bang back and forth against the jamb before it nestled back into place.

I followed Aunt Happy into the kitchen. The house smelled of wood and carpentry. Outside, two-by-twos were piled in the summer sun. The new garden was coming along and Brother was elbow deep in it, picking the first leaves of spinach. My mother was bent over the stove, and Nana was next to her, banging two little tin cups together as if they were cymbals.

When she saw me, Nana grinned and held out one of her cups. I turned away from Aunt Happy, accepted the cup, and pretended to drink from it. Nana laughed. Then I gestured to the door and ran outside. Nana stumbled after me and giggled as I took the old cup into the yard and put just a little dirt inside it. Aunt Happy was talking excitely with Mama, glancing at us distractedly from time to time with her absent-minded smile.

"J'ai trouvé une école pour Catherine," Aunt Happy said. Aunt Happy and Brother always called me Catherine. Mama called me Kitty, and Nana called me Little Kitty.

Nana jumped up and down waving her cup. I put a little dirt inside her cup, too, not enough to make Mama mad, just a few grains on the bottom. Back inside, I stirred my dirt carefully with my finger, and Nana copied me.

"Talk English," my mother told Aunt Happy. Maybe I was deaf, but Nana could hear, and Mama sure didn't want her hearing the language that had caused her so much trouble. It was important that Nana talk American.

"A school for Catherine," said Aunt Happy. "I found a school for Catherine."

My mother, busy stirring the sausage from the night before into a tomato sauce, shook her head and frowned. She didn't look at Aunt Happy and her mouth was tight.

Talk of school reminded her that I could never go where Brother went. Not that Brother thought his public school was that great. First graders, aged six to twelve, sat in his class, he told me, some of them speaking only the French they'd brought from home. They zestfully flunked English year after year until the law said that they didn't have to come to class anymore. "My first grade had the best basketball team in the state, maybe the country," Brother would later joke.

Aunt Happy sighed and continued. "Catherine needs a school," she said.

Next to me Nana spilled some of her dirt on the floor. I glanced up at Mama and Aunt Happy, but they hadn't noticed. Carefully, I scraped the dirt into my hand and put it back into her cup. Nana fussed. The dirt was hers; she wanted it back on the floor. I laughed and picked her up. Mama continued making the sauce that she put on meats. She usually made her own, grabbing whatever ingredients she had in the house or Brother could find in the garden.

"Catherine's fine," said Mama, chopping at the onion extra hard.

Aunt Happy would have none of it.

"Catherine is five years old," she said firmly. "She needs a school."

And, quite by chance, Aunt Happy had found one. That very morning she had driven Uncle Speedy to work and was returning home when she took a wrong turn. She tried to turn around, but one road led to another, and she found herself completely lost. Even though she was technically inside the city limits, the roads were narrow and winding, with dilapidated houses, bushes, and shrubs high on each side. Fortunately Aunt Happy had plenty of gas in the tank. When she came upon a sign, she realized that the large building she saw on the other side of the fence was a school. The sign outside said, "Louisiana State School for the Deaf."

"A school just for deaf children!" said Aunt Happy.

My mother made a great show of whisking leftover tomato soup into the hot sauce.

Aunt Happy sighed, emptied an ashtray—she was always emptying ashtrays—and continued. Although she didn't want to seem too curious or be thought a trespasser, she drove through the gate. Feeling nervous but sure she was doing the right thing, she parked outside the main building. She knocked on the heavy door, and she knew by the hollowness of the sound that she had to go further to gain entrance. Pushing with all her might, she opened the door.

"Opened the door?" My mother was astounded.

"And walked inside," Aunt Happy said.

My mother stopped stirring and stared at her sister. Oblivious to the conversation, I bounced Nana up and down. Her curls flew through the air, and her cup jiggled in the air. Nana laughed and laughed.

"It is a nice place," said Aunt Happy.

"I can't believe you walked inside that place," said my mother.

"It's beautiful really," said Aunt Happy. "It has columns outside, fancy grillwork, and ivy—"

Conversation stopped for a moment as both women searched for a way to continue.

"Where?" asked my mother finally.

Aunt Happy hesitated.

"Where is the school?" my mother asked again.

"Somewhere in Baton Rouge," Aunt Happy mumbled finally.

"Baton Rouge!" my mother exclaimed. It might as well have been Beijing.

"That's not far, Topsy. It's only about seventy-five miles," Aunt Happy maintained, developing a sudden interest in the simmering sauce.

Mama left the pot and stepped over toward the window. Aunt Happy took over stirring, while Mama lit a cigarette and stared through the glass. Aunt Happy stopped stirring for a moment, hastened over to Mama's ashtray and emptied it. Then she returned to the stove, dipped a finger in the sauce and brought it to her tongue, then continued her offense.

"I live right close to it," she told Mama. She and Speedy would visit me often. Of course they would. They would check on me whenever my mother wanted. In fact, more often. Aunt Happy wouldn't let anything happen to her niece. Of course she would check on me.

"Maybe the school can teach Catherine something," she said.

"Baton Rouge!" My mother was disconsolate.

"The people there seemed very nice," Aunt Happy said. "They gave me directions back to the highway."

My mother twisted her apron in one hand and smoked with the other. "This is all my fault," she said suddenly.

Aunt Happy's eyes flew to Mama's face.

"Topsy, don't you go talking silliness."

Nana wanted another cup, but I didn't dare get it for her. A few grains of dirt already lurked on the floor. Not enough for Mama and Aunt Happy to see, but no use pressing our luck. I moved my cup back and forth like Daddy sometimes did with his beer before dinner, then I held it to my lips and pretended to drink again. Nana grinned and copied me. She lifted her cup to her lips, too.

Afraid she would really let the dirt into her mouth, I reached forward for the cup. Her fingers brushed my own and the metal rim clashed into her teeth. A bit of dirt must have made its way into her mouth. She spit and started to cry. Still talking, Aunt Happy came over and reached down to pick her up, but Nana refused to be picked up.

Nana didn't want to be with Aunt Happy, she wanted to be with me. But if Aunt Happy wanted to hold someone, I was willing to go to her. I stood up and raised my arms, but Aunt Happy just laughed and patted my head. Her mouth worked while her eyes rested on me.

"Catherine's a big girl," she told Mama.

I watched her moving mouth without understanding; I had no idea what moving lips meant. My mouth felt dirty and gritty and I wiped my lips against my sleeve. Nana pulled on my shirt. Irritated, I pushed her away. Why do little children get all the attention? It wasn't that Nana didn't deserve attention. She had those curls and chubby little arms. She smiled all the time. She didn't even know that she was so cute. She just ate and burped, and took for granted all the women who circled around her. No wonder everyone loved her. At five, my cuteness was fast disappearing. I could feel it.

I took both cups and turned to go outside. Nana lunged after me and tried to repossess her cup. Angry, I jerked away. Dirt spilled over the floor. I glanced over at Mama and Aunt Happy, but they hadn't noticed. Then Nana's face crinkled up. I knew what was coming. Tears would fall, and adults would gather. I didn't quite understand about noise yet, but I knew that something happened that I couldn't see, and I knew it happened in the throat. And I knew it made people look. Now Aunt Happy would pick up Nana for sure. My sister would be in Aunt Happy's arms and lost to me. Mama and Aunt Happy would probably be mad, too. Even indulged as I was, I wasn't supposed to make Nana cry.

As Nana gathered force to deliver a full-fledged gale of sound and water, I reached over and put my hand over her mouth. She was so tiny that my fingers covered her nose, too. Her face froze under my fingers. She looked so surprised. I pressed and the wail stayed inside of her. Her eyes got bigger and bigger, and her stomach made a series of little jerks. I pushed hard, my hand clamped tight. The look in her eyes changed.

I pushed still harder. Her eyes started to close.

Suddenly I felt the floor tremble. There were adult legs and hands all around us. Aunt Happy grabbed me and swept me to the side. In the same motion, she lifted Nana. Tension like a wave put everything into slow motion. Nana couldn't seem to get any breath into her body. Her lips and mouth worked in choking motions. Her lips were a strange color and her eyes had opened again very wide. Finally a shudder passed through her chest, and she let out a series of sobs. Relief flowed through the room.

Aunt Happy swayed back and forth with Nana and planted kisses in her sweaty hair. She walked as she swayed, patting Nana's back. Nana cried and cried. Without pausing, Aunt Happy worked her mouth and glanced at Mama.

By the stove, my mother was motionless. She didn't even smoke. The cigarette burned unnoticed in her fingers.

There was much clucking and head shaking.

"I'll talk to Alex," said my mother. Alex was my daddy. "He likes Catherine at home," she added.

Aunt Happy shook her head. Nana cried and cried, and I began to cry too.

That night when my father came home from work, my mother told him about Aunt Happy's find. My father resisted. He didn't believe in putting family in institutions, especially institutions so far away.

"It's a school," Mama told him.

Daddy shook his head.

"Maybe a school will help," said Mama.

"No." Daddy could be stubborn. "No," he said again.

"She almost killed her sister," Mama said finally.

Daddy shook his head again. But later that night Daddy talked to his father, who had no formal education at all, and he encouraged Daddy to go see the school. And just like that, my family made a decision that would change my life.

3

꙳

"*I* Don't Think She's Retarded"

Great is Language . . . the mightiest of sciences . . .
greater than wealth . . .
Buildings, ships, religions, paintings, music.

—WALT WHITMAN, "GREAT ARE THE MYTHS"

I don't remember that first visit to the Louisiana School for the Deaf, even though it had repercussions that would resonate throughout my life. I was still five years old when Daddy, Mama, and Aunt Happy packed me into the car, and we left for the all-important interview. In those days, the Louisiana School was adamant about accepting deaf children who were "normal." These were children like their hearing peers in every way, except that they could not hear. Teachers called them "pure deaf" children. I had one boy in my class with mild cerebral palsy, but in general deaf children with disabilities were not admitted. Deaf children who were mentally retarded were not even considered. The school for deaf children was as strict as the public schools in excluding children with multiple disabilities.

My parents must have doubted that I would pass muster. Aunt Happy drove the four of us to the school while Brother and Nana stayed with neighbors. While my mother feared the rejection, my

"*I* Don't Think She's Retarded"

father half wanted it. He still was not convinced that he should send his daughter away to an institution.

In those days, the Louisiana School consisted of several enormous brick buildings on eight acres of land in the shadow of downtown Baton Rouge. The buildings—which used to be an elementary school, high school, swimming pool, vocational building, and dorms—are still there, tucked into greenery and perfectly visible to the most casual traveler who passes by on Interstate 10. The Louisiana Department of Correction uses the buildings now. Only a plaque on the wall and splashes of strategically applied yellow paint reveal the buildings' history.

With the high-rises and businesses of Baton Rouge a fifteen-minute walk away, the old school seems charming, almost quaint. That first visit, I was oblivious. My parents found the structure intimidating and entered the administration building with a mixture of awe and dread. Alcatraz seemed less formidable. Still, my Aunt Happy was right. With Spanish grillwork and columns, it was magnificent.

The corridor closed around us and our eyes adjusted to the dim light. We were led to the office of the principal, Mr. Ken Huff. Mr. Huff had worked at the school forever. His parents were deaf, everyone said, and he was an old hand at deaf education. My parents positioned me between them, so that I would be within easy arm's reach of both. Aunt Happy took up her post next to my mother. They prayed that for once in my young life, I would behave myself.

For the first part of the interview, I did. In this place of strange people, smells, and colors, I stayed close to my parents and Aunt Happy. Then curiosity replaced intimidation, and I trundled about the room, lifting one object after another, and taking each to my despairing parents. Finally I tried to commandeer the ashtray, which happened to be accommodating my mother's lighted cigarette.

Daddy huffed and puffed. Mr. Huff laughed, recovered the ashtray, and put it back on the table. My mother blushed as I chafed and fussed. My daddy figured it was time to rush to my defense. He did

23

most of the talking in the interview. Perhaps his stint in the army during World War II had prepared him, giving him both the confidence to answer the questions of authority figures like Mr. Huff.

"My daughter is good at home," my daddy declared grandly.

I was about to again prove him wrong, when Mr. Huff came to my rescue and saved me from totally disgracing my family and myself.

"There's a class of children outside," he said. "The children are about Catherine's age. Why not let her go play with them?"

Nervously, Mama walked to the door with me. When I caught sight of children, I ran from her side. I was never shy and joined them eagerly. It was the first time that I had played with children who were deaf, and I really believe that on some level I knew that these children were like me. They accepted me as readily as I accepted them. Two girls were drawing houses in the soil with a stick. I grabbed a stick, too and began a house of my own.

Inside the office, Mr. Huff and my parents discussed my situation. Daddy confessed. I was deaf, he said, and full of mischief. A doctor had told them I was mentally retarded, too, he added. Mama said almost nothing but cried a little. Daddy tried to emphasize my good points, though I suppose he had to think hard to come up with them, or maybe he made them up.

"Really, she is a good girl," Daddy said. "Sometimes she helps her mother around the house. Sometimes she takes care of her baby sister."

Mr. Huff was surprisingly reassuring. It was true that mentally retarded children were not accepted into the school, he said. But many times doctors—even those doctors who plied their trade over in Lafayette—were wrong in their diagnosis of deaf children.

"We can barely even measure the degree of hearing loss in young children," he told them, "let alone accurately measure their intelligence."

He paused for a moment and walked over to the window. After watching for a while, he called to my parents.

"Look at her," he said.

By this time, I had joined a circle of seated children where we played a simple game. One child would walk around the circle and select one of the other children with a sharp tap. Then the child would take off running. The tapped child would jump up in pursuit. If the runner made it all the way around the circle to the vacated spot and plopped into it without being tagged, he was safe. But if he were caught, he was out and he couldn't play anymore.

It was Duck Duck Goose, of course, a version of the same game that Brother played with the hearing children at the school near my home. Like most kids, I mastered the rules easily, and as my parents watched, I quivered expectantly in my spot in the circle, just hoping to feel a hand touch the top of my head.

"I don't think Catherine's mentally retarded," said Mr. Huff.

My parents' eyes went from the window to him in unison. Aunt Happy's eyes went down to the floor. The school was her find and her responsibility. It seemed to be paying off.

"I think Catherine's just deaf," said Mr. Huff.

Just deaf. After five years of living with me, my parents had not a clue what that meant. Didn't "just deaf" mean mentally retarded anyway? Wasn't the expression "deaf and dumb"? Surely the deaf people they knew—Daddy's old neighbors, and others who had grown up as far from any school as I had been until that moment— seemed deaf and dumb.

Standing there in the office, my parents must have been too stunned to say anything. In some ways, being deaf is so much more complex than being mentally retarded. How could they articulate an assumption that they had never really defined? Not having defined that assumption, how could they identify the other one— which was that he wasn't quite telling the truth, that they didn't quite believe him.

Perhaps Mr. Huff understood. After all, many of his students were from the Cajun communities west of Baton Rouge. He must have met parents like mine before.

"Deaf people are not dumb," he told my parents gently. "As a matter of fact, most deaf people are as intelligent as you and me. All they can't do is hear."

It was the same old message of deaf educators to a public that didn't seem to want to believe.

Seeing the doubt in my parents' eyes, he nodded.

"Do you have hearing children?" he asked. "What would they be like if you could never talk with them and they could never talk with you? Try to imagine it."

My father shook his head. My mother thought about Brother and Nana and looked away.

"Perhaps we should keep Catherine at home," my father said finally.

Mr. Huff was aghast.

"School is even more important for deaf children than hearing children!" he burst out. "Hearing children learn to talk—they learn *language,*" he amended, "without any schooling. But not deaf children. Deaf children need special training to understand English," Mr. Huff explained.

My parents nodded.

"Catherine has to *see* things," he continued. "What she doesn't take in with her eyes, she doesn't take in at all."

On one hand they already knew this, of course. On the other hand, it is always revelation.

My mother started to cry again.

"Love is a start," Mr. Huff said, seeing there was at least one thing my family had plenty of. "When parents who hear have a child who is deaf, they have to learn new habits. Most folks just keep right on with their hearing habits and hope. Schooling is essential, but she's still too young. Louisiana law requires that she be six by October of the year of entry. So she has almost another year at home."

Then he made the suggestion that may have changed my life. "Try labeling things," Mr. Huff said. "Write names on things in your home—the table, the door, and the bed. Everything."

"Labels?" asked my father.

"Labels," confirmed Mr. Huff.

"Labels will teach her to read," nodded my father, thinking he understood.

"Even more than that. Surely labels will help her to read," Mr. Huff allowed. "Of course. But it will help her with something even more basic. Catherine must learn about names."

By five years old, most kids know all about names. It doesn't matter what country they live in or what language they use. They know about names, and they use them all the time, stringing them together with other words in the mysterious ways of whatever grammar their language happens to require. Five-year-olds chatter away. Deaf kids with deaf parents chatter in sign language and hearing kids with hearing parents chatter in spoken language.

All this chattering provides connection. It connects the kids to their parents, their brothers and sisters, and to the whole world around them. It connects the kids to other worlds, too, not only worlds that are geographically distant, but also the worlds of the past, and the worlds of fantasy and mathematics.

"Civilization," Mr. Huff insisted as he had many times with other parents, "comes to us partly through our stomachs and partly through our words and stories. Grand stories like Peter Pan in Never-Never Land and Jesus Christ saying, 'Let the children come,' and everyday stories like, 'Catherine is outside playing with some new friends.'"

He was right. I struggled and pranced, laughed and cried, in splendid and terrible isolation. I couldn't ask about my grandmother even when she died, or call for my mother. I couldn't tell my Aunt Happy when I had to go to the bathroom. I couldn't say, "I'm hungry," or "Look at the children playing," or "I love you." In fact, I didn't know what any of those words meant. Not *Mama*, not *love*, not even *you*, or *me*.

I was like a computer minus a keyboard, software, and even a plug. So much capacity and no programs to run—and no way to run them if I had them. I was a linguistic disaster, but I was more than that. I was like the famous Helen Keller before she met Ann Sullivan, except instead of meaningless darkness, my world held meaningless light. I didn't know any names, let alone that everything I could see and touch possessed one.

My poor parents. They were overwhelmed.

Mr. Huff wasn't done. He told them—without presuming to build hope that he knew would be misplaced—that some of the students at the school learned to speak. If the literature of the school is correct, Mr. Huff was one of those educators who believed that deaf students should use speech whenever possible. I don't know if he mentioned this to my parents. If so, it might have been the one area where I might not have nodded my head.

When it was time to leave, my parents were overwhelmed again by my reaction to the school, which was as perplexing to them as Mr. Huff's words. My parents had dreaded taking me to the Louisiana School, not just because of their own emotions, but because of what they expected my emotional reaction would be. To consign their five-year-old daughter to what by any other name was still an asylum was almost more than they could bear, with or without the columns and ivy.

To their astonishment, I didn't want to leave. I wanted to stay in that play yard with those children. They promised me that I would come back. I'm told that I understood them, and maybe I did.

☙

My daddy must have had some faith in me because he began writing words on cards almost as soon as we got home. English words appeared on everything, just as Mr. Huff had specified. There was the PORCH, the DOOR, and the REFRIGERATOR. There were SHIRTS, PANTS, and SHOES. There was RICE and TOMATO. The electric LIGHT in the evening gleamed from a single BULB above the SOFA in the middle of the LIVING ROOM.

Within weeks, *I* was writing words too. At first I only tried to copy all the letters arranged as I saw them around me.

KITTY.

Proud to have his attention, I made each letter carefully.

When I was done, he held up the paper and pointed to me.

"Kitty, me?" I asked by pointing to the word and then to myself. It was the first time I had ever used language, rather than gestures and facial expressions, to talk with a member of my family. It was rudimentary, but I got my point across—which is, in many ways, the same way I would continue to communicate with hearing people.

"*You're Kitty,*" he affirmed.

Then he had me write DADDY. I made the letters awkwardly.

"*That's me,*" he gruffly let me know.

"*You?*" I said with a point.

He nodded.

The man before me was DADDY. Then we wrote a new word. That woman was MAMA. I lined up the pieces of paper, one after the next, DADDY, KITTY, and MAMA. Later, I added NANA and BROTHER to my repertoire.

I don't know how I managed to skip the alphabet and the myriad of sounds they say it encompasses and began to associate those static labels with the objects that they represented. But I seem to have done just that, making direct connections between physical objects and the Latin letters scrawled across them on paper.

Soon Daddy began to eschew paper and let the alphabet flow from his fingers. He would write each letter in capitals. I would catch his words through the air. B-E-D, he would scrawl with his forefinger, shaping each letter exactly as it would have appeared on paper, except about twenty times bigger. I would watch the sweep of his hands and know that it was time to go to sleep.

The letters gave me some kind of guidance, a check on my full-speed charge through stimuli and feeling that I still had no way to understand. However rudimentary, communication deeper than points, tugs, and smiles entered my life.

While I learned, my parents learned, too. It was their first lesson on how *deaf* is not *dumb*.

4

&

A Seasoned Student

Elected Silence, sing to me.

—GERARD MANLEY HOPKINS, "THE HABIT OF PERFECTION"

In this day when people believe asylums are so bad even for people who are mentally ill or dangerous, it shocks hearing people to learn how much deaf children loved their deaf schools. There may have been many reasons not to love the school. Many of the personnel may have been untrained. The premise that deaf students were being educated according to the school's own guidelines may have been contaminated by more than a little prejudice against the belief that deaf students were truly the intellectual equals of hearing students. There was a woeful inadequacy in sign language. And the facility itself may have been constantly in need of repairs. Nevertheless, classmates, teachers, staff, the published curriculum, and the values that they represented—all that constituted the Louisiana School—were what pulled me out of my primal isolation and into a human culture. From the Louisiana School, I learned not only how to read and write, but also what it meant to be an adult, and educated, and a citizen in the United States and the world.

Over 1,600 children had received an education there by the time I entered in 1953, presumably many of them going through the same transformation that I did. In 1838 Louisiana was the fifteenth state to pass legislation providing for the education of deaf children; in a time when black people were still locked in slavery, this legislation meant education of *white* deaf children. Deaf children had been educated in Louisiana before, the school's literature maintains, it was just that their parents paid for private tutors. Every time I read this, I think of my own parents, who barely thought school worthy of their hearing children and would have found the thought of paying to educate deaf children hilarious.

Provision for a facility wasn't included in the legislation, so for more than a decade Louisiana's deaf students traveled up the Mississippi River by flatboat to attend the Kentucky School for the Deaf. Eleven children were making the annual journey when the legislature decided to authorize the purchase of a building in Baton Rouge. In 1852, James Brown, an experienced educator, was recruited from Indiana School for the Deaf to become the Louisiana School's first superintendent. He was accompanied by a young teacher, Martin M. Hanson, and a steward, Thomas Wood. Hanson was deaf and a graduate of the Indiana School where Brown had been his teacher. Sadly, both Hanson and Wood were dead within a year, felled by yellow fever. Brown must have valued Hanson enormously for he saw to it that his obituary was published in the 1854 *American Annals of the Deaf:* "His polished and courteous deportment, his efficiency as a teacher, his amiable bearing toward his pupils, all alike contributed to render him universally respected and esteemed . . . His loss to the Institution is of serious consequence."

Brown was an active superintendent. He provided academic courses for students in sign language, contributed to national professional organizations and publications, and in 1856 published *A Vocabulary of Mute Signs,* one of the first sign language books in the United States. Brown also drew up plans for a new, large, beautiful building; purchased a printing press; and launched the first versions of the *Pelican* (then the *Deaf Pelican*), the school's newspaper, which is still published today. In 1863, he was fired, and the entire teaching staff either quit or was fired along with him. His firing left him so bitter, and the bitterness changed him so, that a newspaper editor whom he had successfully cultivated during his tenure as superintendent professed to no longer know him.

When Brown and his staff left, the school, having no teachers for its classrooms, dismissed the students two months early. The ruinous effects for the students endured for almost half a year. Classes resumed in the fall as if nothing were amiss. According to the literature, there was only one student less than there had been when the school closed during that disastrous spring.

All these problems are in synch with the history of other schools for the deaf. The deaf teacher unremembered except with an obituary in a dated file. The battles of politics. The dedicated educators who were summarily dismissed. The subsequent disruption of teaching that ensued on scales large and small.

The school mirrored other residential schools in other ways, too. According to the records, not until 1859 was the first hearing teacher hired. The Annual Report noted "an experienced hearing lady was employed," without noting exactly in what the lady was experienced. Vocational training was introduced the same year. Older girls and boys learned typesetting, presswork, and bookbinding.

In the beginning, students performed yearly for the state legislators, demonstrating the fruits of their education as their teachers made an annual plea for funds. As the nation tumbled into civil war, the school, seemingly oblivious to the turmoil, negotiated to have slaves remain on site. When the war broke out, federal soldiers ventured down the Mississippi River, mistook the school building for the statehouse, and commenced a bombardment. Matron Mary DuFroc and Superintendent A. K. Martin ran half a mile to the riverbank to plead with the Yankee commander to leave the school alone. They were apparently successful, for the Yanks stopped firing with only a few battered doors and cannon balls lodged in the courtyard. Federal troops eventually took over the building and converted it to a hospital, a fortunate event for the few remaining students and staff, for the occupation meant an increase in food rations for all.

After the Civil War, the first speech teacher was hired: a woman named Edith Rambo. She arrived in 1884, having trained at the Clark School for the Deaf in Northampton, Massachusetts, one of the first schools in the United States to set up instruction completely dependent on the deaf students using only lipreading and speech. Teachers of the deaf persist in calling this "oral communication," an application of a perfectly fine Latinate English that I flat-out hate. Precise and honest language may not be the forte of educators, for the opposite of oral communication is "manual communication," another skewed application of Latinate English. The terms *manual* and *oral,* in the controversy among deaf educators, distort something they are supposed to name, and lend lots of heat and little light in every discussion into which they are introduced. In naming the process, the terms misconstrue it. Sign communication doesn't come from the hand any more than spoken communication comes from the mouth. From the head maybe. From the heart certainly. It may be true that the mouth has provided the most common way of instructing deaf as well as hearing children, but equating either body organ with language is like equating a keyboard with writing. Whether one uses a keyboard or a pen, one writes as well as signs with one's hands, but no one ever called writing, "manual communication."

Four years after Rambo's arrival, the superintendent was asking for funds to construct a separate building for the oral students, believing that they should be separated from those who signed. This was considered progressive. One superintendent, S. Walker, noticed that deafness seemed to run in certain families, and he tallied up the students who had deaf cousins, aunts, brothers, sisters, and parents. He tried without success to contact deaf and blind students across the country, writing to each of the sixteen deaf and blind individuals who were recorded in the federal census.

The early educators struggled mightily for the school to be seen as an educational institution as opposed to a charitable one. When in 1908 the legislature changed the name from the Louisiana Institution for the Education of the Deaf and Dumb to the Louisiana State School for the Deaf, it was considered a great victory. By

1913, the school published *A Full Course of Study,* an account of the school's curriculum that made little or no mention of the sign language in which it was presented. Beginning in first grade and continuing through twelfth grade, students were taught the academic subjects of literature, language, and arithmetic. In addition, they were taught agriculture, cabinetmaking, canning, carpentry, cooking, "fancy sewing," harness making, physiology, hygiene, and how to make shoes. In fact, for several years, the cobblery students made all the shoes of their schoolmates.

Increasingly, the curriculum was focused on vocational training and delivered through speech and lipreading. The school's literature for the time when I entered emphasizes lipreading and speech and doesn't mention the use of sign language at all. This doesn't match my memory. There was indeed a class where students who were hard of hearing sat with amplifier headsets and repeated speech sounds. I sat in at least one of these classes, too. Still, all the communication—inside and outside the classrooms—that I remember was in sign language.

While we waited for the next school year, I made it clear that I wanted to go back to the school where I had briefly enjoyed so many playmates. I would look at Mama and Daddy questioningly. Daddy would turn away. Mama would tell me, yes, I would go to school, accompanying the lip information with nods and gestures toward a place far away.

The day finally came when my suitcase was packed with enough labeled clothing to last until Thanksgiving. Mama made beautiful clothes. The Hoffpauirs may have been poor, but we dressed real well. Everyone said so. This was thanks to the stitchery of my mama. I was slipped into a special dress, and Mama and Daddy put on their best clothes, too. Then we all went off in the car together.

In those days, once students arrived at the school we were supposed to stay there. Entry papers specified that "pupils did better" if we stayed at the school except for designated holidays: Thanksgiving, Christmas, and Easter. This may have been one of those rules dating back to the days of the flatboat. There was no interstate and my home was four hours away through swamps. However, I felt that the rule came from habit as much as transportation and that perhaps the citizens of Louisiana didn't want their deaf children roaming loose among them. At the Louisiana School, the rule was most honored in its breach. Some children, especially the little ones, went home almost every weekend. I was among them, at least in the beginning.

Hearing friends tell me that they have distinct memories of their first day of school. Some of them remember the clothes they wore, the parents who followed them with movie cameras, the lay-out of the classrooms, and even the scent of the teachers. Few of my deaf friends claim to have memories like this, though our first school day marked an even sharper watershed in our lives. Vague scenes rise up, but almost all of them come from something I read or something someone told me, considerably after that first momentous day.

Most students arrived by car in the 1950s. We converged in front of the administration building, in an annual ritual. Parents filled out the necessary papers, with their small charges at their sides or in their arms. Eventually the children drifted over to the play yard, where the older kids met their friends and new arrivals like myself looked for ways to be absorbed into the merriment. On the outskirts of the play area, houseparents and administrators stood, watched, and chatted awkwardly.

Most of the children who would become my schoolmates and lifelong friends were there that day. Thelma Scanlan surely was there, probably already laughing and joking with her best friend, Gale. Undoubtedly Thelma and Gale were surrounded by a cadre of girls and watched by another cadre of boys. Thelma's birthday would be in just a few days and perhaps she already suspected her parents were planning to send her a birthday cake. She would have to share it with the rest of us of course, but Thelma never minded sharing.

Yellow-haired Cleve Cormier and James Clement, who would become our school's football stars, were surely there. So was Dale Breaux, already handsome and outgoing—I later found out that he was my cousin. Norris Kraemer, friendly and stocky, who I would date in high school and who would marry my best friend's sister, was probably there. And so was gentle, shy Pat Harsh, who was two years older than I was. So, surely, were my classmates Johnny Fruge, Bill Broussard, Bobbie Clark, and Sharon Foster.

Jeanette Fruge, who would become my best friend, wasn't there. Jeanette was hard of hearing, and her parents made her suffer through eleven years of private school before they realized that she couldn't hear enough to understand her teachers. David Oglethorpe, who married her, wasn't there either. David's mother would bring him to class a few days later.

Our parents slipped away slowly, a few at a time, returning to their vehicles with only each other and any stray siblings for the long ride home. My parents had less far to drive than many of them. But leaving me was still hard. When I glanced up, I saw them standing together on the outskirts of the playground, their eyes riveted on me as if I might any moment disappear. My mother looked fragile. Daddy had his arm around her waist as if he were afraid she would fall.

I waved at them cheerfully, but I was a little puzzled. The other parents had left. Why were mine still there? I turned back to my new friends, but for some reason the silhouettes against the sky troubled me. I looked up again and waved. It was okay, my wave said. They could leave now too.

As it turned out it was a tearful good-bye, a tearful beginning. Daddy said Mama cried the whole way back to Rayne. Nana told me Daddy cried, too. I am told all of us cried during the first weeks of school.

Sarah Val, then Sarah Stiffler, who became a teacher at the Model Secondary School for the Deaf, remembers lots of tears. Sarah entered the Western Pennsylvania School at age eleven after she became deaf from meningitis. She remembers children who played happily in the school yard without her, while she cried alone at the edge of the field. It wasn't until much later that she realized that she'd mistaken the sign for *refuse,* which entails a sharp motion of the thumb over the shoulder, for a point in her direction. She'd thought the other girls were making fun of her.

Then there was Vic Galloway who earned his doctoral degree at the University of Arizona and then administered programs around the country before he continued his career with the federal government. Vic remembers that he read *shoes* on his grandmother's lips when she was trying to tell him he was going to *school*, so he hopped in the car expecting to purchase footwear. After an all-day drive, the car stopped at a strange building: the South Carolina School for the Deaf. Vic and his suitcase were deposited on the pavement and a white-haired stranger restrained him as he rushed, terrified, toward the car while his family drove away.

Almost all the parents rushed away from the school. They were told to. "The sooner you leave, the better," the school officials often told them. Perhaps the parents, as they parted brusquely with their children, were as scared as their offspring.

Anna Gremillion said I cried too, though I have no memory of it. Anna, a graduate of the school for deaf students in New Jersey, taught physical education. She had come to the Louisiana School soon after the war, driving from New Orleans to Baton Rouge, winding through dense swamp where Spanish moss hung so thick that sometimes she couldn't see daylight. When she finally arrived, she cried for days. But somehow she grew fond of the place and made it her home. Perhaps this was partly because of Harvey Gremillion, the social studies and history teacher at the school, who became her husband. Harvey had deep roots in Louisiana. He was Creole, not Cajun, he explained to her, though Anna, like most Northerners and all of us students, never paid any mind about the difference between the Creoles—urban descendants of European nobles—and their rural Cajun cousins. Both Anna and Harvey were deaf, and they became two of my favorite teachers.

"You didn't cry much," Anna told me later. "Only for three days."

Three days? I don't remember crying at all. I don't even remember feeling sad. I remember feeling only intense curiosity and joy. I remember a sense of belonging, too. But this could be the present coloring the past.

My classmate, Helen Dubois seems to remember her first days at the school. Helen was hard of hearing. Her parents came from

Poland and spoke Polish at home. Helen remembers driving with her father all day to get to the school and finding herself alone in a large day room. Another girl was in the dayroom, and the girl pointed to the ceiling where a spider watched the proceedings from its web in the corner.

"You eat spiders," the girl teased.

Helen stared at the girl in something like horror. She knew no sign language, but she looked up, saw the spider, and made sense of what the girl was saying. Still she was unsure of the girl's intentions. Did the girl mean, "You eat spiders" or "You *will* eat spiders"? Was she making some kind of statement or asking a question? Was she suspecting Helen of crass dietary habits? Was she making a prediction? Was it a threat?

Helen shivered. That night she had her first nightmare about spiders and woke up screaming. Spiders are ubiquitous in Louisiana, and their bodies can grow as big as a man's fist. Awake, Helen would run from them, but then they would turn around and chase her in her sleep. After years of being plagued by nightmares about spiders, she finally stopped running away. She killed one and was surprised by how easy it was.

"After that, my nightmares stopped," she said.

I suppose if I could have heard, I would have known that screams and sobs echoed through the dorm those first nights.

❦

Like all the kids, I got a name in sign language. The teachers, all of them hearing, distributed them. Name signs, so important to us, were fashioned primarily as a matter of logistics. The teachers needed a way to refer to each of us, and they knew that the shape of spoken names on lips was problematic at best. Usually they named us with the initial of our first name as represented by a letter handshape placed in a specific position of the body. THELMA was a *T* handshape touched twice against the breastbone. PAT was a *P* handshape touched against the back of the hand. DAVID was a *D* handshape touched on either side of the chin. For my name, they placed a *C* handshape in the palm of the opposite hand. Probably they chose this location because Carolyns, Cindys, and Cathys who had arrived before me had gotten all the best locations.

Carolyn McCaskill, a friend of mine who went to the Alabama School for the Deaf and later taught Deaf Studies at Gallaudet University, had a *C* handshape on the hip as her name sign. Carolyn didn't like the sign, but couldn't get rid of it. It followed her right through college and into her adult life. People said she earned her sign name because she was pretty and walked sexy, swinging her hips. But they were wrong; that wasn't why it was on the hip. The hip was just the last remaining area of the body on which her less-than-imaginative teachers could stake out a popular initial.

When she arrived, Jeanette was assigned an *F* at the breastbone for her last name, Fruge. When she married and became Mrs. Jeanette Oglethorpe, she found her name sign an irritant. A relic of a name she no longer used, it reflected nothing of her current situation or identity.

Despite all the tears, I remember my initiation to the residential school as gentle. With the other children, I moved from one activity to the next, falling into line as we marched from playground to cafeteria to day room to classroom to dorm. Through the elementary grades, we were never alone; we lived and studied as a group.

The elementary girls' dorm was a large room where eight beds lined each wall. Our houseparent was Mary Frances, a deaf woman from out of state who only worked at the school for a year. The older girls had more private cubicles in the H-shaped dorm on the other side of the courtyard.

During one of those first nights, I lay awake in the darkness, wide-eyed and hungry for new experiences, and too excited to sleep. I took comfort from all the bodies around me. Whatever happened, I clearly wasn't alone. Suddenly, lying there watching the shadows of my dorm mates in the adjacent beds, I was conscious of a familiar nighttime sensation. I had to pee.

The bathroom was past three beds and across the hall, just beyond the room where Mary Frances slept. It might as well have been in Texas. I didn't even think about trying to go there. I watched the restless shadows and waited for morning. It was no use. My bladder was as insistent in the dorm as it had been back home. With no Brother to turn to, and no Nana either, I wet the bed. Then I curled up in a dry corner of the mattress and fell asleep.

The next morning all proceeded calmly until Mary Frances spotted the ugly stain on my sheets. Her reaction was instantaneous. I didn't know the signs of course, not even the *C*-in-the-palm that designated my own name, but that didn't matter. No one in the world is better at communication than the deaf dorm staff of deaf residential schools. You bring someone from Mars onto their floor, and those deaf dorm people will apprise the Martian fully of all the do's and don'ts of living in the dorm. Mary Frances was no exception.

My scolding was delivered in elaborate and outraged gesture. First, I was pushed toward the stain from which a none-too-pleasant smell arose. I tried to turn away, but Mary Frances caught me with her eyes and locked me resolutely in place with her glare. Signs followed in rapid succession. DON'T . . . WRONG . . . BAD . . . NO WAY. Then I was led to the lavatory as if I had never seen it before, passing my classmates and roommates in solitary ignominy.

Mary Frances positioned me uncomfortably near the toilet and resumed her gestures and signs. TOILET . . . THERE . . . THAT'S THE PLACE. Then in increased humiliation, I was paraded back to my bed, just in case I'd managed to forget what was still there. The same gesture sign combination flowed again. Then it was back to the toilet, then back to the bed, where I was instructed to pull off the dirty sheets and put them in the chute.

By the end I was too scared to be embarrassed. I simply knew if it happened again, my fate would be worse than the stuff that went into the toilet.

The next night I crawled into bed resolved to go to sleep quickly. It was no use. After only a few minutes, the same urge returned. I lay on my back willing the sun to rise or the urge to subsist. But it was no good. Inexplicably, implacably, I had to pee.

Two terrors confronted me—the darkness and Mary Frances. I chose the least terrible. Sliding out of the bed in the dark, I pressed the arm of the girl in the bed next to mine. She jumped at my touch. Frantically I gestured toward the bathroom and made my first signs: "I have to go to the toilet." In a frenzy of nerves and fear, I waited for her to crawl out of bed and join me.

She held my hand and I held hers, and we made our way past our sleeping classmates, across the room to the lavatory. It was pitch-black in the stall and I hurried, so afraid she would leave. She didn't. She was still there trembling as I finished, and we scurried to the safety of our beds and scrambled between the stiff sheets. I closed my eyes and was asleep. She could have been my friend for life. And maybe she has been. I don't remember who she was.

❧

Life attained a pattern. Every morning we got up at six. We made our beds and lined up to brush our teeth and wash our faces. We each had a towel. They were tiny, but clean. And they were exclusively our own. So was the toothbrush. It was more than some of us had back home.

The older girls departed first. They had chores in the kitchen, cleaning and setting up the tables for breakfast. Elementary girls and boys would line up inside their respective dorms and march the short distance to the cafeteria in single-file lines. We ate family style, sitting at tables that accommodated six to eight children, with an older girl at the head. The older girl cut our food, helped us serve ourselves, and generally functioned as a model for our behavior. The fare wasn't great, but it was reliable. Brother said once that he aspired to make sure that his sisters had milk every day. Here at the school we drank milk at every meal. We had meat almost every day, too. Some Sundays, we even had fried chicken.

Classes began promptly at 8:15. We didn't have kindergarten, but I moved rapidly through three levels of pre-first grade. I attribute this to the bit of learning I'd picked up from those labels back at my home. I didn't know any grammar, of course. But I knew that letters made words, that everything had its own special word, and that this was its name. I intuited that somehow stringing words together, one after another, was critical.

Only a few children knew more than I did. These were the children who had lost their hearing after they learned to talk and children who had deaf parents. We all looked up to those children of deaf parents. They were ahead of us for one thing, amazingly able to understand each other and our teachers, rooted to and through each other in ways that the rest of us were just beginning to understand. Their world was larger than the school. And richer. Those deaf children had grown up with language, while most of the rest of us had gotten along with our points and expressive faces. Though none were in my grade, at least two families of children in our school had deaf parents. One of those families had two girls in the class ahead of me, and a younger daughter would follow behind me. Then there was a family with five kids throughout the grades.

Throughout all my years at the school, laundry was done for us, a dubious luxury that saved us some manual labor but resulted in underwear of various shades of gray, and color bleached out of every piece of clothing that was supposed to have it. All of us had labels with our names sewn into our clothing. This requirement was so strict that for years afterward, we would joke about it. When friends got together, we would pretend to forget each other's name and peer at the back of the other's collar as if to check. I remember one friend who added a twist. "You are Sears, now," he laughed, pretending to confuse the store label with the one that held the former student's name. While we were young, labels, like everything else, were handled with great seriousness.

We didn't take classes to learn sign language. I picked it up naturally, the way hearing kids pick up speech. Despite official emphasis on speech and lipreading, all of us signed. Signing was as natural as breathing, and we were just as unaware of it. We had little recognition of what we were doing. At Gallaudet, researchers were just beginning studies that would lead to the linguistic acceptance of signs, and most of our teachers were tempted to belittle what they couldn't understand. We had very few deaf teachers, and none in the elementary department. Some of the hearing teachers signed so badly we couldn't understand them. One English teacher, Adie Gill, the wife of the head of the nearby blind school, always wore a flower behind her ear and spread the sweetest smell from her class-room through the hallway—and managed to communicate just fine without using signs. I'm the first to admit that communication is a miracle; still, just exactly how Mrs. Gill managed this, I've no idea.

Students, like Helen, who had some hearing were put into spe-cial classes where they clapped on headphones, practiced speech, and tried to glean most of their education without signs. To this day, this seems bizarre to me. Outside the classroom, Helen was deaf like everyone else.

Mrs. Strieby was my first-grade teacher. She sat before us with her chalk and blackboard. We watched her earnestly and even fear-fully. I remember always being a little bit scared. More than once her hands clasped my shoulder and led me to stand in the corner. I don't remember what I did that warranted this. I remember only my impotence and fury, and the smacks that came from nowhere when I tried to steal a glance back into the classroom.

The worst punishments occurred in the dorm. I received my share of these too, especially in the first few weeks. If displeased, the dorm staff told you to place your hands and feet on the ground and keep your body aloft. You would stay in this position until you ached. I forget precisely what I did that merited this, but I remem-ber the pain in my arms and legs.

Used to being a free agent, I faced the new situation like a little warrior. I would master these rules and live within them. Like most students, I saw the mismatch of power and conformed as best I could to the new lay of the land. My outbursts were few.

Lunch was at 12:05. When class was over at noon, we had five minutes to line up, boys in one line, girls in the other, and walk to the dining hall. We ate in separate rooms, girls in one dining hall, boys in the other. Our feet weren't even touching the floor as we sat in our child-sized chairs, but already we stole looks in each other's direction, and explored the communication possible in glances and gestures. Already we were figuring out how to make such commu-nication invisible to the adults that surrounded us.

At 1:00 we lined up to march back to our building. Classes resumed at 1:05. Physical education was scheduled for 2:25, the last class of the day. The younger students had free play at 3:30, and the older students were free at 4:00. At 4:30, the kitchen and dining room crews reported to help prepare and serve our meal. Dinner was at 5:30 and study hall was 6:30 to 7:30. We studied like we did everything else—boys and girls in separate rooms.

Back in the dorm, we selected our clothes for the following day and folded our selected blouses and skirts neatly over the chairs by the beds. Prayers followed, and then it was lights out. The older girls got to stay up until 9:00, but we were in bed by 7:30. Throughout the night Mary Frances or another supervisor checked on us. The literature says that they made their rounds hourly and I believe it. The only times we tried to have night conversations in the bathroom, we were promptly caught and sent back to bed. Once we hung sheets from the ceilings in an attempt to insulate the walls and muffle any sound of our meeting. To no avail. We were caught and sent unceremoniously back to our beds. Little subterfuge was possible, and at least in elementary school, almost none attempted.

The school literature says that mail call was at 10:15 A.M., but I remember getting letters at the end of the day. If a letter arrived, the day sparkled in retrospect; if not, its cast was gloomy. When I was too little to read, Mary Frances read my letters to me. Mama wrote to me often—almost every day in the beginning. Mostly her letters asked how I was. Mama could ask how I was so many times and in so many different ways that she would fill a whole page, and a whole page constituted enough writing to warrant a stamp. Thelma had glorious mail calls. Invariably the packages that arrived for her contained at least one tin of candy, cookies, or some kind of treat. Thelma was generous, and we all tried to be standing somewhere in her vicinity when it was time to pick up the mail.

Each day of the week had its special designation. Wednesday was for club meetings. Friday was movie night, with the script rendered into on-screen captions by the federal government. Saturday was for forays downtown. Boys and girls took turns making their expeditions on alternating weeks. Sunday was church, and we lined up again, girls in one line, boys in another, to proceed on foot. We had a choice of churches: Catholic or Baptist.

A few days after I started school, an older girl showed up in my dorm room. It was a Friday, and the other kids were getting ready for one of the captioned films. Mary Frances made it clear that I would not stay for the film, but go with this older girl. Although I had never seen her before, I held her hand as we walked outside the school grounds. We talked only a little. I had just begun to learn signs and was a little intimidated to be the single charge of someone who seemed far older and wiser than I could ever aspire to be.

The girl took me to the bus station. She led me on board, and I watched as she paid. We took our seats as the bus rolled out of the station, through the city, and into the countryside. The road wound on for what seemed like forever. When the bus finally stopped, Aunt Happy, Mama, and Brother were standing outside the window. I was back in Rayne, and everyone was happy to see us. Mama gave us both a big hug.

The older girl was my cousin Velma Savoy. She came to my dorm several times during my first months at school to take me home. I quickly grew weary of the journey. I didn't like the long bus ride, I didn't like leaving school, and most of all, I didn't like being back home. After only a few weeks, I wanted to be where I could communicate, where I had friends and connections beyond those that suffice for dogs. The school was my home now. The other students and teachers had become a kind of family. I was a seasoned student.

"I don't want to go home," I told Mary Frances.

"Please, let's not go home," I begged Velma.

At first I thought Velma had problems understanding me because of my inexpert signing, but slowly I came to realize that sometimes she couldn't see my signs. By trial and error, I learned to hold my hands quite close to my face to communicate with her. If my signs were too large or they moved outside out of this circumscribed space, she couldn't understand me. When I fingerspelled, she would sometimes take my hand and steady it before her eyes. Once when we arrived together in Rayne, she crashed into the trash can at the bus station. I guess it made a racket because all the hearing people turned to look at us. Velma just kept on walking as if she hadn't even noticed.

"Tunnel vision," the other students told me. Velma had tunnel vision and so did some of the other students at the Louisiana School.

"You don't have to go home again until Thanksgiving," Velma told me one day as the bus began its winding course through the streets of Rayne and back to Baton Rouge.

I smiled up at her.

"Better to stay at the school," I said.

She nodded.

I hadn't realized how much communication had changed me until several weeks into the term, when a new boy entered our classroom. David Oglethorpe was from Monroe, a town in the north of Louisiana that is even tinier than Rayne, and he was hard of hearing. His mother had sent him to school in nearby Columbia, but David's hearing was just bad enough to keep him shut out of the conversation that transpired in public school. He might as well have been totally deaf. At eight years old, he spoke only the simplest words and didn't know his alphabet, let alone how to read.

When his mother had become ill and was hospitalized, his grandmother packed him up and the two of them traveled to Baton Rouge on the bus with the intention of finding the Louisiana School. They walked together from the bus station and someone led them to the principal's office. Mr. Huff brought them directly to Mrs. Strieby's classroom. It must have been during one of my rare speech classes because we were seated in a semicircle, earphones around our heads, listening and speaking as best we could.

Unprepared for his journey and innocent of its purpose, David stood at his grandmother's side having no more idea about what was going on than the chalk did. When his grandmother turned and left, he ran after her. Finding the door locked, David kicked it in fear and fury. Mrs. Strieby rushed to restrain him, and he turned and kicked her, too. He didn't stop there, but crashed about the classroom like a mini tornado. All about him books and papers went flying. On the wall hung drawings that we had produced the day before. Before Mrs. Strieby could stop him, David reached up and tore them off the wall one by one, crumpled each, and dashed it to the floor. Mine was the last to go.

It was a few minutes before Mrs. Strieby forced David to sit in his chair and restored order to the classroom. Even in his seat, David couldn't be still. He wriggled and cried.

Looking at my crumpled paper on the floor, I wanted to cry too. I didn't. I put my eyes back to Mrs. Strieby. Her eyes remained hard on David.

"Don't you dare get up," Mrs. Strieby said with her eyes. "You sit right there."

After a few minutes, she returned to the lesson. I stole a look at David. His eyes flitted about the room as if he were looking for an escape route. I remembered the old woman who had dashed from the room. I was sure she hadn't wanted to leave. The woman had gray hair, but she had the same haunted face and stricken eyes that I'd seen when my mother left me at the school, and she looked like she wanted to cry.

Yes, she was like my mother, at least in her grief. I looked over at the squirming angry boy. And I had been just like David.

5

❦

$\mathcal{H}$ome and School:
Ever the Twain

And nothing I cared at my sky blue trades
that time allows, in all its tuneful turning, so few
and such summer songs.

—DYLAN THOMAS, "FERN HILL"

"Look!"

Thelma was sitting in the grass holding a bee on her bare knee. I watched the stinger extend and penetrate her skin.

Gale was sitting next to her. She grabbed a bee and placed it on her arm. We watched again as it stung her.

I looked at Pat. She shook her head. She wanted none of this foolishness.

"What for?" she asked.

But then her own hands slid along a flower and closed over a bee. We watched her as she encapsulated the living bee between her palms and raised her hands skyward.

"Feel it?" Thelma asked.

Pat's face made all sorts of motions, one of which was a nod.

I nodded back, my face mirroring hers. The bee must really be exploring the territory in the dark of her closed hands. Pat raised her hands over her head, opened her hands, and the bee sped free, rising and disappearing in the air above us. Relief spread over all of our faces.

Then they looked at me.

I reached out and caught a bee, too. It buzzed around inside my hands before I placed it on my wrist. Out came the stinger, and I felt a prick.

"Ouch!"

It was quick. A little raised flesh and redness.

Thelma had another bee. Gale and a few other girls trolled along the edge of the bushes looking for bees. Pat watched as I went searching for another one, too.

Catching the bees and letting them sting us was just one of the games we invented. White flowers grew in the wild area near the fence. We picked their stiff petals and found they made handy toothpicks. More than pedagogy, more than methodology, more even than the books that came and went in our classrooms, these events are the ones that seem most precious.

For teachers, administrators, and I suppose taxpayers, schools focus around classes. Even for students, academics—reading, writing, and arithmetic—are the structural center of the day. Still that center is a tiny spot, only six hours of any given twenty-four. In some ways, especially in the beginning, our lives surrounded our classes without having much relationship to them. Just as for our hearing counterparts, class was just one long event in the course of the day.

The focus of deaf education, especially in the first grades, has never wavered. The goal is to get us to understand and be able to use the spoken language of our parents at least in its printed form. Thus in class my classmates and I worked on English, which we approached primarily through the mysteries of the Fitzgerald Key, a system invented years before by a deaf teacher to help deaf students write. Edith Fitzgerald was valedictorian at Gallaudet College in 1903 and taught before she became the principal of the Virginia

School for the Deaf. At the Virginia School, she developed and promulgated use of what became known as a "Key," which specified that students be taught to write subject, verb, object, and finally an adjectival phrase, in a linear march across the page that would result in grammatically correct sentences. The Key meant construing sentences through this structural understanding. This may have been like trying to create a tree from the appropriate placement of various-sized pieces of wood, and of course a person could cobble or whittle wood into whatever they chose, but they'd never get an oak. At about the same time I was wrestling with the Key, Noam Chomsky was publishing work that would change our understanding of learning language and of teaching grammar, and would help consign the Key to the dustbin reserved for educational approaches that were supposed to work and didn't.

But I liked the Key; it helped me. I had no idea how to arrange this language that hearing people sent forth into the air around me, and the Key gave me clues about which words to put where. I don't know exactly why I felt it worked. Perhaps it was the modeling, usually done by the teacher at the blackboard, that use of the Key entailed. Seeing these sentences scrawled out in consistent patterns helped me understand a system that was as new and difficult as any I would face. The teacher stood by the board or bent over me at my desk and told me, "Now you need the action word." There was a lot more to it, of course, but that would come later.

Language, Chomsky and later Stephen Pinker and others would go on to say, is a kind of human birthright. People develop language almost like ducks develop webbed feet. Ability to learn and use it is practically programmed right into our genes. For most of the world, of course, language is spoken. This singular fact seems to account for the fact that right up until the 1980s, in most texts language was equated with speech.

So the kids who were hard of hearing worked on pronunciation, and I tried to decode sentences with my Key, and the educators looked at the words we were able to generate with our mouths or our pens and despaired. Our understanding appeared so feeble. What they didn't see was that we were developing language just fine. It was signed, not spoken, and it blossomed as we got along and grew up together in the school. The intent of the school was fulfilled, and the teachers had no idea.

Here is an article, probably heavily edited, that I had published in *The Pelican,* the school newspaper. It was April of 1958, so I must have been nine years old.

> We jumped the rope yesterday afternoon. Thelma won. She jumped 447 times. She was not tired. I was surprised. I asked her if her side hurt. She said that it did not. I jumped 33 times without missing. When I was a little girl, I jumped 500 times. My side hurt. We had a good time jumping rope.

As we grew older, the center of our lives shifted from school to each other. We cavorted. We had fun. We yanked more laughter out of our school day than people looking through the iron fence from outside could ever imagine.

❧

The first time I saw Jeanette Fruge, she was talking with the supervisor, using her voice and chatting away nervously. She was looking at the floor, not at the supervisor's face, and moving her mouth just as if she were a hearing girl. I was with Sharon and we were taken aback. Who was this new student? Why did she act so hearing?

When the supervisor left, we approached her. This was our turf, and we wanted her to know it. I can't remember what we said, only that we teased her. I don't remember the teasing as hostile, but Jeanette said we were mocking her and she felt humiliated.

She was hurt, I could see. Probably lost and scared, too. Her mother was gone, instructed, as all our parents had been, to leave "the sooner the better." When she saw her little sister in the cafeteria, they hugged each other and cried. She cried in the dorm too. In fact, she cried every night for three weeks.

I felt ashamed of teasing her. Talking may be a neat trick, but it does a student no good in the dorm of a deaf school. My heart went out to this shy new girl who could talk but couldn't hear. We asked her if she wanted to come with us to the captioned movie. It took a few minutes and the help of the dorm supervisor to get her to understand, but she nodded her head, and when Sharon and I ventured off, she followed.

Because of her private school education, her little bit of hearing, and her very good speech, the school officials initially placed Jeanette ahead of her grade level. She stared at the work in horror. She couldn't do any of it. They moved her into the next younger class, and then the next. Finally she was in my class as well as in my dorm. Me, Sharon, and Jeanette became a trio. Sharon and I got along tumultuously—sometimes arguing, competing, disagreeing. Not so Jeanette and I, we stayed fast friends.

Because of Jeanette, I picked up a way of signing that was different from that of many of my classmates. Used to trying to cope with hearing people, Jeanette initially matched her signs with spoken English, the only communication system she knew. I brought my lips into my sign language to facilitate communication with her, mouthing the English words that matched my signs.

Our deaf teachers who had attended Gallaudet signed this way too. Mr. Corbett, Mr. Freeman, Mr. Ray, and even Mr. Gremillion sometimes moved their mouths when they signed, as if speech were coming through their mouths at the same time signs flowed through their fingers. So signing with Jeanette had helpful ramifications. I would use this method of signing with people who were learning sign language, and when communicating at the same time with people who could and people who could not sign. I would use it with teachers, and I would use it with bosses. It was a helpful addition to my signing skills, all because of Jeanette and my desire to talk with her.

✣

David Oglethorpe saw Jeanette before I did. She hadn't entered the program yet, and was touring the Louisiana School with her mother and younger deaf sister. David was sitting next to John Fruge, who was Jeanette's cousin, though he didn't know it when he saw the family enter the classroom. David gave John a quick poke at the sight of Jeanette.

"She's mine," he signed swiftly, so the teacher would not see. "I'm going to marry her."

Jeanette was my best friend, and I wasn't pleased to see David Oglethorpe chasing her around. I was even less pleased that she enjoyed it.

❧

Our school camaraderie spread to our parents. My mother learned that Helen's family had financial problems, and some of our money and her time went to sewing Helen a new skirt. Probably made from scraps like most of our clothing, it had successive colors of material fanning out from the waist to the hemline. Helen was ecstatic. I was jealous, and I didn't hesitate to let my mother know. Next time, she made a smaller article of clothing for me to take to Helen and made sure I got one for myself.

My mother aspired to keep me connected to deaf friends, and the other deaf people who lived in and around Rayne. I remember Brother made Geraldine Thibodeaux and me some wooden stilts, and the two of us spent a summer trying to learn to walk with them. And James Guidry, who we all called Jimmy, became one of my best friends. Jimmy and I learned that we lived near each other when we rode the bus back from school. We each got off the bus, only to find ourselves face-to-face at the bus stop. Jimmy lived on a 300-acre farm where his great-aunt raised crawfish, cotton, and rice. He had five brothers and two sisters. He was the only one in the whole family who was deaf. Jimmy was shy and cute and loved movies. After that first astonished greeting, we were instant friends. We'd meet at the movies on weekends, and if I didn't show up, Jimmy would walk to my house to find me. Sometimes he would walk to my house even when he didn't go to the movies.

Then there was Alpha and his brothers and sisters. Alpha came from a family of ten children, half of whom were deaf and blind. His parents, like my daddy, had hesitated in sending their children

away to school, and as a result, Alpha's older siblings had little education. Alpha went to the Louisiana School though. And sometimes Jimmy, Alpha, and myself got together during vacation days.

Alpha had tunnel vision too, so I signed to him like I signed to
Velma, directly in front of his eyes. But his poor sight didn't stop him
from walking the few blocks between our homes and making his way
to my house. There he would jump up and down on the stoop until
someone opened the door. He jumped so hard that if Nana and Mama
weren't home, I would feel the floorboards tremble and let him in.

Then there was Lenora Heinen. She and her husband Charles
were both deaf, and they lived in Branch, a town even smaller than
Rayne just across Interstate 10. I met Lenora one Saturday in
August, when deaf people descended on Baton Rouge for our
annual picnic. It was a spontaneous gathering, as far as I know,
without official sponsor or organization. Everyone knew about it,
and everyone came. We gathered in a park by the lake and it was
there that I met Lenora. I was a small girl, but I had heard of her
long before that. Tall and gracious, she had been the first woman
president of the deaf club in Baton Rouge. At the picnic, I had gone
up to adult after adult, fingerspelling her name.

"Do you know L-E-N-O-R-A?" I asked one person after another.

Everyone knew her. They assured me that she would be there
soon. Finally one of the women I approached nodded.

"Lenora?" she responded, using her name sign: an *L* handshape
on the back of the opposite hand. "That's me."

After that, if there were a deaf community event, at church or
club or school, Lenora was going—and taking me along with her.

All of my friends, especially Jimmy and Alpha, loved Mama.
They could read her awkward fingerspelling, and they appreciated
that she took the time to use it. Sometimes Mama gave Jimmy a
ride home from the station, and several times she drove him to
school. Daddy overwhelmed Jimmy. Once, my father arrived to
pick me up, all in a rush with his taxi waiting outside the bus station. He grabbed my suitcase with one hand and told me with the
other how he had come instead of Mama because she was busy with
Grandpa. Jimmy stared at us in amazement.

"What was that?" Jimmy asked after my father disappeared into the taxi. His signs were curious and careful. He didn't want to offend me.

I knew exactly what he meant. While Mama and Nana had learned some true fingerspelling, Daddy maintained his singular system, tracing Roman letters through the air at me with a solitary finger.

"That's my daddy's sign language," I told him.

"It's backwards!" he noted.

I thought for a moment, then I knew he was right. Not only did my daddy maintain his allegiance to Latin letters, but he lined them up in space in the opposite way of American Sign Language.

I nodded and grinned.

"Backwards fingerspelling," I said.

"I understood nothing!" he exclaimed, and we both laughed.

I understood my daddy fine. He had been telling me about Grandpa. After I climbed into the taxi next to him, he continued the saga. My grandpa had lived in the little house in back of our home. First he couldn't find the keys. Then he couldn't remember where he lived. Now he was really sick. Daddy said now that he wasn't sure of his name, and he didn't want to wear clothes anymore.

"No clothes?" I spoke and gestured. Both at school and at home, a naked human body was scandalous.

"Walked down the street naked," Daddy said, all matter of fact. *"Mrs. Richard had to call your mama to go get him."*

Even with her children almost all grown up, Mrs. Richard took it as her mission to keep an eye on the neighborhood.

When we got home, I was surprised at how thin Grandpa had become. His chin had a little straggly beard. He was restless, and his eyes looked constantly angry. Worst of all, he stared at me like I was a stranger.

When I walked into the house, he moved his mouth like he was trying to either talk or chew a big wad of gum.

"Did he say something?" I signed to Nana.

"Yeah," said Nana. "But I don't know what. He didn't make any sense."

With that, she took me around back and opened the door to Grandpa's house. I gasped at its transition. Daddy had nailed plywood sides to Grandpa's bed and spread chicken wire across the top. On each side were restraints for Grandpa's arms and legs.

"It's a cage," I said.

"That's where he sleeps," Nana explained.

First it was where he slept. Then it was where he lived. It was our job to bring him food, drink, and sometimes help him eat and drink. As he grew sicker and angrier, Grandpa spent more and more time lying in the bed, his arms and legs tied down, his naked feet hanging out over the mattress.

Sometimes when no adults were watching, I would creep over, Nana at my side. I would stretch out my forefinger and tickle his feet with the tip of my fingernail. Oh, he would be so mad. He would thrash and holler. But he was tied up and couldn't get loose. I would giggle, knowing we were safe from his wrath. Nana would look excited and scared. Mama would invariably sense something was up and come running. She would shake her head at the both of us and make us leave.

And we would leave, until we got bored, when we sneaked back to do it again.

Sometimes Grandpa got loose, and Mama or one of her sisters would have to go chase him. They could almost always persuade him to return home with them. Other relatives came to help, too. The shadow he cast over our house was a weak one. He was too old and frail to cause any real problems.

※

I began teaching Nana signs. My little sister was my only playmate and, when she wasn't fussing at me, my adoring acolyte. She had toddled after me ever since we were little.

"Sit here," I told her.

She understood and watched me expectantly.

"A," I told her with my lips and shaped the letter with my hand. "Now you do it."

She held her hand up eagerly, a perfect *A* formed with her tiny fist. I nodded.

"B," I continued, again forming the letter with both my lips and my hand.

For some reason that was a harder handshape for her. I reached over and took her hand in mine and molded it for her into the proper shape.

Poor Nana. She was in no mood for a lesson, especially one that didn't seem to have any point. She wiggled around and tried to get up.

"No!" My rebuke was sharp, using my voice as well as my lips and hands.

Nana sat back down, both scared of me and willing to help.

Children younger than four are supposed to be geniuses at learning languages—and this was sure true of Nana. Before long, she knew all her letters. By the time she was eight she would meet my eyes and interpret without me even asking. She picked up some Cajun French, too, though Daddy and Mama swore they never used it with her. It wasn't without reason that everyone loved Nana.

❧

Mama was looking worriedly over where the chickens scratched near the barn. I had followed her outside in boredom. Watching Mama's face, I immediately knew what was wrong: Mama hated killing chickens.

I waved to her to get her to look at me. Startled, she turned around.

"I'll do it," I mouthed at her, pointing toward the chickens.

She didn't understand at first.

"Me," I repeated, pointing dramatically at my own chest. *"I'll do it."*

She looked puzzled for a moment, then shook her head. The sadness returned to her face just like it always did when Daddy wasn't there to do the killing. Her jaw thrust out a bit, and she clenched her teeth real hard. My father was at the mill or he would have done it, and Brother was nowhere in sight. So the work was left to my mother—and she didn't even like cleaning fish.

I waved at her again.

"I'll do it," I insisted, when she finally turned and looked at me again. *"Which one?"*

Mama coughed and turned back to the hens, fixing her eyes on what was soon to become our dinner. Wearily, she pointed to the old orange hen nearest the barn.

I shooed the birds away as I walked towards the hen. The rooster, angry and arrogant, watched me warily, but I wasn't afraid of him anymore. I glanced at him briefly, made some strong noises, and waved my hands. He wouldn't move away, but he wouldn't advance either. Throughout the whole ordeal, he just eyed me from his spot on the fence.

Long past laying, that hen had never been my favorite. I was happy to help my mother in dispatching this old chick to a well-deserved resting plate. At the last minute, the chicken tried to flee, but I was too quick. I grabbed her neck with both hands, held tight, and lifted. That old bird struggled mightily. Her wings flapped crazily, her beak and claws coming toward my eyes. I tried not to be scared. Daddy usually held the birds with a single hand and twirled them off to the side like Charlie Chaplin with his walking stick, but the chicken was too heavy for me to manage this. I managed to swing it though, making ever-increasing circles in the air. My daddy just stood in one place, but I found I had to move about the yard just to keep from falling. I got into a rhythm when I swung it over my head.

I remember my mother in the doorway and Nana inching toward her, eyes big and wide as if she were scared of something. I remember Aunt Happy looking at me through the window and Grandpa's head next to hers staring straight down at the floor. But mostly I remember concentrating on copying my daddy, swinging and swinging that bird, its neck vibrating and its orange feathers flying. When I felt something go loose in my hand, I knew I was done.

The hen hung still, limp as a wet towel.

I smiled and turned proudly to my mother. Her eyes moved to the sheets hanging in the yard. Her lips moved.

"Oh, no," she said.

It took a moment for her to reach out and take the dead chicken. Then she snatched it from my hands like it was some kind of poison toad. She did give me one of her quick pats though, before disappearing back into the house.

Nana, using the signs I had taught her, showed me what was wrong.

"They need to be washed," said Nana. She pointed to the clothesline.

I looked and saw that in its death throes, the chicken had emptied its bowels, and the excrement had flown across the yard and landed on Mama's newly washed sheets. With a sigh, I walked over to get the dirty sheets.

❧

One day, Mama saw me teaching Nana signs and came over to learn, too. Her attitude was so much better than Nana's, but her fingers were so much worse. She copied the shapes of my hand slowly, achieving only approximations of the letters. *R,* with its crossed pointer and middle finger, proved a downright impossibility. Like the other letters, *R* rises from the hand like printed letters rise from lines on a page, with the wrist held almost perpendicular to the floor. Most letters don't fully achieve the 90-degree ideal, and none of Mama's letters did, but *R* was a complete failure. No matter how many times I reached over and righted her fingers, Mama's *R* shot out parallel to the floor, pointing squarely at me. Worse, she crossed her pointer finger on top of her middle finger, an exercise in fine-motor movements that I find difficult to this day. Nana, my helpful accomplice, grabbed her fingers with her little hand and tried to rearrange the *R* and point it to the ceiling. I nodded. Mama laughed and understood. But the next time she rolled from *Q* to *R,* or tried to spell the name of our town, the handshape came out backward and pointed forward like a fleshy cigar.

As the long summer days dragged on, I took up my pencil in boredom, and wrote out the names of each member of the family on a piece of paper. When I finished, I showed my work to Mama. She pointed at each name and nodded. Then she arrived at

Brother's name and shook her head. Leading me back to the table, she reached over and scratched out *Hoffpauir.* To my mounting horror, she wrote a new name, a completely strange one, *Istre.*

"Brother's name is Istre," said Mama.

Then she scratched out *Brother* too. *James Grady,* she wrote. Then she lined up all three strange words together: *James Grady Istre.*

I stared at her. Who was James Grady Istre?

Mama just smiled and got up and walked outside.

But I was beside myself. How could Brother be Grady and Grady be Istre? My name was Hoffpauir. So was Daddy's. So was Mama's. So was Nana's. What was an Istre doing in a Hoffpauir house? And how could he be Brother?

I looked at Nana for clarification, but with a single year of school to her credit, she could hardly be expected to negotiate such complexities. Still, I had to know.

"Ask Mama about Brother," I told her. "Ask about his real name."

Mama had gone outside to wait for the mailman. She was rocking back and forth on the porch swing, smoking a cigarette. Nana looked over at the open window and let her lips fly. Mama stopped swinging and looked over at me again. And sighed.

Getting up from the swing, she came back in the house. She tried to tell me about her first marriage.

"I was sixteen," she began.

"Sixteen?" I was appalled.

"Sixteen," she nodded.

I shook my head. That was too young.

"Aunt Happy was thirteen when she got married," she laughed.

"Aunt Happy was thirteen?!"

At school, I looked up to the teenage girls. They flirted with boys, put on make-up in the evenings, and were full of secrets. By sixteen, they knew how to look really glamorous, but none of them were married. The only people who were married were the teachers. Marriage was for grown-ups.

"That's what girls did then," Mama said gently, abandoning her crippled fingerspelling and trying to talk into my face. "What was I supposed to do?" she asked me. "Hang around the kitchen and help my mother cook?" She looked over at Grandpa, sitting in a stupor near the stove. Her mouth moved in his direction, and she must have said something in French, for Grandpa allowed himself a weak smile. Mama laughed out loud, and that caused a coughing spell. As soon as the spasms stopped, she laughed again. But it was not a joke to me.

"What about school?" I asked.

Already I knew that school had saved me. Mama just laughed.

"We quit school long before that," she said.

Brother—Grady—bounded up the steps and rustled through the kitchen. We watched him through the window as he laid his hands on frog-catching equipment. He barely looked at us, but I saw his lips move.

Nana turned to me.

"Brother said not to feel bad about not knowing his name," she said. "He didn't know it himself. At least not the James part."

"It's not important," Brother said.

He came out on the porch, cheerfully jabbing at the three of us with his special stick.

"You going after frogs tonight?" asked Nana, signing as she talked to him.

I loved when Brother caught frogs for Mama to cook, but now I wasn't interested. I just wanted an explanation. Mama's eyes were on Brother. I knew I had to be patient, but I was a little mad at him for stealing attention from me. I tugged at Mama's sleeve. Mama turned to me and sank down to be on my eye level again. Brother's real father was not my daddy, she said. I was so shocked, I could only look at Brother to see what he would say. Nana looked at him too. He just shrugged and nodded.

"My real father was no good," he elaborated.

Just then a black car pulled up, and Brother was down the walk in a leap. Uncle Frank got out of the driver's seat and his mouth moved at Mama, and Mama stood up to see or hear him better. She smiled and nodded. Then Uncle Frank and Brother were back in the car, and a few minutes later, they were off.

I turned to Nana and she confirmed what Brother had said.

"His father was no good," said Nana. "At least not to Mama."

Mama didn't tell me much more about it. Nana was the one who told me most of what I know about Mama's first marriage—and only much later. Brother's real father drank a lot. He beat my mother. There were other women. At first, Mama pretended not to hear the stories. Then she pretended not to care. But one day when he beat her, she ran all the way to my grandma's house. And she asked to stay.

She was a disgrace. Her mama and daddy didn't call her that, but other people did. Still she wouldn't go back to her husband. She stayed in the house with her parents. She raised my brother and began a new life. After a while, she resumed dating. She and Aunt Happy went dancing with other young people in the music clubs. That's where she met my daddy, Alexandre Hoffpauir.

Nana didn't seem surprised or upset as this came out. She seemed to have known it all along. Nana just absorbed the information from the air, soaked it up like a cloth soaks up oil. For one thing, Brother never called our daddy *Daddy,* like Nana and I did. Brother called him *Alec,* giving the name *Alex* a French pronunciation. For another thing, Nana knew everything about all of us.

I never could find out all I wanted to know about my family and home. I was always in some kind of bubble: I could see everyone and everything, but I was alone. For me everything about my family was shocking and new.

I could see Mama always coughing and smoking, but it was Nana who said Mama smoked too much. It was smoking that made her cough all the time, Nana said. Sometimes I patted Mama's back as she coughed. Nana made a gesture at snatching away her cigarette. Mama laughed and caught Nana's hand.

"Bronchitis," Nana explained later. She wrote the word down because it didn't flow easily from her fingers. "The doctor says Mama has bronchitis. And the stupid cigarettes make it worse."

At that time, even with school, Nana, Mama, Daddy, and Brother and the dilapidated houses of Rayne were what made my world safe. My daddy's parents were still alive, and we went to visit them often. Grandma always gave me buttered bread with a little sugar on it. Daddy was a foreman at the nearby rice mill, and he went to work every day, taking a taxi or hitching a ride with friends. Most days, he stopped at Grandpa's on the way home and read him the newspaper. My grandfather had joined a special state reading program for French-speaking adults. At seventy-two years old, he was learning to read. We still never had any money, but no one seemed to care about that.

Brother had become a hunter. By the time he was seventeen, he was probably one of the best hunters in the state. I never heard his duck call, but he's famous for it. He hunted in the swamps and rice fields, and brought home ducks, geese, rabbits, and squirrels. It was Grady who kept meat on our table.

Nana helped Mama around the house and kept up on the Rayne gossip, which she shared generously with everyone.

Mama would say she didn't want to hear it. Nana would tell her anyway, and me, too. As she became fluent in sign language, Nana was my conduit to the lives and talk that flowed around me. Almost all the information that came to me from family and neighbors came through Nana's hands.

Some of our favorite family times were spent down in Hackberry where JoJo lived. Her real name was Joelyn, and she was my favorite cousin—one of the people I loved most in the world. Two years older than me, JoJo knew how to communicate with me better than any hearing person except Nana. She could do the whole alphabet with her fingers.

JoJo would use a letter handshape for the first letter of a word, then speak the rest of it so I could lipread. She would hold up her hand shaped like the letter *C*, wait for me to look at her, and say slowly and carefully, "Would you like a piece of chicken?" She'd add a little point too, so I'd know which chicken she was talking about.

JoJo and I had sign names for everybody. JoJo's mother was Aunt Eva, and we signed her name by miming filing our fingernails. I could read the names of Aunt Olivia and Aunt Happy easily on JoJo's lips. I could read Aunt Mae's name on the lips, too, but we gave her a name sign anyway—we would slide our hands in an arc over our chest in imitation of her giant bosom. The doctor's name sign was a gesture for a mustache and briefcase.

JoJo's Hackberry was a little town that made Rayne look like a metropolis. Four of my mother's sisters lived among the families there. They called it Hackberry Island, because with the bayous, the marsh, and the gulf, it was completely surrounded by water or soggy ground. Originally the home of the Attakapas Indians, Hackberry was fought over by the French and Spanish, and became a haven for outlaws, rustlers, and pirates. It was the center of my mother's heritage. Here, where a church had been rebuilt three times since 1895, and a single road trundled merrily along the seven-mile stretch along the Calcasieu River without the benefit of any stoplights, I lived for weeks at a time in summer.

To get to Hackberry, we'd drive west almost to Texas, turn off on Highway 27 just before the border, and follow a single lane for miles. The lane was made of shells, and they flashed in the sun, hurt the eyes, and threatened constantly to mangle Aunt Happy's tires. Still the road wasn't as bad as the ferry. Waiting for the ferry, wrote Hackberry's Reverend Theodore E. Brandley, gave folks "a very good notion of eternity," especially in the summertime.

The local kids called themselves river rats. They were proud of it, too. By then most everyone in Hackberry worked for the oil companies. Cousin Buddy worked for oil companies, but that didn't stop him from hunting in the swamps every chance he could get. The marsh still held game, and it was Brother's favorite hunting area.

Hackberry would have been paradise, a perfect place even in the wintertime with the tangled gray swamp, if it weren't for its savage prejudice against black people. I never saw it, but I've been told that a big sign stood by the entrance to this fair community that said: "Nigger, don't let your ass be caught here after sundown."

One family believed to be of African-Indian heritage lived there for a while and went through hell. They were called "Redbones." Their children were not allowed to attend the island's small public school, and the husband, who was white, let it be known that he would eat neither with his wife nor his own children. I guess I accepted and even adopted the racism, though I want to deny it.

Still, some of our best times happened in Hackberry. The whole family would pack up and go to the banks of the Calcasieu, where the men would fish, crab, and shrimp, and the women would cook everything in a pot on the beach. The stories from these outings tumble together in piles that I can't untangle. One time, Brother got bit by a rattlesnake, and Uncle Frank sucked gasoline from the car to clean his wound. There were turtle heads decaying in a heap outside Aunt Olivia's fence, and she threatened that they would come back alive and eat the children.

So, as much as I loved school, many of my best times were still at home. We never dreamed that they wouldn't last forever.

6

❧

$\mathcal{M}$ama

And the crack in the teacup opens
A lane to the land of the dead.

—W. H. AUDEN, "AS I WALKED OUT ONE EVENING"

During my elementary years, the focus of my life was increasingly my friends and school, though my family remained my security. Then I was yanked back forcefully to my family in a terrible cloudburst, a storm of sadness, when I hadn't realized that there was a cloud in the sky. I was thirteen.

First my poor weakened grandpa died. My parents were each the youngest in large families, and as a child I went to many funerals. I don't even remember my grandpa's. All I remember is that he was gone.

Then there was Brother's wedding. I was shocked when Nana told me he was getting married. The girl was pretty, I guess, but I didn't like her. She looked at Daddy, Mama, Nana, and me as if we were unsavory, some kind of side dish that no one had ordered. Her family owned a drugstore and lived in Opelousas. For a long time, I thought they might be old-fashioned city Creoles, looking down their noses at us Cajuns. Brother says no, the family was Cajun just like us and not all that rich until much later. Only the girl was crazy, he says, and he loved the rest of the family even after he couldn't stand her.

For me—for all of us—the relationship was a mystery from the beginning. Brother says Mama knew the girl wasn't right for him. He says she even tried to talk him out of the wedding. She waited too long though. When Mama came to his room, Brother was to be married the next morning. She sat on the edge of his bed, just like when he was little. She asked him flat out if he loved this girl.

Brother allowed as he sure thought so.

Mama thought for a while, and then told him that being married and living with someone was hard work. "If you don't love the person, it's just about impossible," Mama said.

Later Grady heard this as a warning. But before the wedding, he couldn't hear anything, except maybe the roar of his loins. Otherwise why would my brother, who loved hunting and fishing and the marsh that surrounded our home, move away? Why else would he accept a stuck-up girl who wasn't nice to the rest of his family? I was excused from school to go to his wedding—a fancy one by our standards. Brother's new wife glared at me and I glared right back.

I was glad to get back to school, and I didn't go home again until summer.

꩜

At first, I had no inkling that anything else was amiss. I was in my usual state of ambivalence about leaving school, partly excited, partly nervous, and dismayed when Aunt Happy, Nana, and Mama arrived to take me home. My friends and I said tearful good-byes, promised to get together sometime over the long holiday, and wondered how we would pull it off. Thelma said her mama had promised her a car when she was sixteen, and that was just a year away. Jeanette Fruge had become my best friend, and she lived in nearby Crowley. Perhaps Mama would take me to see her. Surely David would be there. I always had to put up with him.

As hard as I tried to deny it, David and Jeanette acted like sweethearts. Last summer, David had hitchhiked all the way from his home up in northern Louisiana to visit Jeanette. And I knew that she was hoping he would come again. There just seemed to be no separating those two. I didn't have a boyfriend. Boys, however, had become new and ever-blipping lights on a radar screen that I didn't know I had. They seemed to demand my attention, even while I vehemently denied their existence.

I was pleased that Mama and Aunt Happy brought Nana with them. If Mama's face was paler, I didn't notice it. I didn't even notice her cough right away. I guess I'd come to expect it. The cough would begin with just a little catch below her throat, a small motion as if she had caught her breath too quickly, like the motions I've see adults make at church. Except it wouldn't end there; instead it would build. Each cough harder and stronger than the next, until she bent over and grabbed hold of whatever was stable and nearby. She would continue coughing, her body wracked in convulsions until you'd think her body would simply give up for lack of air.

After it was over she would smile, almost apologetically, as if to say she was sorry for the jolt of thunderclaps and gales, and for the worry she'd injected into the day. She apologized as well for whatever it was in her body that made her sick. Then she'd pull herself together, take a draw on her cigarette, and continue as if nothing had happened.

As we pulled up to Aunt Happy's house, Nana tried to slip the pack of cigarettes from her purse.

But Mama just laughed at her. "Thank you," she said almost gaily, removing one and lighting it while Nana glared.

"It's bad for your bronchitis," said Nana sternly.

"I know, honey," agreed Mama, still smiling and patting Nana's hand.

I was surprised to see Aunt Happy pulling my suitcase was from the car.

"We're staying with Aunt Happy because Daddy drinks too much," Nana told me.

"Daddy always drinks too much," I said. "He's been drinking too much all along."

"Mama said we would stay here for a while," said Nana. She didn't look pleased, but she didn't look sad either.

"Maybe this will teach Daddy a lesson," I said.

But the news disconcerted me. I missed Daddy and wondered when we would see him.

Aunt Happy and Uncle Speedy seemed glad that we were there. Nana and I had our own bedroom and shared a bed, just like at home. As the days passed, I heard nothing from Daddy, Jeanette, or anyone else. Summer lay ahead, a tedious expanse of heat, humidity, and loneliness, a three-month desert to be negotiated.

I'd been back from school about two weeks when Aunt Happy rushed into our bedroom in the middle of the night, pushed at my body frantically, and roused me from sleep. Something was wrong. The light was on, and in its arc Nana was throwing on her clothing and crying. Confused, I began to get dressed, too, pulling on my skirt and T-shirt. Once she saw me moving, Aunt Happy dashed from the room. Nana rushed from the room behind her, and I, still pulling at my clothing, followed in her wake.

In the light of the living room, I could see Aunt Happy and Mama. Mama was slumped around Aunt Happy's shoulders, her head bowed and her whole chest concentrated on pulling in and letting out breath. She wore only her pajamas and robe, and they were soaked in sweat. Aunt Happy was trying to help her walk. Uncle Speedy must have been working so it was the three of us, Mama in the middle, who stumbled out to the car.

Nana was sobbing; I was stiff with terror. Aunt Happy got behind the wheel, Mama slid into the passenger seat, and Nana and I crawled into the back. Aunt Happy handed me a damp cloth and made motions with it. I understood. I took the cloth and stroked my mother's dripping face. Aunt Happy and Nana were moving their mouths at each other.

"Don't die, Mama," I prayed. "Please don't die."

Mama's head swayed for a moment then fell heavily back against the seat. She remained like that, her chest heaving, her eyes closed, her mouth wide and gasping. As Aunt Happy drove the car through the darkness, I wiped Mama's head again and again. Each time, the wet film returned. Aunt Happy was on the highway. I assumed that she was headed toward the hospital. Next to me, Nana fell asleep, tears still on her cheeks.

It seemed like forever before the car stopped. To my chagrin Aunt Happy had pulled up in front of our house in Rayne. I shook Nana awake.

"Tell her we have to go to the hospital!"

Aunt Happy refused to pay attention to Nana. She insisted that Nana and I stay at home. She would take our mother to the hospital, but we would stay at the house. I protested vigorously. Nana interpreted for me, adding her own protest.

"We want to go with Mama!" she cried again and again.

Aunt Happy was adamant.

"This is how you can help your mother," she said. "She wants you to wait for her here."

Daddy was still at work but the door was never locked, and Nana and I entered the empty house together. Nana fell asleep in the living room, but I sat by the window and watched. Sure enough, Daddy came home with the sunrise. He had worked the late shift. I watched as he took a small bottle from his trouser pocket and pressed it to his lips. He opened the door and turned to the bedroom and saw me.

"Why are you two here?" he gasped.

I woke Nana, and we told him what happened. Alarm filled his face.

"Let's go," he said to me. "You're too little," he told Nana, as she came to my side. "You have to stay home."

Nana dissolved into tears again.

Suddenly Aunt Happy appeared at the door. Nana and I watched her talk to Daddy. Then Daddy gestured to me, and I headed for the door. As Nana started to cry again, Aunt Happy walked over and hugged her.

"There's nothing we can do, baby," Aunt Happy said. "It's the hospital's rules."

I took notice of my increased age and responsibility and felt a touch of pride. The sun was coming up as I watched Aunt Happy and Daddy from the backseat, and wondered about my mama. Before too long I poked at Daddy.

"Who's watching Nana?" I asked him.

"Cecile," he said, his fingers slicing through the air. Cecile was my aunt, his sister. I suppose he had called her.

When we arrived in the hospital, we were ushered immediately into Mama's room. She was lying on her side in the bed. A tube protruded from her chest and a pink fluid seeped through it. Ethel, her best friend, sat beside her. When she saw me, Mama motioned for me to leave. She didn't want me to see her like this. I couldn't leave though. I sat in the chair next to Ethel and wondered what to do.

Our relatives began to fill the lobby. Whenever we left the room, aunts, uncles, and cousins greeted us with hugs and pats on the shoulder. I waited while they talked for a long time with my daddy.

I had no idea what was going on until we got back home. In the living room, Daddy explained to me, via Nana.

"Someone has to be with your mother every minute," he said. "She is too sick to be alone."

I nodded.

"Aunt Happy will stay with her most of the time," Daddy continued. "But you are a big girl now. Perhaps you could just watch Mama for a few hours in the afternoon, too. Would you be willing?"

I had been watching Nana's face and hands, but now I turned to Daddy.

"Yes," I said firmly with my lips. I was eager to help, even proud.

Daddy nodded, patted my head, and moved his lips. I looked back at Nana.

"He says he knew you would help," she said.

I had no idea what awaited me. Back in the hospital, Mama had become a different person. My mother was gone and in her place was a stranger who lay on the bed, weak and pale, her stomach and chest rising and falling as one painful breath succeeded another. It hurt to see her like that. Sometimes she would writhe in pain, curling over her pillow in a fetal position. Most of the time she slept. What I couldn't bear were those moments when she woke up and raised strange eyes to mine. Those eyes had little to do with Nola Granger Hoffpauir and everything to do with suffering. They were pools of pain and desperation. Her eyes and then her mouth cried out in pain, pleading for relief.

I held a straw to her mouth so she could sip water, but she jerked too much to swallow. I tried to stroke her cracked lips with moistened Q-tips, but she twisted away from me, rolling and thrashing, and gnashing at the pillow with her teeth. In desperation, I pushed the button to call the nurse. Finally she came, but when she saw my mother she just shook her head, pointed to her watch to explain it was too soon after the last dose of pain medication, and left the room. Horrified and helpless, I watched my mother continue to thrash in the bed. When she stuffed the pillow into her mouth, I pulled it out. Other than that, I didn't know what to do. It seemed like forever until the nurse returned. This time, she held out the needle and gave Mama a shot. Mama returned to her sweaty sleep.

"She ate the pillow," I told Aunt Happy tearfully when she arrived.

Aunt Happy took one look at me, conferenced with Aunt Cecile, and told my father that I couldn't take care of my mother anymore. Aunt Happy would stay a little longer in the evenings, and Aunt Cecile would come a little earlier. Of course, my father stopped by every day after work, devoted and utterly helpless.

I was so relieved to be back at home with Nana.

The two of us spent part of our time at home, part of the time with relatives. We were at Grandpa Hoffpauir's house when Aunt Happy drove up. She said a few words to Grandpa and then came over to us. Her mouth moved at Nana, and Nana got up and turned off the TV.

We faced Aunt Happy expectantly.

"You tell Kitty what I say," she told my sister. Nana signed the words as Aunt Happy spoke them. I read each clearly from her fingers.

"I've come to tell you about your mother," Nana signed, interpreting for Aunt Happy like the ten-year-old professional she had become.

"Your mother is very very sick."

We nodded; we knew Mama was sick.

"She's going to have to stay in the hospital," continued Aunt Happy.

Again we nodded.

"She's had many different tests—"

Nana's hands stopped abruptly. I glanced at Aunt Happy, whose lips continued to move. My line of communication had snapped. I tapped desperately at my sister.

"What did she say? What did she say?" I asked her.

Finally, Nana turned to me with tears running down her cheeks.

"She said Mama doesn't have long to live." With that my sister ran from the room.

I started to go after her, but Aunt Happy gently stopped me. *"Let her go,"* she gestured.

Aunt Happy and I never understood each other easily, but somehow I followed what she was saying. *"Your poor dear mother has lung cancer,"* Aunt Happy explained.

Later, Nana and I learned that other acute episodes had occurred. Mama had known for some time that she was dying. My father knew, too. So did Aunt Happy and Uncle Speedy, and Aunt Cecile, Daddy's sister. In fact, all of the adults knew. Even Aunt Adele, who I only saw on holidays, knew.

They just didn't tell my mother's children—not even Brother, Mama's only son and a married adult. Perhaps they had thought to lessen our sorrow by postponing it. Still, I felt betrayed. I cried in anger as well as grief. Nana spent the night alternating between crying and sleeping.

"What will become of us?" I asked Aunt Happy.

"You'll come live with me," she answered, stroking my forehead. *"We—your father and I—promised your mother. You'll live with Uncle Speedy and me. I'll take care of you."*

Aunt Happy gave me a rosary, and I began to pray. Later my daddy came to see us at Grandpa's house, but he didn't take me home. Instead I found myself at Jeanette's house. She lived in Crowley, very near the hospital. Even with my mother sick it felt like a treat to be there.

"It will take your mind off things," Aunt Happy promised.

Daddy said he would take me to the hospital, and he did, almost daily. He arrived in a taxi because he still refused to drive. On the days he didn't come, sometimes Jeanette would walk to the hospital with me. Jeanette would wait in the lobby. She understood a lot of speech with her hearing aid, and she seemed to get along comfortably with the clan that seemed perpetually encamped in the lobby.

I never saw Brother, but he says he came and I am sure he was there. Aunt Happy was probably the one who called him at work and told him that Mama was in the hospital. He picked up his wife and drove to see her right away. Brother loved Mama, no doubt about that. When they performed the biopsy, Brother took the tissue sample to the lab in Lake Charles. When they told Brother that the results of the biopsy were positive, he cried tears of joy, thinking that positive had to be good. He didn't know that it meant they had found cancer.

Already thin, Mama grew still thinner. Sometimes she tried to smile at me when I arrived. Never again did I see her so bad as that afternoon when I had to take care of her. I said the rosary every night, and I prayed that she'd come home.

June slipped into July. I got used to traveling between home, Grandpa's, and Jeanette's house. It seemed I'd always had a mother in the hospital and always traveled back and forth to Crowley and the Fruge home. It seemed like Mama had always been sick and dying, like she would be sick and dying forever.

One morning, I looked over at Jeanette and made a sudden decision.

"Let's go to the hospital," I said.

Jeanette nodded and the two of us walked the few short blocks.

"Where is everyone?" I asked, nodding toward the deserted lobby. Usually it was filled with my uncles and aunts.

"Maybe it's just too early," said Jeanette.

She took a seat while I made my way to Mama's room. It was a familiar trek by now. Down the hall, through the double doors, and then right, just before the nurse's station. My father was standing in her doorway and saw me coming. He touched my arm and ushered me inside. To my surprise, Mama was sitting up. She looked right at me when I came in. At first I thought she was better. Her best friend, Ethel, sat there before her. Pale light from the window illuminated her face and the statue of the Virgin Mary that stood by her side.

"She's in a coma," my father said.

Her eyes held no recognition, but they looked calm and clear. I approached the bed to hug her, but my father grabbed hold of my dress and stopped me. Resistance was useless. Every time I would venture toward my mama, Daddy would tug me back to the door.

"Time to go now," he said finally, pointing to his watch.

I didn't want to leave. Something felt even more askew than usual. I tried to get my father to explain but he was agitated.

"Go," he said. *"Go."*

With his hands on my shoulders, he walked me back into the hallway and then down to the lobby. Then he returned alone to my mother's room. I caught a glimpse of him as he entered, old and bent, though still as stubborn and strong as an oak. Jeanette smiled when she saw me and jumped up to go.

"No," I said.

I was going to stay. I was going to wait.

Jeanette saw my face and sat back down.

"We'll wait together," she said.

How much time passed? Maybe thirty minutes. Maybe an hour. I looked up and saw Daddy's face at the end of the hallway. He beckoned and I got up. He shook his head. He didn't want me. He pointed to Jeanette; he wanted Jeanette. She and I looked at each other and I shrugged. Jeanette made her way down the hall to see Daddy.

I saw him bend down to talk to her. With his face directly in front of hers, he moved his mouth and carved through the air with his finger.

Although she had some ability to hear and could understand speech well, Jeanette would never understand my daddy's one-finger alphabet, I thought. I began to walk down the hall to interpret.

Jeanette turned and walked quickly away from my father.

"Let's go outside," she said, not pausing even for a moment as she drew abreast of me.

I hesitated, puzzled. Then I saw the priest, a slight figure in black at the other end of the hall. As I watched, he turned into my mother's room.

I turned to Jeanette and she burst into tears. Then I knew. Mama was dead. *Dead.*

I shrieked and ran toward my father. He was crying. I tried to get back in the room, with its light and its statue, but Daddy wouldn't let me.

"No! No! No! No!" I screamed. It couldn't be. But it was.

Arms tried to restrain me, but I was too strong. Determined, horrified, I remained in the doorway.

"In nomine Patris, et Filii . . ." I couldn't hear it, but I know what he said. I saw the movement of the black sleeve, of the hand.

My father caught me as I fell forward. I collapsed into his arms screaming. A nurse loomed suddenly before me, a hypodermic needle in her hand. She was looking at me meaningfully, and I quieted down.

I don't know who called Nana to tell her. When we returned home, I climbed out of the car wearily, aware of the stillness of the street, feeling the neighbors watching me from their windows. Aunt Happy and Daddy were at my side when an enraged Nana ran out the door. I didn't even have time to wonder why she was so angry. Before Aunt Happy or Daddy could stop her, she attacked me, her fists flailing.

"It's not fair!" she cried as she hit me. "You saw Mama and I didn't! It's not fair! *It's not fair!*"

Adult hands restrained her.

"You saw Mama!" she cried again and collapsed.

I could think of nothing to say. I had nothing to do with rules that barred children from visiting their dying parents. Nana knew that later. Her anger was crazy, she said.

And so was her silence. After her outburst, Nana didn't cry any-more. Not at the viewing, not at the services, not at the funeral. Not when we came home to the house that would always be empty.

"Are you okay?" I asked her again and again. She only shrugged and looked away.

Her system must have closed down completely because she said later that she didn't remember any of it. I, on the other hand, remember everything. I remember Brother arriving at the funeral home, red-eyed and devastated with his wife right next to him. I remember he wouldn't enter the room where Mama lay, but stayed among the visitors in the lobby. I remember rubbing Mama's hands in the coffin, soft and ice cold. I remember the funeral, the deceitful caress of the July sun, the feel of my best dress, the grimace of the priest. I remember Daddy moving like a dead person, crying and crying. I remember praying again and again over my rosary beads. And I remember Nana's small stone face and the dark circles under her red-but-always-dry eyes.

7

Life After Mama

Why should a dog, a horse, a rat have life,
And thou no breath at all?

—SHAKESPEARE, *KING LEAR*

Nana and I were going to stay with Aunt Happy and Uncle Speedy.

Just as well, I thought. I didn't want to stay in my own sad home.

The five of us—Aunt Happy, Uncle Speedy, Daddy, Nana, and I—went home first so Nana and I could pack some clothes. As we crossed into the living room, I realized that Aunt Happy and Daddy were arguing. Their faces, weary and tear-stained from the funeral, suddenly flushed with anger, and Nana stared at one, then the other as if she were watching two ghosts. Aunt Happy didn't like her staring because she suddenly stopped talking to Daddy and spoke directly to Nana. Then Daddy gestured at me, trying to shoo me into the back room like I was some kind of chicken. Aunt Happy was shooing, too. They didn't want us to see them fight.

Nana and I stumbled over each other as we left the room.

"What are they saying?" I pressed Nana to listen.

She stood like a small soldier in front of me, wearing the same blank expression that she had worn since her outburst the morning that mama died. Now she turned away without responding.

"Pay attention!" I scolded, grabbing her and turning her to face me. "What are they saying?"

I knew she heard everything despite the walls.

Nana maintained her blank stare. Despite the hard little front she put forward, I suspect she was even more hurt and frightened than I was. Too much was happening too fast. Mama, the central person in both our lives, was gone. Furthermore, adults weren't supposed to argue, and now the two adults closest to us were arguing violently. To bury our mother and see our father fight with our aunt, all on the same day, destroyed any feeling that there might be reason to stay alive on the planet.

"They're arguing," Nana said finally.

Of course, they were arguing. Why else would they have sent us back here? I shook my head, exasperated.

Nana, who in our former lives always did as I asked, wouldn't tell me what they were saying—or maybe she couldn't. She was so determined to remove herself from stimuli, I'm not sure how much she heard; if she did hear, I'm not sure she could understand.

Aunt Happy finally came back to our room, her make-up smeared and her eyes red. In a new outburst of tears and pain, she managed to explain.

"Daddy wants us to live with him," she said. Yes, indeed he had promised our mother—and Aunt Happy, too—that we could stay with her. But our daddy had changed his mind. We were his girls, he said. We would stay with him.

Nana, her eyes hard and swollen, interpreted for me without expression. As soon as she finished, she turned back to Aunt Happy.

"I want to stay with you!" she told Aunt Happy, wearing the same flat look.

I nodded. I wanted to stay with Aunt Happy, too. We were used to women taking care of us, and neither of us had any idea how to proceed without one in the house.

Aunt Happy sighed. She did get Daddy to compromise on one thing, she said.

"Uncle Speedy and I are headed for a vacation in Colorado. Your daddy said that you both could come with us. It's the best I can do," Aunt Happy said.

I sank wearily to the floor. Nana sat down next to me and put her head against my shoulder. Aunt Happy hesitated a moment, then joined us on the floor. She hugged us and stroked our hair.

I don't remember much about that trip, a surreal adventure in green, rising lands that shielded us at least temporarily from the flat, gray landscape that our lives had become. I couldn't shake the grip of sadness. At night, the tears would come. I never believed the human body could produce so much salt water. I gripped my rosary. I repented every sin I'd ever committed. I begged God to take care of my mother, and I begged him to let her come back.

I don't think Nana saw much either. She didn't cry, and she didn't laugh either. Nana faced the mountains just as she faced the flat marsh—with the same impervious stare. We all tried to be gentle, though, with each other and with Aunt Happy.

When we returned home, Daddy informed us that Aunt Mae, another of our mother's sisters, was coming to live with us. I hated Aunt Mae. She—whose sign name honored her great bosom—was in between husbands (she would have seven) and needed a place to live. The little house out back, where Grandma and then Grandpa had lived, was empty. Aunt Mae would sleep there, my father explained, but she would take her meals with us.

I begged Aunt Happy to stay. Nana watched me talking to her without even offering to help. She might as well have still been staring at the landscape as it passed her window. It was as if we had nothing to do with her.

"I'll stop by," Aunt Happy promised.

It would have to do. Brother said the same thing, but he had moved to New Orleans. He had bought an auto shop there, and he was always busy working on cars or customers. He owned the shop by this time, I think, and we almost never saw him. However, Aunt Happy made her way to our home often.

Aunt Mae showed up as promised. She took over the small dwelling in back of the house, ordained herself the female presence in our home, and quickly lived up to my most devastating expectations.

Until she was hospitalized, Mama had handled the housework. Nana and I chipped in as requested, and we weren't requested very often. We saw no reason to change the way we lived. Aunt Mae saw different. She took a shine to the idea that the debris of everyday living should be stationed out of sight. Dishes should appear only when it was time to prepare for eating. They should be washed immediately after the last morsel of food was lifted away. Glasses should never, ever be left to dry on their own; the drying process should be speeded up by overt human assistance. Immediately upon completion of meals, we—by which she meant Nana and me—should wash, dry, and return the dishes to the cabinets and place the towels in the laundry basket, so that the next meal we—again, Nana and me—could begin the whole process once more.

Whereas Mama required little cleaning and did most of what got done, Aunt Mae required major scrubbing and purging and did none of it. She never saw herself as one for manual labor. Manual labor was for her nieces. She had better things to do. Nana was amenable, but I rebelled. As a result, Aunt Mae was on a constant broom with me, flying after me wherever I went, demanding that I stop whatever I was doing and attend to some chore she specified.

Worse, I couldn't understand her. I couldn't read lips; she couldn't read signs. Not one word was ever successfully communicated to me directly from her mouth. Neither of us had much patience for writing either—and with all the stuff perpetually tucked out of sight, we couldn't find a pencil anyway. Aunt Mae was especially irritated because hollering at me was useless. She could make Nana jump just by booming a command from clear across the room when Nana wasn't even looking. She had less control over me because I was deaf. She had to extend to me the artificial courtesy of coming into my field of vision before she issued orders or reprimands. These then had to be repeated, not once, but multiple times, and sometimes shifted through the hands of Nana for me to understand them. Meanwhile, as she strove each time to communicate, her authority dissolved. Important overtones—that she was the queen and mistress of the house and we its unhired help—were therefore totally missing. She couldn't order or scold with appropriate impact. It does people like Aunt Mae no good to yell at someone if the someone is deaf. You don't get any more deaf than me, and my deafness inconvenienced her.

This made her even angrier. Once I was bent over, washing the kitchen floor, when she spied a spot that my rag had missed. Perhaps she yelled to call my attention to it. I don't know. She got my attention by walking over to where I was washing and giving me a kick in my shoulder. I was in a constant state of outrage.

I complained to Daddy to no avail. Daddy was a problem, too. His drinking seemed to be worse. Fridays were lost days, sometimes setting the tone for lost weekends. Knowing that we disapproved—no, that we passionately hated—his drunkenness, he hid the alcohol. We were always finding bottles in his clothing and under the house.

"Mama used to let him sleep overnight in the police station," Nana murmured to me darkly.

"I wish he'd find his way there instead of here!" I answered.

❧

I thought I could change him. I walked him over to the refrigerator on Friday morning before he left for work.

"Look," I commanded, holding wide the door. Except for a half-empty can of Coke, it was empty.

"It's payday," I told him harshly. *"We need money. You bring that money home."*

Daddy looked embarrassed.

"Don't drink it," I continued.

"I promise," he nodded. He looked so sad and unhappy.

"Maybe all would have gone just as well if I had stayed quiet," I told Nana after he left for work.

"Maybe we've been quiet too long," she said.

We so looked forward to Daddy coming home that night. Our joy was heightened further when Aunt Mae left the house all dressed up in the late afternoon.

"Date tonight!" she proclaimed gaily.

I missed what she said, of course, but Nana flashed it to me with her swift fingers.

"Hooooray!" Had we ever been so happy? Surely not since Mama had died.

Nana began a grocery list.

"Milk," she wrote.

"Debris," I wrote. Heck, debris—the organs of animals ground together and packaged like hamburger—was almost meat. I could fry up a whole pan of it, mix it with some free rice from the rice mill, and maybe have enough food to last the week.

At five o'clock, Nana and I met each other by the window.

"He's getting off from work," she said.

At half past five, he wasn't home. We felt stupid standing at the glass, so we pretended to be busy with other things. Still, we contrived reasons to pass the window. And every time we happened by, we'd glance up and down the street, looking for Daddy's cab.

Nana finally grabbed the doorknob.

I almost stopped her. *No use letting the neighbors see us waiting like this*, I thought.

But it was warm and sunny outside. Avoiding each other's eyes, we walked out the door. It was impossible that he'd be treating us like this. The neighbors had to know we were waiting for Daddy, and they had to know why.

I glanced down at my watch. Minutes ticked by. He had promised that he would come home this time, and I was so sure he'd be there soon.

At eight o'clock, dusk gathered and none of the cars that trundled down the street held our daddy. The mosquitoes began buzzing.

"People say if you just let the mosquitoes sting, there'll be no itch," I told Nana, who had begun swatting at her body as if possessed.

She put her stony eyes on me for a moment.

I nodded emphatically. "The mosquitoes will completely remove the poison they inject in the skin," I said. "They inject the poison to thin the blood so they can suck it better . . ."

"Kitty!" Nana motioned for me to shut up.

"It's this poison that causes swelling and itching." I had read this in school. "But sometimes if you just give the mosquitoes enough time, they'll suck it all right out and your skin will never be the wiser."

Nana shook her head. She was batting at the air now, and doing an unmerry box step in hopes the constant motion would keep her skin free. Just watching her was making me itch.

I felt like swearing. Maybe I would have sworn, too, if I'd been with anyone except Nana.

"Let's go back," I said finally, heading toward the house with a final glance down the empty street.

"I hate Fridays," Nana said morosely.

"He promised!" I was fierce.

"Mrs. Richard saw us for sure," said Nana.

"All the neighbors saw us," I shook my head.

It was dark now, and Nana turned on the TV. I kept my eyes on the window and fumed.

I don't know where he went or what he did. When he finally showed up, chauffeured right to the door in a friend's car, it was almost ten o'clock. He got out of the car and swayed. His mouth and neck were moving in the strangest way. Nana had fallen asleep watching TV, and I poked her to wake her up and get her to look at him.

"What's wrong with him?" I demanded.

"He's singing," she said wearily.

He sang and danced and sashayed his way up the pavement until he reached the doorway. It was not yet locked, so there was no key to negotiate. That was fortunate because the handle proved elusive enough. Nana looked away, her lip out and her eyes set, but I watched him angrily. After a few minutes he was able to coordinate his movements and successfully negotiate the entry.

"Daddy!" I met him as he entered.

What else could I say? I used my lips only, sure they were visible in the faded circle of light. I was beginning to make out his features in the lamplight. His mouth hung open and his eyes looked trapped. Crestfallen. The cheer evaporated.

"Where's the money?" I asked bluntly. I stretched out my palm for emphasis. *"Where's the money so we can eat?"*

He was a vague silhouette swaying in the doorway and looking down at me.

"Where's the money?" I asked again. I shook my hand, partly in anger and partly as if shaking it would help him fill it.

He didn't answer. He looked at us, held onto the doorframe, and threw up. Nana ran from the room. I stepped back. The smell was overpowering. I had an urge to vomit, too.

"Don't you clean it up!" I told Nana, when I saw she was getting rags from the kitchen. "Don't you go near it!"

Daddy certainly didn't want to get near it. He stared at the pile like some dog had put it there.

"You drank the money!" I accused my father. *"You drank the money that was supposed to be for our food."*

It was no use. He wasn't looking at me. He couldn't understand sign language anyway. And my voice had utterly failed.

Holding on to the wall, he stumbled back toward the bedroom.

"Let him clean it up!" I ordered Nana, who stood by the vomit with the rags poised in the air.

"It's no big deal," she said in her flat way.

I began crying then.

"Better face it now than in the morning," said Nana. Her mouth was positioned as it had been at the funeral.

I searched her eyes, looking for tears. There were none.

"It's already almost morning," I said, turning to get a rag to help her.

When he was sober again, Daddy was apologetic, and I was implacable. He'd let us down. There was no excuse.

The scenario repeated itself week after week. I threatened him mightily. He promised not to spend his paycheck. I learned that

Mama had been picking him up from work on Fridays to try to ensure that he would not spend his paycheck on alcohol. Other members of the family confronted him. Once, I saw his brother, who worked with Daddy at the rice mill, give him a good scolding. He repented all week long, but come Friday, he wouldn't come home.

I stopped being hopeful and stayed watchful and angry.

❧

Aunt Happy was our bright spot. We loved when she came. Nana wouldn't smile, but she always ran to the door when she heard Aunt Happy's car. For some reason, we felt we needed to tell her how well we were doing. Aunt Mae, of course, told her we were doing just grand.

But the home that I had loved was a place of discord and tension. I felt I was only adding to the dysfunction, stirring around in the mess. And in just a few weeks it would be September. School, usually a bastion of comfort, felt like a sentence to a faraway prison. I couldn't bear the thought of leaving Nana.

At night, I lay awake planning. I was too young to get a real job, but I'd heard that sometimes kids picked cotton for money.

"I'm not going to school," I told her one day. "I'm staying home this year."

Nana was horrified.

"You have to go to school," she said.

"No," I told her forcefully. "I'm staying home."

"It's the law to go to school," Nana said. I didn't even wonder how she knew about the law.

"Who'll be with you?" I asked her bluntly. "I don't want to leave you here with that slimy, wiggly Aunt Mae."

"Remember, I'll be going to school too," Nana said.

"I'm staying right here," I tried to sound like I meant it.

Through Nana, I told Aunt Happy of my fears about leaving Nana alone. She knew that I hated Aunt Mae and thought my anxiety was exaggerated, since according to what we'd been telling her, things were going so well.

"Mrs. Richard will keep an eye out," said Aunt Happy. "And I'll stop by too, of course."

I had not really seen Mrs. Richard since Grady moved out. Still it was true, and I was grateful for our neighbor. She would be watching out for Nana.

"And Aunt Mae," continued Aunt Happy, destroying my reverie. "Aunt Mae is taking good care of her."

I pretended I didn't see that.

"Maybe Aunt Mae will move her bed into the house," said Aunt Happy.

"No!" I cried.

Nana looked at us warily.

"It doesn't matter," she said finally. She signed and talked at the same time with no expression at all.

I shook my head. I couldn't imagine myself leaving. There was no way Nana should be home without me. But when the autumn came, I felt as helpless as the earth when the sunlight grows shorter. The leaves turned brown, the days got short, Aunt Mae stayed in the little house out back, and I went off to school.

8

❧

*T*wo Revolutions:
My School, My Soul

To exist humanly is to name the world . . . to say the true word . . .
is not the privilege of some few persons, but the right of everyone. . . .
Only through communication can human life hold meaning.

—PAULO FREIRE, *THE PEDAGOGY OF THE OPPRESSED*

Sick and shaken with grief, I returned to the Louisiana School.

"A lost soul," said Mr. Ray, one of my teachers.

It was as if fibers, before so ready to fire and tingle, had died. I couldn't respond to my friends and teachers who hugged and teased, and generally tried to cheer me. During the day, I felt nothing. At night, I was consumed by waves of grief and pain that left me sobbing and sleepless. I prayed for my dead mama, and the little sister who was back home in Rayne.

I, who had treated religion as just a pretty drama, clutched at my rosary, prayed, and cried.

"You're a changed person," my roommate Thelma said. "Before you would laugh and smile—now all smiles have stopped."

She sat with me during the nights I couldn't sleep.

"You can't change it about Nana," she'd tell me sorrowfully. "Nana will be okay," she said again and again. "You can check on her next weekend," she would offer when all else failed.

School felt like a foreign place. Its buildings rose up ominously, manmade mountains against the flat landscape. But even mountains erupt from time to time. Transfixed with grief, I hardly noticed the eruption under way at the Louisiana School. I felt like it was happening to a school in a distance city. Still, not even I could avoid it. It assaulted me on my very first day back.

Black block letters graced each step with a single word: STEP. Jeanette called my attention to it, touching me on the shoulder and pointing downward. I stared at the writing. STEP. STEP. STEP. Jeanette tapped my arm again. This time, she pointed to the door where similar block letters proclaimed DOOR. Just as quickly she pointed to the rainspout, on which letters proclaimed in capitals: RAINSPOUT. Thelma had our attention now and she was pointing to other words, ROAD, SIDEWALK, FOUNTAIN.

Inside the building, labels continued. The FLOOR, the CEILING, the WALL, the WOODWORK, and even the small WINDOW above each door. Just as at my house when I was small, each item introduced itself with its own printed label. Altogether, the labels announced the arrival of our school's new principal. Mr. Ed Scouten, whose name sign was an *M* handshape on the forehead, which looks like the sign for "salute" and can also mean "scout," had arrived.

Mr. Scouten had been teaching deaf children since two deaf boys were assigned to him at a Nebraska Boy Scout camp where he had been a seventeen-year-old counselor. Having learned the manual alphabet from his scout manual, Mr. Scouten learned his first signs from his deaf campers. He was fascinated with sign language; he said so himself. And people said that he signed beautifully. This may be true. I don't know because I've never seen him sign.

With me and with every other deaf student that he would meet during his five years at the Louisiana School, Mr. Scouten communicated exclusively with the tiny portion of sign language that is fingerspelling. And the language he aimed to fingerspell was not sign language at all. The language that Mr. Scouten chose to finger-spell was English.

Why would a person who loves a language decide not to use it?

It's a mystery to me, but this was Mr. Scouten's philosophical and pedagogical decision. Ed Scouten thought sign language was bad for deaf children.

He might not put it quite that bluntly himself. He would probably say that he avoided sign language because he believed deaf students should learn English. He would say that while he sometimes enjoyed using signs with deaf adults in social situations, he felt that children have to use a language to learn it—and the only realistic way for deaf children to use English was to code it through fingerspelling. QED, Mr. Scouten and the teachers and students at the Louisiana School would fingerspell English. As he implemented this decision through-out the campus, Mr. Scouten made the Louisiana School the latest bat-tleground in the skirmishes and feints of what has been known as the methods war in deaf education. Like so many administrators before him, he had become one of the war's victims and perpetrators.

The methods war that had broken out two hundred years ago, during the first days of systemic deaf education, was still raging. Should educators use lipreading and speech to teach deaf children, or should they use signs? The disagreement was pursued by parents and educators, each mustering assistance from philosophers, lin-guists, religious leaders, and psychologists in a grand dispute. In my day, few deaf individuals were involved in such skirmishes—we were mostly off the field, mostly cheering from the sidelines for those who supported signs. A few deaf people supported communi-cating through speech and lipreading, but even those people who had understandable speech managed to produce conversations that to the rest of us seemed inane.

"What floor do you want?" a hearing friend heard one oral deaf person inquire of another oral deaf person on an elevator, in En-glish that was pronounced as precisely as any she had ever heard.

"Thursday!" was the equally precise response.

Nevertheless discussion remained heated and it is still going on today. Perhaps we students at the Louisiana School had been lucky to be free of its currents and counter currents for so long. Perhaps it was just indifference that left us down there on our own, using sign language as if it could, like spoken language, be both the currency of education and social life.

No one could doubt Mr. Scouten's intentions. After he worked with the deaf campers, he went to the Nebraska School for the Deaf in hopes of starting a Boy Scout troop there. It was 1931 and the Nebraska School superintendent was Frank Booth, the hearing son of Edmund Booth, a well-known deaf publisher who had helped to found the National Association of the Deaf. Son Frank was an old colonel in the methods war. Perhaps he was even some kind of general. This man, the son of deaf parents who had lived in sign language as long as he lived in spoken language, was, Mr. Scouten believes, the mastermind behind the 1911 law that prohibited the use of sign language in the classrooms of the Nebraska School.

When Mr. Scouten met him, Booth was an old man. He sanctioned Mr. Scouten's troop, and Mr. Scouten, still a teenager, had no prohibition against signing to his scouts. At the Nebraska School, Mr. Scouten would remember later, signing flourished outside the classrooms and fingerspelling was used in the chapel. A few special classes for "slow" students used fingerspelling, but in most classes, deaf students and teachers pursued communication through speech and lipreading.

Intrigued by the issues of deaf education, the deaf students themselves, and sign language, Mr. Scouten decided to become a teacher of deaf children during a time when instruction was primarily through speech and lipreading. He trained at California School for the Deaf in Berkeley and then went to Rochester School for the Deaf in New York. In Rochester, he learned the technique of supplementing instruction through speech with fingerspelling. In 1941, he trained to become a teacher at Gallaudet College and earned his master's degree at the college. Back when Mr. Scouten was a student, cows and chickens were raised on Gallaudet's campus, only hearing people were admitted to the graduate school, American Sign Language was called "*the* sign language" and described as a nonsystem of gesture, and training for teachers was primarily in the technique of using speech and lipreading with deaf students.

Mr. Scouten was a devoted teacher. Busy on the campus of Gallaudet, not until he was forty-six years old did he marry Eleanor Powell, whom he met while conducting a workshop at the New Mexico School for the Deaf. In 1962, he was chairing the department that prepared incoming students for Gallaudet's four-year program, and Eleanor was taking care of their first son, still an infant, when Dr. Powrie Doctor, another Gallaudet professor, recommended him for the position of principal at the Louisiana School.

In the 1970s, several people, deaf as well as hearing, would snatch the signs from sign language and suggest that they be formed and sent through the air in accordance with English structure. In Mr. Scouten's day, however, the only way to make English visible on the hands was through the method he had learned in Rochester, sometimes called the Rochester Method, where an individual fingerspelled each word as he or she spoke. Mr. Scouten called this system Visible English (VE). He conceived VE as using every way possible to present and use English visually: fingerspelling, writing in class, on the blackboards, overheads, flashcards, and labels, and with younger children, using gestures, demonstration, and pictures.

According to Mr. Scouten, Lloyd Funchess, the superintendent, gave him a free hand to implement whatever he thought necessary to raise the academic standards at the Louisiana School, including insisting that fingerspelling—VE—be used by all the students. Mr. Scouten was eager for the opportunity. As he saw it, he had a chance to bring English to deaf students through a new surefire technique. Once we accepted the constant spelling that the new method entailed, we could see English, and therefore use it. Our understanding of the language would no longer be lacking; gradually our test scores would go up. It was a given.

Mr. Scouten's expectations were high.

He instituted fingerspelling more thoroughly than Booth had ever dreamed. He pledged that it would be the single means of communication on campus. From seniors to preschoolers, all of us would fingerspell. We would fingerspell to ask for the butter at the table and we would fingerspell as we figured out our social studies homework. Older students would fingerspell to ask for dates and younger students would fingerspell—or at least try to—to request paint brushes and tricycles. We would explore everything from the day's gossip to civilization's literature, through spelling on our fingers.

"English for every act," Mr. Scouten told people.

I think he meant well. Mr. Scouten and his wife had an appreciation for students and an appreciation for subject matter that can lead to great teaching. Mr. Scouten once described how he encountered a primary student bent over the grass, watching something intently. Curious, Mr. Scouten approached him.

"W-H-A-T A-R-E Y-O-U L-O-O-K-I-N-G A-T?" inquired Mr. Scouten.

"N-O-T A W-H-A-T. A W-H-O," responded the little boy.

On closer scrutiny, Mr. Scouten saw the boy was observing an ant, and he knew enough to be proud of him.

"That boy knew that he was looking at something animate," he explained. "Not merely an inanimate object. An ant is living. The boy was right. An ant was 'not a *what*. It was a *who!*'"

Now he had a chance to revolutionize the communication of a people and in doing so bring them into the hearing community. As a result, the biggest change in the campus was not in the nouns that unceremoniously labeled everything throughout the facility and its grounds. We would effect the biggest change ourselves. We would converse in a different language using the code through which it is committed to paper. We would transmit and decipher it through its alphabetic components in the milieu of sight and air, and presumably learn to do all this as quickly as deaf people sign and hearing people talk.

That was quite enough, but the plot thickened.

The deaf adult staff was to model the change by fingerspelling every conversation.

Yvonne, the new houseparent for the high school girls' dorm, introduced it first. A steaming mountain of a woman who had graduated from the Louisiana School years before, Yvonne began work as a houseparent almost directly after her own graduation from the Louisiana School. She would work there forty-three years and die soon after she retired.

Tall, single, and filled with energy, Yvonne confronted us as we arrived. She shepherded us about as we unpacked, brushed our teeth, and got ready for bed. From now on, Yvonne said, we must all communicate differently. Before, we had communicated in sign language. But now that would change. From now on, she proclaimed, we would communicate in F-I-N-G-E-R-S-P-E-L-L-I-N-G.

At first, we didn't understand. We already fingerspelled. The littlest children used fingerspelling before they even knew what it was. I've seen kids as young as four fingerspelling. "H-A-H-A-H-A-H-A," one four-year-old boy chortled to his friend. I'm not sure the child knew that his handshapes represented letters of the alphabet and those letters represented words for the sounds that hearing people make when they laugh. But he knew full well that expressing those shapes over and over displayed his merriment. By the time he grew up, he would use fingerspelling as we did, to render the names of people, towns, or streets, or to mark phrases in our conversation.

Yvonne usually performed the welcoming lecture half in sign, half in mime for the new students who had just entered the Louisiana School from public schools. But this year would be different. Yvonne told us that from now on we would have no signs at all. N-O-T I-N T-H-E C-L-A-S-S-R-O-O-M, N-O-T I-N T-H-E D-O-R-M, N-O-T I-N T-H-E L-A-V-A-T-O-R-Y. Fingerspell, fingerspell, fingerspell—and I-N E-N-G-L-I-S-H!

It may seem like a contradiction in terms to fingerspell English—transmitting a language based in sound and hearing, through a code dependent on sight and seeing—but why should it be? You can write English. You can represent English on paper with a pen. So why not represent it through space with spelling on your fingers? Yvonne explained that Mr. Scouten had decided that we, the Louisiana School's students, teachers, and staff, would take the language of print off its pages and transfer it to our fingers and generate it letter by letter through the air.

Yvonne sweated as she modeled her first all-fingerspelling S-P-E-E-C-H. We would get one S-H-E-E-T, one T-O-W-E-L, and one W-A-S-H-C-L-O-T-H every three days, she said. And there was to be no more wasting of toilet paper. We were allotted three sheets a squat. She held them up, pointing to each of the little squares. O-N-E. T-W-O. T-H-R-E-E. That was it. N-O M-O-R-E. And we could thank the State of Louisiana for those.

Even in my disassociated state, watching this speech was hard. One word bumped into the next, and sentences seemed to extend for miles. Fortunately the toilet paper speech was made every year, and I knew it by heart. My eyes wandered from Yvonne and found Jeanette.

"Is David back?" one of the other girls was asking in the signs we had been told we could no longer use.

"He's here," said Jeanette. "I saw him."

Too distracted and depressed to participate, I noticed, as if they were on television, a spate of conversations springing up around me. Thelma was talking to Gale and Carol was talking to Helen. Jeanette had sprung into one of her David stories. As Yvonne tried to interpret her spiel into English and think of spellings for each English word, the students renewed acquaintances and recounted episodes from the summer break. Yvonne's communication was breaking down. Before long, our stalwart houseparent, who usually was capable of holding all eyes in submissive attention, had lost the entire room.

And I had lost interest in the whole production. My eyes slid to my shoes and I wondered if I could go home this weekend. Nana started school at the same time I did. Who was there to prepare her dinner? Perhaps Aunt Happy would come to get me. Suddenly a gust of air wafted through the warm room and the floorboards trembled. All eyes returned to Yvonne, who stood next to the door she had just slammed shut.

Yvonne hesitated a minute, sweat pouring from her forehead. Finally with a glance in either direction of the dorm room as if some spy might be hiding under one of the beds, she resumed her oration. This time she signed. With the door closed, she expressed herself forcefully and kept our attention with ease.

Yvonne's attitude proved typical of many of the deaf teachers in the school, and a few of the hearing ones, too. Out of sight of the administration, a small rebellion occurred. Students and some teachers and staff would sign to each other until an administrator was glimpsed, at which point hand movements returned to finger-spelling until the administrator was out of sight.

Only one man seems to have publicly positioned himself against the new system. This was Max Ray, our teacher from New York City, who had earned his undergraduate degree at Gallaudet College and his master's in education from Louisiana State University. He was one of my favorite teachers, even though he taught the distinctly unalluring subject of math. Mr. Ray was an old-time deaf teacher who believed that his obligation to students extended beyond the classroom. Whether the problem concerned algebra or quarrelling in the dorm, we felt we could approach him for help, which he was always willing to extend.

Mr. Ray was adamant that VE had no place in his classroom or any math class. The idea was laudable, he said. The reality was a disaster. Maybe VE would be useful in teaching other subjects, he told Mr. Scouten in an effort to appear open-minded. But not for his subject. Not for math. It was hard enough to teach math when he had a full array of signs to choose from. Lord knows, hearing teachers didn't fare any better, and they used voice. Verging from conciliatory to defiant, Mr. Ray told Mr. Scouten he would not use the system.

"*You* teach with VE," he told Mr. Scouten.

Thus it was that Mr. Scouten appeared before Mr. Ray's students ready to teach a math class.

It must be said Mr. Scouten was no slouch as a teacher. In fact, I believe it may be argued that he was a gifted teacher. At Gallaudet, he had beguiled students into memorizing whole paragraphs of Shakespeare, and he was soon to give me a grammar lesson that would last me a lifetime. But even Mr. Scouten was helpless with only the letters of the alphabet and a class of restless teenagers reluctantly sitting in an algebra class. Mr. Ray says Mr. Scouten made it partway through a lesson before giving up. But give up he did. Mr. Ray was given permission to use signs in his classroom. Mr. Scouten had one caution: The classroom door would have to be closed. It wouldn't do for other teachers to see him.

Without either the credentials or analysis of Mr. Ray, but with all of his passion, Anna Gremillion also tried to resist the finger-spelling dictate in her physical education classes. She didn't stand a chance. Within a few more years, Mr. Scouten would be questioning her preparation for teaching and asking for her resignation. Her husband, Harvey Gremillion, handled the new system with the accomplished grace of an aristocrat. He seems never to have questioned it, either in his classroom or with the administration. Perhaps he hoped that Mr. Scouten's theory was correct and the pain of it all would be worth it. In any case, he kept us interested as we made our way through world history, despite the fact that he could only present it in alphabetic doses.

Ronald Nomeland, who had taught at the Louisiana School several years before, also learned the method of fingerspelling English at the Rochester School. Nomeland, who would get his doctorate from the University of Syracuse and teach at Gallaudet University, discovered that students exposed systematically to fingerspelling learned and used the names of the tools in the print shop. The deaf child of deaf parents, he also noticed how students' fingerspelling conformed to principles of sign language. I W-E-N-T L-A-S-T W-E-E-K, the students would sign with the last group of letters sweeping over our shoulder, in the same direction and shape as the sign LAST-WEEK.

At the Louisiana School, the grumbling continued. When some of the deaf teachers were asked to fingerspell their conversations with each other "as an example," one of our alumni stepped up to the plate. Rose White Barbin was a graduate of the school. Her mother had been homecoming queen and her daughter would later graduate slightly before I did. Rose offered her pledge that the deaf teachers would fingerspell all of their conversations if the hearing teachers did the same. It was a fair offer. Of course, no one seriously expected hearing people to limit themselves to letters in space. They might flutter their fingers as they tossed words back and forth from their lips. But the finger-flutter was for show. Connected through sound, hearing people never had to decipher the message from their fingers. But not even Mr. Scouten dared to try to enforce Mrs. Barbin's offer, and the idea simmered to a standstill. For the deaf staff, the challenge was real—and it was enormous. Two interpreters attended meetings of teachers and administrators; one interpreter fingerspelled what transpired, the other interpreter signed it.

Aside from his pedagogical obsession, Mr. Scouten maintained a lively interest in the students and staff. One day, I encountered him unexpectedly in English class, where I was in a misdirected dialogue with the teacher. Despite my determination to maintain a wall between myself and the world, I was struggling to understand something that I had written incorrectly. I had asked a question and the teacher was trying to answer it, but in truth, we were both hopelessly lost and unable to understand each other, when to my astonishment and horror, Mr. Scouten ambled to the front of the class. He had been in the back of the room observing the whole proceeding.

I wilted immediately. Retracting my question and trying to hide my confusion, I tried to slink back to my seat. It was too late. Mr. Scouten was intrigued.

I don't remember exactly what he said to me, and I've no idea how he used the fragile tool of fingerspelling to accomplish so serendipitous a grammar lesson. The construction that stumped me is one that has frequently stumped deaf students—the passive voice. Passive voice, the joy of administrators and the bane of writers, permits the subject of a sentence to duck into its bowels. Native English users know immediately that "Jane *hit* Paul" and "Jane *was hit by* Paul" mean dramatically different things. This convolution isn't so naturally understood by those who learn English as a second language. Mr. Scouten paused on his appointed rounds to explain.

"If you see both the past tense and the word *by*, it is a different kind of sentence," Mr. Scouten fingerspelled at me gently. "The word after *by* becomes the subject of the sentence."

Without pondering the peculiarity of this language, I simply suddenly grasped what Mr. Scouten was saying. The tip-off was mostly in that tiny word, *by*. Mr. Scouten had me demonstrate with a few more sentences, just to prove that I understood. This was an auspicious achievement for a ninth grader, and Mr. Scouten helped me accomplish it on the spot. That he did so makes me think he was quite extraordinary and could have been more so if he would have signed.

Then there was another time when we were all outside playing, and one of the young children needed to run inside to use the bathroom. I took it on myself to tell the adult in charge about the situation, and Mr. Scouten saw me as I conveyed the information.

"Don't say it in the sign way," he admonished me. "Say it in fingerspelling: S-H-E H-A-S T-O G-O T-O T-H-E B-A-T-H-R-O-O-M."

Yes, that's what he said: Code the sentence in English and produce each letter of each word, rather than indicating the child and making a single sign.

I nodded politely.

"By the time I got all that out, the poor girl probably would have wet herself!" I flashed the signs to Jeanette in the time it takes to blink an eye as soon as he turned away.

Jeanette glanced around to see if anyone was watching. She didn't laugh.

We complained about it and we laughed about it, and we complained some more. Later, I was told that some of the Louisiana School graduates at Gallaudet College considered signing a petition of protest. I was told some students and teachers at our school did sign a petition. But while I was a student any protest stayed so far underground that I never felt any rumblings of it.

Mr. Scouten instituted another change too. He looked at our curriculum and he looked at its claims, and he saw a grand mismatch. Our high school not only wasn't providing an appropriate curriculum to juniors and seniors, it wasn't providing appropriate curriculum to anyone. A parent complained that his sixth-grade hearing son and eleventh-grade deaf son were using the same textbook. To correct the situation, Scouten proclaimed that our twelfth grade was now our ninth grade, and each grade was bumped down accordingly. We would add a new grade every year, he announced, until the Louisiana School really did have the high school it claimed to have.

There was grumbling about this, but at least a few teachers supported it. Max Ray, for example, embraced Mr. Scouten's reconstruction of our program. Mr. Scouten was only recognizing what already existed, he said.

"Scouten raised standards," Ray maintained, and not just by restructuring the curriculum. Ray and other teachers believed that Mr. Scouten's labels—so like my father's—were helpful, especially to the younger students. Today, with a department of the Louisiana state government using my old school, yellow paint covers those block letters, like so many embarrassed band aids. Few people know why they are there.

While many of us accepted the ubiquitous labels and came to accept the elimination of the high school in order to create it anew, no deaf student I ever met supported the idea that we should communicate always and only through fingerspelling.

Although this was a convulsion in my program, I'd be lying if I said that this was my strongest memory of my first year back at school after my mother died, or even if I said that it was the most important one. My memories are vague, stilted, and gray. I didn't pay attention when my friends made jokes with me. I had to remember to laugh when I saw other people laughing.

Still, I performed my schoolwork, and the character that the school was molding into mine became obvious in some of my writing. *The Pelican* published student work in those days, just as it did one hundred years before and just as it does today. *The Pelican* published a story I wrote based on an experience with my brother, whom the teacher insisted I call Grady.

A Cruel Girl

When I was a young girl, I did not understand right from wrong. I was a mischievous, mean, and vindictive girl.

One Sunday afternoon, my aunt drove all the way to Baton Rouge to bring me back to school. There was heavy traffic that made Aunt Happy nervous at the wheel. I was sitting between my aunt and Brother Grady. I knew I was going back to school. I was excitedly watching the cars pass by on the busy highway, when I got a glimpse of Aunt Happy hurriedly replacing something shiny in its socket in the dashboard. I was curious and stared . . . it was a cigarette lighter. Quickly I looked up at Aunt Happy, but she was paying close attention to the traffic . . . I grabbed the lighter and examined and toyed with the shiny thing.

I noticed my brother was sprawled and sleeping on the seat beside me. I thought it would be a thrill to play a trick on him. I pulled the end of his T-shirt up and pressed the hot end of the cigarette lighter hard on his bare stomach.

Poor Grady flew in the air and howled with pain. Aunt Happy was terrified and pulled over to the side of the highway. As soon as she discovered the trick I had played . . . she blew her top at me. I did not understand her.

Poor Grady suffered all the way to Baton Rouge, while I was sitting . . . and pouting.

Now that I look back at my childhood days, I feel ashamed about picking on my brother.

I don't remember writing this or much else about schoolwork. My strongest memory is of crying at night and not being able to sleep. I wondered how Nana was doing and if Aunt Happy and Mrs. Richard were taking care of her. I wondered if Daddy were drinking too much.

"You don't laugh anymore," Jeanette said.

"You don't eat much anymore either," said Thelma.

Mr. Ray asked the other teachers to cut me some slack in the classroom, and Anna Gremillion stood by with her hugs.

Word of my incapacity got around to Mr. Scouten. He called me to his office one day to ask me to explain. I told him about my mother's death. In my agitation, I told him about my father's drinking and about Nana, the little sister whom I had left behind. But he could do no more for me than my teachers and friends.

9

❧

$\mathscr{A}$t Home At School

I am he as you are he as you are me and we are all together.

—JOHN LENNON AND PAUL MCCARTNEY, "I AM THE WALRUS"

We may have been too young to explore the mysteries that sparkled like firecrackers around and inside us, but we sure knew they were there. David Oglethorpe called the enclosed sliding board on the playground "the kissing hall." To this day, he claims to have been a kind of elementary schoolyard masher. I never met him—or anyone else—on the sliding board. Either he was after older prey, or perhaps he was dreaming.

Once, David went right to the principal to ask the definition of a new word. We'd all seen it. It was scrawled on the walls of the buildings by the river. David, still making up for the time he'd spent in public school in terms of his English vocabulary, encountered it in a public bathroom in downtown Baton Rouge. None of us knew the word that so puzzled him, though in this day and age every fifteen-year-old certainly knows it. The word was *fuck.*

Lillian Jones, a former supervising teacher, was the principal when David needed to know the definition of this word.

"Look it up," Mrs. Jones told David, when he entered her office to question her on the subject.

Reluctantly, David dug up a small dictionary from the English department. Repeated checking revealed that the dictionary chose neither to supply the definition he sought, nor even another look at the word itself.

Unabashed, David returned to Mrs. Jones. Quite abashed, Mrs. Jones sent him to a male teacher. The teacher sent David back to Mrs. Jones.

Giving in to the inevitable, Mrs. Jones scrawled another word on a piece of paper.

"That word means this word," she said,

David looked down and saw: *intercourse.*

"Now look up that word," said Mrs. Jones.

David returned to the dictionary and progressed in the subject that used to be called the facts of life. He even pursued the subject in speech class. This class was the cause for considerable complaint for David and the others who attended it. I don't doubt that speech is important, maybe even terribly important, but sometimes poor speech is worse than no speech, and the emphasis hearing people put on tone and pronunciation is a constant source of irritation to deaf people. People hear whatever it is that makes our accent "deaf," and look at us like we've sprouted broccoli from our eye sockets. In school, speech class meant time spent doing exercises that were neither pleasurable nor meaningful.

David was somewhat mollified, however, when the speech teacher turned out to have very big breasts. He was totally reconciled when the weather turned warm and the teacher turned to low-cut clothing. Remonstrated for taking too overt a peek, he was unrepentant.

"I may be deaf," he told the teacher bluntly, "but I am sure not blind. I can see!"

We were all teachers and all students of this subject, and we pursued it avidly. Jeanette returned from Christmas vacation with a lesson from her mother.

"Adam and Eve didn't eat an apple," she told me. "That was not the sin that got them kicked out of the garden."

Oh, no?

"They had sex," she said, her signs very small.

Sex? Could any word be more explosive?

I stared at her too astonished for words.

"It makes sense," I decided at last, after turning the thought around in my mind, though I still wasn't quite exactly sure what sex was.

It was Pat Harsh, dear serene Pat, who tumbled into the most trouble. Pat, the most quiet and innocent of all of us, was asked to be a lookout for the students who were necking in the dark hallway near the laundry. Apparently for some students, necking turned into more extensive involvement. When they were surprised by an adult, they were all summarily suspended. Pat was rounded up in the same bust, although she stood outside of the main arena of action, and virtually alone.

Deeply shamed, she was sent home. Only her mother's trust and understanding kept her from despair. To return to school, a letter of apology was required. At first Pat wouldn't write it. She was innocent, she protested. Her mother knew that. Still she counseled her daughter to write the letter. She even helped her. Getting back to school was essential.

Once back on campus, more humiliation waited. A school assembly was called. Pat and the other recently readmitted students were forced to stand on stage for a public chastisement. Mrs. Jones delivered it personally. Deeply outraged by the event, she approached each student for a personal scolding.

Pat felt the sting throughout the rest of her years at the Louisiana School.

"I felt everyone knew," she said much later, though I couldn't even remember the incident. "I felt people thought I did something dirty."

She ran afoul of Mrs. Jones one other time. This time it was because she was repeatedly late for her first-period class. In frustration, the teacher sent her to the principal's office, where an indignant Mrs. Jones greeted her. Pat explained that the reason she was late was that she always had to run back to the dorm after breakfast to go to the bathroom.

Mrs. Jones jabbed Pat in the chest, her fist closed but the center knuckle extended. After a few jabs with her knuckle, Mrs. Jones solved the problem.

"Don't eat breakfast!" she said, with a thrust at Pat's breastbone.

Once back in the class, the teacher followed up with a punishment of his own. Pat had to write a sentence one hundred times: "I will not go to the bathroom."

She did it. She wrote one hundred times that she would abstain from a totally unavoidable act. We laugh about this now.

We laughed about a few things even as they occurred. Once, the school received a donation that made it possible for us all to go see the new movie, *Cleopatra*. David was entrusted with the task of buying the tickets. He walked to the movie theatre with an air of importance.

"How many?" asked the sleepy attendant in the ticket box.

David tried not to smile.

"Sixty," he said.

Soon afterward, we marched to the movie theatre in downtown Baton Rouge in our sex-segregated rows and filed into our sex-segregated seats. The movie roared to life and we sat transfixed by the colors, the clothes, and the passion. There were no captions, of course, and we usually had no background for understanding the story line and the dialogue. Only much later did I realize that Egypt was a real place and Cleopatra was a real queen, that Elizabeth Taylor, Rex Harrison, and Richard Burton portrayed people who had actually lived in a faraway, not make-believe, land.

The dorm sometimes sprang to life after the lights went off, with students laughing, partying, and tossing pillows at each other. One student would serve as lookout, and when a houseparent was spotted, everyone would flop quickly back to her own bed. The deaf houseparents weren't fooled at all. They simply placed their hands on the backs of the supposedly sleeping girls. At the touch of those gentle hands detecting rapid breathing and wildly beating hearts, the girls knew they were in trouble.

❧

When I was sixteen, I saw a knot of girls crowded around the window and went to join them. As we watched, a large car slid through the gate and wound through the campus. It was an enormous vehicle with dark windows.

"L-I-M-O-U-S-I-N-E," spelled Thelma excitedly.

The car stopped in front of the boys' dorm.

"Maybe a movie star," someone signed surreptitiously.

The driver, wearing a uniform and a small cap, jumped quickly from the car. His appearance brought our speculations to a halt. The man negotiated his nimble way to the rear of the car and opened the passenger door.

A boy, a bit younger than I was, got out. He put his hands on his slender hips and his eyes swept the campus.

Understanding rippled through the crowd at the window. This was no stranger, but Jim Hynes. As he arrived, we watched in something between alarm and enthusiasm as suitcase after suitcase emerged from the enormous vehicle out of which he had sprung. Furniture, collected from one of his mother's apartments, would arrive later. Now Jim surveyed the campus like a small deaf Warren Beatty.

Jim was in his early teens, not tall, but already muscular. His mother was of French heritage, one of the descendants of Europeans that had dominated Baton Rouge society since the 1700s. These French were different from those that settled the small towns and bayous where the rest of our families lived. They had laid claim to New Orleans in the same way the English had laid claim to Canada. While most of our ancestors had fled as refugees, Jim's ancestors had come, settled, and conquered culturally. Just how eminent his family was, Jim was always in the process of discovering. When he was a child, he understood that his grandfather was treasurer of the Cathedral of St. Louis, the oldest and grandest Catholic church in Baton Rouge. When he grew up, he learned that his great-grandfather had been one of its founders.

His father knew nothing of all this prior to meeting his mother. He had been a student at Georgetown University Law School in Washington, D.C., far from his own home in Michigan, when a friend asked to borrow his car. The friend's sister was participating in some kind of pageant at the White House. At the word *pageant*, his father pricked up his ears. *Pageant* meant pretty girls. He said his friend could indeed have his car, and he could have a chauffeur, too—Jim's father himself would drive. When the two men got there, they found Jim's mother was one of the participants. After she returned home to Baton Rouge, Jim's father went to visit her.

Love was born.

They had five children. The oldest, a girl named Kenny, was born deaf. So was Jim, the youngest. In between were two hearing sisters and a hearing brother.

While most of our parents turned to the Louisiana School with gratitude and relief, Jim's father had determined that his son would never be enrolled there. Raised in Baton Rouge, Kenny and then Jim initially went to a private Catholic school in St. Louis, where speech was emphasized and signs were banned. Jim was the demo kid, as he tells it, the boy whose speech was so good that it was used to advertise the school's program. Jim hated his success. It meant performances that he felt were demeaning and private tutoring for which his parents paid extra and, more importantly to Jim, which occurred during what was supposed to have been his recess. While his friends cavorted on the playground, Jim practiced making the sounds of the English language. Again and again he would say the same sentences, rehearsing for his next performance.

"Marco Polo went to the Far East," he remembers intoning, while prospective parents and interested adults listened and nodded. Only much later did Jim learn who Marco Polo was or where the Far East was.

"The meaning of what I said wasn't important," Jim would say, his genial face contorted briefly in irritation. "What was important was pronunciation, pronunciation, always pronunciation."

From the time he was a small child, he flew back and forth regularly to his private school. He came to know the stewardesses, the pilots, and even the planes. He accepted the trip as the only way he could get an education.

Yet the Louisiana School was just a few miles from his home. This irritating fact, Jim says, his father took great pains to keep secret. Even after Kenny, eight years older than he, enrolled at the Louisiana School, Jim knew nothing of the program in his hometown. It was left to Jim to discover the Louisiana School for himself.

As Jim tells the story, when he was about thirteen, he arrived home from his school in St. Louis and was taken to his father's downtown office. His father had one last client, and he told Jim to amuse himself in the city for an hour or so while they finished up. Jim was wandering around in the streets when he caught sight of a group of older teens signing. Jim didn't know sign language. At his school, sign language was forbidden. The children used only gesture, and then only when the nuns weren't looking. Jim was attracted to the signs and the other kids immediately. Friendly and curious, he approached the teens.

"Are you deaf?" he asked, using gestures he'd used at school and with his sister.

Assuredly they were deaf, they replied.

"I'm deaf, too," Jim proclaimed, but he must have spoken the words along with his gestures.

"Oral," they responded, half mockingly, pounding one their fists against an opposing elbow, demonstrating the way spoken language bounces off without penetrating the understanding of human beings who are deaf and in oral classrooms.

He talked with them by pairing hand and mouth gestures, communicating much as he did with his sister. A little work yielded comprehension. When the teens said that they went to a nearby deaf school, Jim was intrigued. He followed as they made their way back to the Louisiana School campus.

Passing through the gates, Jim's eyes took in little children, kids his own age, and teens on the verge of adulthood. In the dorm, the richness intensified. Supervising the dorm was a contingent of deaf adults. Jim had never seen deaf adults who signed, and he had never seen deaf adults in positions of authority. The experience was overwhelming.

"I thought all the deaf people in the world went to my private school," he said many years later. "The school was located in the middle of the country, and we had students from all over the United States, as well as Jamaica, Cuba, and other faraway lands. I never guessed that there might be so many other deaf people, especially not in Baton Rouge."

His father's son, he remarked on the number of pretty girls. Pretty *deaf* girls. Still another surprise awaited him. On the wall were photos of boys playing football. Jim recognized one of his new companions.

"You, football?" he asked.

Grinning, the boy nodded.

Football and pretty girls. Where had he been all his life?

"What's wrong?"

Jim's father had finished with his client and was driving him home.

"Why didn't you tell me about the school?" Jim demanded. He couldn't help it. He was frustrated and angry.

"The school?" his father asked. *"What school?"*

"The school with deaf students. Why do I have to go away when there is a school for deaf students right here in Baton Rouge?"

Now his father was angry. He pulled the car over and stopped so that he could talk with his son.

"How did you find out about that school?" he demanded.

"I want to go to that school!" responded Jim, ignoring his question.

"I told you to go for a walk that *way,"* said his father, gesturing toward the quadrant of Baton Rouge in the opposite direction from the school.

Jim explained about meeting the teenagers.

His father shook his head wearily. *"That school is no good,"* he said finally.

Still, Jim's father didn't ignore his son's desire to stay near home. He took him out of his private out-of-town program the very next semester, so Jim could stay in Louisiana.

His father had found an oral school in New Orleans.

"My father meant well," Jim would say later. "He just didn't understand."

Perhaps Jim's dad's mistake was the same mistake that so many parents make. He may have confused speech with talking and with language itself. I wonder if Jim's father was one of those people who have a kind of aching love of language—in sound, in print, in stories, and in song. I wonder this because Jim credits his father with helping him discover reading. Reading, like speech, was the focus of schooling for deaf students, and Jim had spent hours in the classroom confronting sentences and short paragraphs of print, and answering questions about what they meant. He was already a teenager, with many days of such programming behind him, when his father tossed him *Catcher in the Rye.*

"You'll like it," his father said. *"It has dirty words."*

Jim did like the dirty words. He could recognize them easily. But he pulled meaning from the other words, too. Somehow the sentences fell together and Jim read Salinger's classic. He says it was the first novel he ever read.

Another novel followed, and then another. For the first time it occurred to Jim that reading had a purpose beyond pleasing anxious parents and teachers. As he made his way through literature, he discovered that print could be the source of information and—even more startlingly—pleasure.

Jim was named after his father, who had a special affiliation with the son who bore his name. That affiliation was strengthened by their shared love of golf, and he invested in Jim's talent. Golf was not a minor undertaking in Jim's family. It was a somewhat sacred tradition, and tradition held the family together like warm handcuffs. When they had father-and-son talks, it was usually in the country club that both considered a kind of second home. Once when Jim expressed frustration at the social limits imposed by being the only deaf person in that whole hearing place, his father responded with a science lesson.

"There are five senses," he explained. *"Hearing, seeing, touch, smell, and taste. You have only four. Now say we are each an hourglass, and some of us have five senses, others have four. For those with five senses, the sand filters through faster. It takes longer for those with four senses, but all the sand gets to the bottom sooner or later."*

The older and younger Hyneses played golf regularly, together and separately, enjoying the fairway, discussing the greens, working on hand position and putts. Jim grew from the little boy who would walk nonchalantly through the country club kitchen, picking up slivers of bacon from an indulgent cook, to the boy who showed promise with his swing.

When his father transferred him to the school in New Orleans, Jim rebelled the only way he knew: He refused to play golf. When he came home on weekends, he hightailed over to our school to hobnob with his signing friends.

The boycott didn't last long.

The father told the son he could attend the Louisiana School.

❦

His new school friends from the deaf school became Jim's guides to the world. He was as taken aback with us and our way of life as we were with him and his life. By the time Jim was fifteen, he had his own car, a 1957 Chevy. With great gusto, everyone in the vicinity would pile into it and off they would go for a treasured spin. Sometimes they would stop and Jim would buy everyone ice cream. I never joined them, but these trips were highlights for his classmates. Most of us chuckled about having such wealth embodied in one of our fellow students. We reveled in his money almost as if it were our own.

On Jim's initiative, he came to our homes and saw how we lived. He met the country farmers with the same open friendliness that he brought to meetings with school officials, financiers, and priests. He pulled up to one small home, several miles down a gravel road, and walked carefully into the living room, where light seeped between the floorboards and chickens scratched in the ground underneath. To his amazement, he found two sisters slept together in one room, four brothers slept together in the next, and the parents in the third. And all of them shared the same bathroom.

"Enough! You're teasing!" he told his friend, when he learned the parents didn't only share the same room, but actually shared the same bed. Assured it was true, he sought out his hearing brother when he returned home. His brother affirmed it: *Most married couples sleep in the same bed; it is only our family that is different.* Thus Jim learned that most people lived differently than he and his family did.

He learned about cultural prejudices firsthand, too. Jim had a rare grace, which went something like, "I'm deaf, you're deaf, so what's the big deal?" He took our beloved math teacher, Max Ray, to the country club to play golf, oblivious to the fact that Mr. Ray was Jewish.

Jim vaguely noticed that once inside the club, no one waved. He was used to seeing smiles and *"How ya' doin'"* on the faces of the other members, but he didn't see the welcome this time. He and his teacher kept on golfing anyway, talking in signs and having a grand time. Finally his father, summoned from his office by someone in the pro shop, drove up in his golf cart.

"There's an emergency at home," Jim's father said.

"An emergency?" Jim was horrified. It must be something very serious to cause his father to leave work and come to get him.

"Yes," his father assured him. *"We have to go now."*

Jim turned to Ray and apologized.

"No problem," Ray smiled as Jim hurriedly explained.

Jim met his father after they returned their carts, only to have his father tell him that he was heading back to work.

Confused, he asked about the emergency.

"I'll explain later," his father said.

In the privacy of their home, Jim's father noted that there were many Jewish people in Baton Rouge and many stores owned by Jewish people downtown, but did Jim see any of these Jewish people in the country club?

Jim shook his head. No. He had never seen any of these people in the country club. He had never really thought about it.

Jews were fine people, his father allowed; in fact, Jim's sister's friend was a rabbi's daughter. There was nothing wrong with people of different religions. They were fine people.

Jim waited. He knew everything his father had told him. The exact connection with golf and Max Ray was still not clear.

Finally the words came out of his father's mouth.

"Jews are not allowed to play golf at the country club," he said.

The ludicrousness struck Jim immediately.

"Who decided that?" he demanded.

His father became vague again.

"We should change that!" insisted Jim, outraged at the injustice.

His father was clearly unsure what to say next.

"Who's the president of the country club?" demanded Jim. *"I'll write to the president!"*

His father groped again for a way to convey to his deaf son what his hearing children understood with no words seeming to transpire whatsoever.

"Who's the president?!" Jim said again.

"I'm the president," his father admitted finally.

As Jim's astonishment rose to incredulity, his father talked slowly and carefully.

"It's not me that makes the decision," he said. *"It's the board. The board makes the decision. They voted."*

Voted. Jim was silenced by the grandeur of democracy in action.

Democracy eventually wended its way into the operating philosophy of the country club board. Jewish people and black people were eventually allowed to join. Max Ray himself returned there to play golf—twice with Jim's father.

Poor Jim. He was only a year at the Louisiana School before the sign language he had gloried in was relegated to darkened nooks and crannies of the campus, just as gestures had been in his oral school.

10

❧

$\mathcal{J}$eanette and David

Since feeling is first . . .

—E. E. CUMMINGS, "SINCE FEELING IS FIRST"

"See?" demanded David. His finger slid along the lines of tiny type of the September issue of the *Silent Worker,* the nation's magazine for deaf people published by the National Association of the Deaf. It was a story on the Louisiana School track-and-field squad by Art Kruger, a graduate of Pennsylvania School for the Deaf and Gallaudet College, who would chronicle sports in the deaf community for fifty years. Jeanette and I focused on the picture in the left-hand corner.

"There!" Jeanette said, pointing to a tiny face in the middle of the group. She'd found David of course, but David wasn't interested in the photo. His eyes were elsewhere in the article. At his urging, Jeanette and I fixed our eyes on the text. Here's what Kruger wrote:

Oglethorpe, sensational 16-year-old junior, pole-vaulted 12 ft. 6 inches . . . for another national standard as well as a new American deaf record.

"You're sensational!" gushed Jeanette.

Kruger noted all four of the national deaf prep records that year occurred at the Louisiana School. Senior Jeff Lambrecht earned the Deaf Trackster of the Year award, and John Shipman, who later became superintendent of the Wisconsin School for the Deaf, earned Coach of the Year. Kruger called our team, the Mustangs, "powerful."

> The Mustangs competed against five other schools this year and they were superior in every event except the shot put and perhaps the discus throw and high jump . . . they won the second annual Mason-Dixon Deaf Relays in cold, drizzling weather they encountered in Jackson, Mississippi. Results: Louisiana 69, Tennessee 46.5, North Carolina 44.5, Mississippi 40, and Alabama 24.

Jeanette and I didn't pay much attention to the numbers. I was busy trying to make out the features of the other faces in the photograph.

"Norris Kraemer," I pointed at Norris's picture. But Jeanette had eyes for no one else.

"You're sensational!" she told David again.

David grinned, his bravado mixing with shyness.

Oh, what a fake! I thought to myself. *He pretends to be embarrassed when he himself showed us the article!*

I looked at Jeanette in frustration. Why couldn't she see through him? In truth, lots of girls were smitten with David. He was tall and handsome, good in class, and a superstar in sports. In 1965, David would compete in the World Games for the Deaf. He won third place, making him the third best deaf pole-vaulter in the world.

David had returned to the Louisiana School after another stretch in public school, where he had been miserable because he couldn't communicate. After almost a semester among all that sound that he couldn't hear, feeling like he was inside an impenetrable bubble, and working hard just not to be laughed at, he asked to come back to the Louisiana School. Perhaps as a result of this break in his education, in addition to the early years that he had already lost while in public school, David was so far behind that he was never able to take English with his age group at the Louisiana School. He began to excel in math, however, and sometimes he and John Fruge would stay in class during recess for the sheer challenge of solving math problems.

He had suffered from bronchitis and asthma from the time he was a baby, and as a child he had recurrent infections in his sinuses and ears, which may have caused his hearing loss. He was the only person I ever knew who believed his hearing improved as an adult. Perhaps he simply outgrew his allergies. When he was little, he was so congested that the doctor refused to let him play sports, but David convinced his mother to sign papers releasing the school from liability and giving him leeway to join the football and track teams. He became a star on both.

At sixteen, he broke the national deaf record for pole vault. At seventeen he beat his own performance, and set a new national record. In 1962, the National Association of the Deaf named him National Track Champion. A year later, the *Silent Worker* named him National Deaf Football champion.

I didn't have much to say about all this, because I wasn't very interested in sports. And I couldn't get Jeanette to see David as the short-tempered, immature rascal that I conceived him to be ever since he threw that fit in my preschool classroom. I had warned her about him many times. By now I knew she wouldn't listen. Except for her fascination with David, I thought Jeanette was perfect.

Jeanette says she knew all along that David liked her in a special way. She says she took notice of him only after he expressed interest in her. Of course, no one could say that David was only interested in Jeanette. Quite the opposite. By high school, David had ushered a few of the older girls to the bowling alley, where a long dark hallway made necking a strong and easily seized possibility. Still, he remained stuck on Jeanette.

"She was very pretty," David remembered years later. "Maybe not the prettiest girl in the school, but always the prettiest to me."

Not even the death of a mother and devastation of a family can freeze forever the blood of thirteen-year-old. Slowly I began to feel my life taking form again at school, and despite rigorous efforts to keep us apart, the opposite sex was definitely part of the formation. Cleve and Norris were vying for my attention and both gave me a peculiar interest in responding. Jeanette and David were alternately loving and fighting. Helen quietly pursued her work off campus. And all the boys were after Thelma.

I remember lots of group outings. The most exciting was to the Texas School for the Deaf for a football game. The Louisiana School and the Texas School met every year across the scrimmage line in celebrated rivalry. We hated Texas and couldn't wait to beat their team. I was on the pep squad, which was made up of cheerleaders who didn't use voice. Jeanette, of course, was a cheerleader.

The schools took turns hosting the event and that year the Louisiana School team—players, cheerleaders, and pep squad members—piled into buses to go to the Texas School in Austin. The eight-hour ride was too far to consider mixing bodies that belonged to opposite sexes in the same bus, and two buses were chartered to make the trip. Girls piled into one bus, boys into the other, and we followed each other along the highway in high spirits. We hadn't gone far when the boys' bus broke down. Both buses pulled onto the shoulder of the highway, and the male staff explored beneath the hood to establish basically that the bus was beyond immediate repair.

The girls were told that we would have to return to school. The boys would commandeer our vehicle and continue on to the Texas School in the girls' bus. Needless to say we girls were outraged and distraught. After all, we, the cheerleading and pep squad of the Louisiana School, were certainly as essential to the spirit of the Mustangs as quarterbacks and linemen.

As the girls exited the bus in tears, pity descended. The staff made a call to the school for special permission to allow both groups of students to share the same bus. Permission was granted, and girls as well as boys climbed on the bus.

Justice had been done. Jeanette and David would improve upon it. They made their way past the rest of us to the very back of the bus, even slipping past the cheerleader uniforms that hung neatly across the aisle in the last seats. Among the generation that raised the art of necking to new heights, David and Jeanette now perfected the art across the flatlands. They kissed and pawed, and swatted away curious friends for miles.

Most of my trips were less flamboyant. Pat Harsh, now a senior, had permission to go off campus once a week into downtown Baton Rouge. Allowed to take someone with her, Pat chose me. Joyfully the two of us set out from the school to venture through the streets of Baton Rouge. Sometimes we would make small purchases. Sometimes we simply did our laundry. Laundry may present a chore to most people most of the time, but for teenage girls it's a delicious activity, second only to shopping. In washing one's clothes in a public laundromat, one pursues an adult activity among other adults. One operates large public machines. One dabbles in chemistry, measurements, detergent, and color separations. One manages one's own wardrobe. One takes charge.

The boys sometimes went to the levee, the fortified embankment along which the Mississippi flows through Baton Rouge. Pat and I only walked there once. We sat on the bank and watched the muddy waters and swollen cypress, and dreamed. We made plans. It never occurred to either of us that our best times might be happening right then.

We continued to make discoveries, wresting time-honored truths from the cocoon of regulations that the adults had infused throughout our school. All of us were at the age when energy beats through veins incessantly, responsibility and urges that feel adult begin, and rules are understood enough to sometimes circumvent.

I had Mrs. Boles for typing. Bless Mrs. Boles. I adored Mr. Ray and Mr. Gremillion, but Mrs. Boles was a woman—a frank and practical woman. She was one of those few hearing people who ended up teaching in a deaf school for reasons other than having a deaf family member or wanting to help deaf people through some kind of educational rehabilitation. She first learned of our school while playing high school basketball. Her team came to the Louisiana School to play against our Mustangs, and she was fascinated by sign language and the deaf basketball players.

Mrs. Boles was the one who explained why some of us were bleeding every month and how babies came about. She also, in answer to Jeanette's troubled question, assured her that taking off one's girdle did not cause a woman's body to explode. She also explained how one became pregnant: one kiss, then another, and boom. Contraception was a dirty affair. We would remain pregnant-free through abstinence. A boy couldn't really think or even see straight when it came to all the events that led to pregnancy, so abstinence was the girl's responsibility. If a boy truly loved us, he would understand. If he were the right boy, we would marry. We simply had to wait until then.

Where Mrs. Boles' explanations stopped, the older girls filled in. Thelma, my roommate when I lost my mother, was a font of knowledge. Two years older than me, she was vivacious and popular. Sometimes she exceeded the bounds of warm-hearted and spontaneous, and became downright adventurous. David told Jeanette that he adored Thelma, but he wanted *his* girlfriend to be "not quite so wild."

If anything, the division of students by sex was even more rigid as we grew older. But in at least one way it relaxed. This was due to John Lopez, another graduate of Gallaudet College, who was hired as dean of student life. For the first time, boys and girls were allowed to get together after class. We were supervised, of course. But every Sunday we could converge for a few hours in the recreation room and talk with each other about issues other than reading, writing, or arithmetic. Flirting—signed by touching thumbs, holding the hands parallel to the ground, and wiggling the fingers merrily—flourished.

We found ways to circumvent the restrictions. For one thing, we had signals. A girl who wanted to show a boy she liked him would brush her hand quickly against his neck, circling the back of his collar. Boys did the same thing if they liked a girl. We had special signs, too.

ONE FOUR THREE! We would flash each numeral in sign language across the dining hall. The numbers were a code. Flashed one after the other, they meant, "I love you." The logic behind this was: *I* is one letter, *love* is four letters, and *you* is three letters. Of course, lots of other combinations could make up a similar code, but we always knew what was meant. As feelings deepened, the code lengthened.

ONE FOUR THREE FOUR FOUR! All the students who caught sight of the long-distance communication knew that one student was telling another, "I love you, very much."

Most of the teachers were clueless. Many barely understood, "Please let me go to the bathroom," let alone an encrypted code. If they were really skilled, they might have recognized the numbers being signed across the dining room. Perhaps they thought it was the answer to math homework. Anna Gremillion figured it out mighty quick though. From time to time, she scrawled out the numbers on a slip of paper and slid it under the door of her husband's classroom. Just in case he didn't know who had written it, she signed her name.

At the Texas School, similar sex segregation sparked a similar secret code. Instead of flashing the letters as numerals, the students would hold three fingers—the thumb, the forefinger, and the pinky—aloft simultaneously. This became the internationally famous "I love you" sign. The pinky represented the *I* in finger-spelling, the thumb and forefinger together formed the *L* of love, and the thumb and pinky together formed a *U* for you. Ruth Phillips, a Texas School graduate who taught sign language at Gallaudet University, told me that girls and boys—standing in separate lines waiting to get into the dining hall—used the *I love you* sign as long ago as 1925.

I never saw the sign until many years later when I was working in Washington, D.C. Soon after I learned it, the sign skyrocketed to some kind of fame. Hearing as well as deaf people began to use it. U.S. presidents Jimmy Carter, Ronald Reagan, and Bill Clinton were each photographed using the sign. When a group of deaf students—winners in an oratorical contest sponsored by Gallaudet University—met George Bush in the Oval Office, he asked them, "How do you form that sign for 'I love you'?" It took a minute to get his stiff hand into the correct position, but the students reached out, gave his fingers a lift, the president got his fingers into their correct position, the doors opened to the press outside, and cameras flashed away.

From its secret use as private communication among students segregated by gender, not even recognized by most of the teachers who saw it, the I LOVE YOU sign became an icon first for us and then for the whole country. It even worked its way onto two versions of a U.S. postage stamp. On one stamp, a white male hand made the sign; on the other stamp, a white female woman signed I LOVE YOU to her baby. By the time the stamps came out, I was a little bored with it. Attached to jewelry and printed in stationery, I LOVE YOU was overused, tired, trite. Whether it's a waitress in a restaurant or a tourist in the adjacent seat on a bus, that's the sign they've caught and want to make. So I grimace at the sign now and I rarely use it, except maybe to hearing people who don't know how out-of-fashion it has become.

David, a senior while Jeanette and I were mere sophomores, was selected to take a special test to see if he were eligible to enter Gallaudet College. Gallaudet was the only college for deaf students in the United States, really the whole world. It wasn't just a coincidence that so many of our deaf teachers had gone there.

Taking the Gallaudet test was a rite of passage in every residential school in the country. When compared with other schools, the Louisiana School was unusual neither in its extravagant claims— greatly tempered since the arrival of Principal Scouten—nor in its limited program. Gallaudet offered a preparatory program for students who graduated from their high schools without attaining college-level proficiency in reading or math. The entrance exam attempted to determine which students should enter as preps, which as freshmen, and which should not be admitted at all.

In 1960 the test was a combination of the Stanford Achievement Test and a written test developed by Gallaudet's English department. In 1964, Gallaudet established a separate office of admissions, with Dr. Bernard Greenberg as its director. Greenberg replaced this combination with a new series of tests that focused on vocabulary, grammar, writing, mathematics, and nonverbal intelligence.

Of course, a lot of pre-test screening happened within each school. At the Louisiana School, it was not merely an honor to pass this test, it was sometimes almost a miracle to even take it. The system of tracking was quite deep at the Louisiana school. School officials determined a plan for each student's future—college or a trade—then designed each students' course work to prepare them for that future. The curriculum gap between the two tracks was profound.

Scheduled to take the test, David came down with one of his bouts of bronchitis the evening before. His temperature spiked so high that he had to sleep in the infirmary. The next day, they wouldn't let him out to take the test, but he heard about it from his friends, who told him it was easy.

Two days later, a confident David marched in to take the make-up.

He passed. He was going to Gallaudet.

"Write to me!" he told Jeanette.

She promised. Of course she would write.

The next year, Jeanette and I were juniors and David was a freshman at Gallaudet College. He found the classes boring. And every day he checked the mailbox. And every day, he found no letter from Jeanette.

"I kept wondering, *What's the point?*" he said years later. David wrote his mother for money to come home. When she sent it, he walked to Union Station and bought himself a train ticket. He held onto it only long enough to check his bags, then he sold it to a passerby. While the train carted his baggage to Baton Rouge, David hitched rides along the highways, using the money from selling his ticket to buy food, and enjoying the scenery and roadside cuisine of his native country.

He came directly to the Louisiana School. He arrived proud and excited.

When Jeanette saw him, she was shocked, not thrilled. She was dating the captain of the football team. She sought for ways to explain, but explanations don't matter sometimes. David left almost immediately. He went to New Orleans to work and play, and he did both real hard. Still, he didn't forget Jeanette, nor did she quite forget him. He visited her occasionally, hitchhiking and later driving himself to her parents' home.

2&

"I'm pregnant." Jeanette whispered to me, when we arrived back from spring break.

She was near tears.

I was horrified.

"David!" It couldn't be anyone else.

She nodded, crying now.

He had come to visit her at her home. For the first time, the kissing, stroking, and messing around went farther.

She'll have to get married, I thought.

But I couldn't bring myself to tell her so. I just stood next to her and watched her try to talk, while she cried and explained.

Later in class, I couldn't get my mind off Jeanette, David, and the baby growing inside her body. That scoundrel! I'd always thought he was no good for her. Now look what had happened. The thought of abortion never crossed my mind. I'm not sure I even knew the word. I did know the word *murder,* which was what I'd do to David if I saw him.

Across the room, Jeanette bent over her book, her brown hair tucked behind an ear, a finger raised to her lips, and her face as innocent as ever. I watched as she studied a text, and I thought how weird that there were now two beings in that chair, one very young and the other even younger and growing bigger day by day. A baby. A nightmare and a miracle. As I watched, she placed her hand over her stomach protectively.

"We need help," I told her after class.

We sought out Mrs. Boles.

She met us at the door of her classroom and, struck by our expressions, asked, "What is it?"

Jeanette burst into tears.

"She's pregnant," I said, near tears myself, but knowing no way to broach the topic except straight ahead. "David!"

Mrs. Boles stepped back into her classroom and motioned us inside. She put her arms around Jeanette and looked her square in the face. Could it be true?

Jeanette wiped tears from her face and nodded.

"David," she repeated. There was no anger or blame in her hands, only quiet acknowledgement, and, I guess, a desire to affirm that even though she'd been dating other boys, of course she hadn't really been with anyone else.

"How long?" asked Mrs. Boles. Jeanette's body was slim as ever.

Jeanette didn't answer. She just continued to cry.

Mrs. Boles looked confused. I watched the two of them fumble helplessly through facts and options, all the while wishing David were there so I could strangle him.

"When did you last have your period?" Mrs. Boles asked finally.

"My period?" asked Jeanette.

"Your period," pursued Mrs. Boles.

It was important to know. It meant adding or eliminating options. It meant how long we had to plan.

"I have it now!" Jeanette exclaimed through her tears.

"Now?"

"Now."

Mrs. Boles stared at her a moment, then burst out laughing.

"Then you can't be pregnant." She said matter-of-factly, still smiling in relief. "It's impossible."

I thought about it a moment.

"If you're pregnant, you stop your period," I affirmed.

Jeanette was watching us hopefully.

"Nine months, remember?" I remembered it from Mrs. Boles' Friday health classes. "You stop bleeding for nine months until the baby is born."

Jeanette definitely looked relieved.

"Stay away from him!" I told her.

I might as well have told Grady to stop catching frogs, or the frogs to stop laying eggs, or the sun to just stop coming up. Mrs. Boles was more practical.

"Talk to your mother," she said.

Jeanette nodded. We knew all about what hearing people call "the Pill." It seemed a daring sort of undertaking. But love was love. And even though both of them dated other people, they couldn't seem to leave each other alone. And just because she wasn't pregnant this time didn't mean she wouldn't be pregnant in the future.

On the way back to the dorm, I told Jeanette what Mr. Gremillion had told me that morning.

"He says I should take the Gallaudet test next year," I said.

Jeanette wasn't the least surprised. David thought it was easy, she reminded me.

"Why don't you take it?" I asked her.

She just shrugged. She wasn't interested.

I was interested. But I was also nervous. I'd been nervous about the Gallaudet test since I was a sophomore, even though I didn't think I would ever take it. Sure I knew that I was fortunate to be on what Mr. Scouten called "the academic track." That meant I took college preparatory classes. College prep meant college, and college meant Gallaudet—no other postsecondary institutions accepted deaf students in those days.

"You'll do fine," Mr. Gremillion assured me.

Other teachers, all of them deaf, chimed in with support over the next several months.

"Don't waste your time here," Mr. Corbett, our senior class sponsor, told me again and again. "Go to Gallaudet."

Most of the time I nodded, but in my heart I didn't even let myself consider it. For one thing I was scared to death of the test. For another, even if I were a deaf Alberta Einstein, ready to set the world on fire in some important way with some important theory, my daddy would no more let me go to Gallaudet than he'd let me go to Mars. My daddy didn't even like for me to go to school in Baton Rouge. The neighbors said that he still cried every fall when I left.

My daddy wanted me at home. Nana still needed me, too. Home in Rayne was where I was meant to be. But with anxiety, curiosity, and no small amount of hope, I decided to take the test and see how I would do.

Of all of us, only two took the Gallaudet test that year, Charles Luther Green and myself. We were both supremely nervous when we arrived in the cafeteria for the exam. We didn't talk at all. We sat down at our respective desks with several other desks between us. I pulled out my No. 2 pencil and blackened the best boxes I could.

In those days, it truly was a case of now or never. The window opened and then it closed. Helen, such an able student, already had a full-time job in a printing shop. She didn't know about the testing because no one told her about it. She resented her exclusion for years afterward.

"I didn't have a chance to try," she would say.

Jim Hynes stayed at the Louisiana School an extra year and prepared for the test. His tutor, Ed Corbett, who later became the superintendent of the Ohio School for the Deaf, got the job after impressing Mr. Hynes with his intelligence and good humor. But most of my friends couldn't do that. Thelma, Pat, and Jeanette were in the same boat as Helen—they did not have the opportunity to take the test. "I would have gone to Gallaudet," Thelma said later, "if I could have taken the exam."

"I wasn't smart," Pat said flatly, explaining why she wasn't chosen for the test. No arguments from me could convince her otherwise. A piece of her might have questioned a label brandished and slapped on by authorities, but never out loud. Most of us accepted the decision of the administrators and followed the course they had put before us.

Charles Luther and I both passed.

"It doesn't mean anything anyway," I told Jeanette. "There's no way I'm going to go to Gallaudet."

It might as well have been Beijing.

11

"You Should Be Proud"

I am a dance—Play up there! The fit is whirling me fast!

—Walt Whitman, "The Sleepers"

At home, my relationship with Aunt Mae remained locked in enmity. I complained about her steadily to Daddy.

"She kicks me to get my attention," I said.

"You exaggerate," he said.

"I do not!" I insisted.

"You girls need a mother," he told me.

"What?!" I was livid at the thought.

"No way is Aunt Mae our mother," Nana told Daddy quietly, in her perfectly grown-up way.

But Daddy wouldn't pay attention. Daddy couldn't believe the world was different from the way he saw it, and as he saw it, Aunt Mae was a well-meaning if misguided family member who could fill in for an absent mother for his two young teens. She might be a little overdramatic with men. She might be a little overstrict with me. But her heart wasn't bad, he thought. Daddy could never see that the simpering act she put on with him was just that—an act. She minced and parried and slithered around him to ingratiate

127

herself and keep a bed, nothing more. She had him utterly convinced of her virtuous intentions.

But one day she went too far.

I was ironing Nana's dress when the insurance man knocked on the door. He came every third Tuesday of the month to collect on the policy we had to insure the house. As I recall, the monthly premium was $1.50. It doesn't seem worth making the journey now, but it was fairly common back then. He would stop at other homes besides our own, and people would hand over similar amounts of money.

The sight of a male figure in a suit and tie was too much for Aunt Mae. She went flying out to the porch to see him, tugging her blouse a little lower and hefting her skirt a little higher. I watched their faces through the doorway, trading raised brows and smirks. I was so irritated by the scene. Why couldn't Daddy see through Mae's act? It was so plain. Why couldn't he see what I saw? I didn't even care if they saw me staring at them. Maybe if they realized they weren't in a private cubbyhole, they would stop carrying on so before the neighbors.

The smell of burning cotton interrupted my thoughts. Alarmed, I glanced down at the ironing board. Steam was rising from Nana's dress. I tried to lift the iron but it was stuck to the material. Frightened, I pinned down the material down with one hand and pulled up the iron with the other. Unfortunately, Aunt Mae was giving the insurance man a sudden oily farewell and hurrying back inside. The burning smell was strong and the material still smoldering when I hoisted the dress, looked through the spade-shaped hole with a crisp, black border, and met Aunt Mae's eyes.

It's a good thing that looks can't kill; I'd have died that day for sure. Not only had I interrupted her interlude with a receptive male, but I'd burned an enormous hole in my sister's dress. Glowering, Aunt Mae came toward me, tearing off her belt as she gathered speed. I pulled out the plug to the iron, propped it upright, and ran. We circled the room, Aunt Mae thrashing the belt through the air, and me a measly few paces ahead of her. The belt caught me several times. I felt leather rip across my shoulders and back, and once it curled like some kind of snake around my arm. I felt nothing. Adrenaline rushed through me, and I was only dimly aware of the blows.

After a few laps, I headed for the door. I burst outside into the sunlight and ran to the end of the sidewalk. Just as I had hoped, Aunt Mae stopped at the doorway, somewhat abashed at the thought of the neighbors watching as she whipped her niece. Finally safe, I stayed at the edge of the sidewalk and cried. My tears dried but I refused to go inside. I waited until my daddy came home. He saw I was upset, put his arm around me, and we walked inside together. Once the door closed behind me, I burst into tears, pulled up my shirt, and showed him my back. I could see by his face that the welts were still red. I told him the whole story. I held up my arm. An ugly red welt slithered from the wrist to the elbow.

Aunt Mae hovered on the periphery, trying to get Daddy's attention. Finally she got it.

"*Out!*" Daddy roared, quite plainly within my sight. "*Get out!*"

She tried to argue, but it was no use. My daddy had finally seen the light.

I was relieved. But like so much in life, her departure left us with a new problem: food.

It turned out that Aunt Mae had been contributing financially to our household; it was her money that enabled us to buy groceries. Her departure didn't improve Daddy's drinking, and no funds were forthcoming. Nana and I briefly reinstated our pleas to get his money from him, but Friday nights remained a lost cause. Sometimes he brought home free rice from his job, but we had no vegetables. The garden had been Mama and Brother's project, so it was long gone. So were the chickens, lost in a hurricane. The refrigerator was empty. And we never saw Brother. I wracked my brain.

"Cotton," I told Nana finally.

Nana, by now eleven, looked at me respectfully.

"We're going to pick cotton," I elaborated.

She nodded. If I said we would do it, then we would do it.

Somehow we found enough coins to take a cab to the fields where cotton grew in all directions. Our job was to reach down and scoop out the tuft from the tough brown pod. Nana and I picked until we ached. Then we picked some more. Each of us filled a single bag. We threw our bags over our shoulders and took them to a large man, who weighed them and then counted out our money. Barely cab fare home.

I tried to be positive.

"We can buy some milk," I told Nana. "And after we pick some tomorrow, we'll buy some cereal."

Nana looked at me, wordlessly, her face blank.

We arrived home with swollen, sunburned faces. Too tired to eat dinner even if we had had some, Nana plopped into bed. I tried to wait up for Daddy, thinking to tell him about our work, hoping he would be pleased with us. I couldn't hold my eyes open though, and when he arrived home, he found me slouched against the wall of the living room.

Instead of looking pleased, he took one glance at my face and shook his head.

"We picked cotton," I told him.

"Don't pick cotton," he said.

"Don't drink," I told him.

He looked hurt.

"You stop drinking, we stop picking cotton," I said.

He nodded. *"Friday,"* he said, remembering suddenly to write his letters in the air with his forefinger. *"I'll have money for food on Friday."*

I looked at him without hope.

The next day, Nana and I were in the fields again. The day after that, too. We picked every morning and every afternoon. Our faces blistered and peeled, and still we returned. Daddy couldn't really protest. Nana was in bed and I was asleep by the time he got home.

We lasted one week.

Nana looked sick all the time, and I was exhausted. And we weren't making enough money either. Truth to say, after we paid our cab fare, our pickings didn't amount to enough money to feed ourselves.

That night we were close to despair.

"Maybe we should send for Aunt Mae," Nana said it in the same wooden way she said everything else. I knew she didn't really mean it, but I still couldn't believe she would say that. It stiffened my spirit.

"That mean old witch," I said.

Nana picked up the corner of the blanket and swished it back and forth in imitation of Aunt Mae's hip-sliding walk.

"A wiggly witch, a wiggly witch," she was almost smiling for the first time since Mama had died.

"A vicious, wiggly witch," I said, not at all amused.

"Wiggly witch. Wiggly, wiggly witch," Nana was giggling now, and parading about the room, slashing the corner of the blanket back and forth rhythmically.

It was so good to see her smiling, even I had to laugh.

The next day, I devised Plan B and we moved ahead with it.

"Welfare," I explained to Nana.

The two of us went to a church in Rayne where food was distributed from a back door. They seemed to be expecting us. They didn't ask for identification, and we didn't have to fill out any forms. We walked out of there with flour, cheese, milk, and bread. All we had to do was sign our names.

"No good," said Nana when we got home.

The bread was dry and pieces of it were gray.

"Moldy," I gasped.

"Disgusting!" said Nana.

She threw it toward the trash can.

"Nana!" I lunged for it.

She understood. We couldn't throw away the bread. There was nothing else to eat.

Together we trimmed off the mold, put cheese on the hardened white remains, and ate the bread.

Soon afterward, Aunt Happy arrived. I don't know who called her or what they said, but it was just the beginning. Somehow word had gotten out. Our relatives came to our rescue. Food began to arrive with some regularity. Aunt Adele, who worked in a department store, brought us clothing as well.

We would never eat or dress lavishly, but we knew we wouldn't starve.

"I don't want to leave," Nana cried, as I returned to the house from visiting a friend.

"Leave?" I put down my suitcase stunned to see her crying. I hadn't seen her cry since our mama died.

"They're taking me away," she wailed.

"Who?" I demanded.

I admit I thought it might be our relatives, and I thought it might be good for her to live with them, especially if she could come home during my school holidays. Nana signed well by now, and our communication was quite easy, but the signs that assaulted me made no sense.

"Never touch me. Never touch me," her hands said.

"Nana, I don't understand," I said finally. "I'm not going to touch you. Sit down. Sit down."

She wouldn't sit down.

"Welcome home!" exclaimed Aunt Happy. She walked in through the side door, her arms full of groceries, and her smile proclaiming all was glorious in the universe.

Nana ran to her in tears.

"She's talking crazy," I said, but of course Aunt Happy couldn't understand my signs and Nana didn't see me. She was too busy crying and babbling to Aunt Happy.

Aunt Happy told me that Nana was talking about our daddy.

"You're not going anywhere," she told Nana. *"You're staying right here with us."*

Nana sobbed. She and Aunt Happy continued talking. I couldn't ask Nana to interpret. I didn't know what was going on, but I knew she was too upset to try to explain it to her older sister. After Nana felt better, she could tell me.

Aunt Happy turned to face me.

"Kitty, I have a question for you," she began.

I didn't understand her, but I knew that whatever she was saying was terribly important. My eyes went frantically to my little sister.

"She has a question," Nana said, wiping tears off her face.

I nodded. I was open to any question.

"Did your daddy ever . . ." Aunt Happy paused, not quite sure what to say. Nana's hands paused in midair, and I grew increasingly upset. "Did your daddy ever touch you?" asked Aunt Happy. Nana's hands moved swiftly.

"Touch me?!" I knew immediately what she meant, though I couldn't believe she would ever say such a thing.

Aunt Happy's lips moved, and Nana watched her face. Then her hands moved again.

"Daddy's a good man . . . everyone knows he's a good man . . . but he drinks sometimes . . . and when he drinks . . . does he . . . touch you?"

"No!" I roared it back with my voice and lips and hands.

Both of them jumped. Aunt Happy held out one hand apologetically.

When I calmed down, the two of them moved their lips at each other again. Then Nana explained. Aunt Happy's lips moved while Nana was signing, so I don't know what came from Nana and what came from her. Nana's hands said that someone had accused Daddy of molesting us. A social worker had come to the house and talked to Nana. They might want to talk with me, too.

"He never touched me!" I exclaimed again. "Never!"

Neither of them seemed to doubt what I said. Both kept nodding their heads, while their lips wiggled on and on. Finally Nana turned to me.

"I was mad because I thought you told the social worker a lie about Daddy," she said.

Then I remembered the conversation that I'd had with Mr. Scouten. Why had I ever talked so foolishly? I hadn't said one word about touching, but I'd talked about other things. Drinking. Hunger. Too much; I'd said too much. More than I ever should have told anyone. And I'd done it all in fingerspelling. Maybe Mr. Scouten had misunderstood. I felt my face grow scarlet.

Aunt Happy and Nana didn't give me a chance to confess. They both were hugging me hard, and I hugged them back hard, too, pushing the guilt as far down as it would go. Aunt Happy went to fix us some sandwiches. We joined her in the kitchen. Nana washed off the dishes from the night before, and I pulled a tomato from the bag and began slicing. For a few minutes, home felt almost like it had when my mother was alive.

Later that night, Nana and I were watching TV when Daddy came home. Nana knew he was there first because drunk people make a lot of noise. I saw her eyes on the doorway, and sure enough, a moment later it opened and Daddy veered through it. We watched as he went to the refrigerator and pulled out a beer. Nana shook her head, but she didn't say anything.

Daddy sat in a chair, put up his feet, and his lips moved. I glanced at Nana, but she ignored him. Then I think he pretended to notice what was on the TV. A moment later his eyes closed and his chin sank to his chest.

"Out cold," Nana signed.

She got up and poured the rest of the beer into the sink. Anger made her gestures jerky and harsh. She threw the beer can into the trash.

I watched her return to her chair and collapse into it. I waved for her to look at me.

"Nana, come here," I said.

Puzzled, she got up, and walked to me.

"Has he ever touched you?" I pointed to the sleeping man in the chair.

She just looked at me in irritation and exasperation.

"Did he?" I demanded. "Did he ever touch you?"

"No!" My little sister could not have been more firm.

Our eyes returned to the TV set. She didn't seem to be lying, I thought.

Nana waved for my attention.

"Did he ever touch *you*?" she asked.

This time it was my turn.

"No!!"

I couldn't blame her for asking. Such is the power of official accusation. It made both of us wonder about our own daddy. I blamed myself for a long time for being weak and cowardly in front of an authority I should have known better than to trust, and I'd almost destroyed my family. It was only as an adult that Grady told me that it hadn't been my fault at all. Mr. Scouten never distorted what I said, nor does it seem he repeated it to social services.

"It was Aunt Mae," he said. "Aunt Mae told Social Services." He said it was her revenge for Daddy kicking her out of the house. But fortunately, Social Services never came back.

Soon after that, Daddy announced he was getting married. The lucky lady was Irene Broussard, a widow with grown children, who lived nearby. Daddy's wedding date was the same time as our senior class trip. He offered to postpone the marriage, but I wouldn't hear of it. In truth, I would do no better with Irene than with Aunt Mae. I think Irene spoke only French, so of course she couldn't write to me. Thus cut off from any communication, the two of us lined up on separate sides of my daddy's life and tried to ignore each other.

Most of my life was at school anyway. Even during vacation I spent more and more time with my school friends. I would go to Thelma's or Jeanette's. Sometimes I would visit Lenora or we would go to church or community events.

I didn't see Nana so much anymore. She was busy with her separate life. She was dating, too. His name was Gerites Cormier, and we all liked him.

"I'm going to marry him when I graduate," Nana told me.

"You're too young!" I protested.

"I'll be seventeen," she noted.

"You have two years to change your mind," I smiled.

In truth, I was relieved that she seemed active and busy and happy. It was good for her to live like a normal teenager and not like some old woman. I was a little bit jealous, too. It seemed everyone had a sweetheart but me.

I had met no one special. There was sweet Norris: my age, athletic, a football star. Then there was Ben, down in New Orleans. Already graduated and working, Ben always had money and plans. I liked them both. Still, I didn't feel like marrying either of them, and I sure didn't feel like I knew what that word *love* meant. What I felt was that I wanted more.

Now here was my little sister, with her face lit and her eyes twinkling, and one man's name always on her lips and fingers. She seemed to have found what all those books and movies were about. My other friends seemed to find it, too—Pat had just written about a man named Bobby. He was hearing, but he had a deaf mother and two deaf uncles, and he signed well. She had met him at a deaf picnic. Pat said she was thinking of getting married.

I wish I could write that I returned to school thinking about graduating and the glories of college and traveling to Washington, D.C., if only I could persuade my daddy. In truth, I had a lot more on my mind; thoughts about college and travel were just some among so very many. College was daunting. I was helpless before the thought of it. Perhaps it was just as well that Daddy wouldn't let me go.

❧

Throughout the year, the deaf teachers had urged me to talk with my father about going to Gallaudet.

"Go to Gallaudet!" said Mr. Gremillion.

"Go!" said Mr. Ray.

"Don't waste your time here," said Mr. Corbett.

They didn't seem to understand that it was out of the question. I tried to quell my restlessness and still my curiosity. And I didn't mind staying in Louisiana, really. Except for Charles Luther, my friends were here, and Daddy said he could get me work at the rice mill. After this multitude of success, I would return home to Daddy and Irene, to Nana, to visits from Aunt Happy. Home was where I belonged. I could find a way to be happy there.

At least that's what I thought.

During the Easter holiday, I looked out the window to see Mr. Albert Seal approaching my house. Mr. Seal was a long way from the Louisiana School, where he worked as a vocational counselor, helping students find and keep jobs. He was hearing, white-haired, and a bit awkward with his sign language. I hadn't had much to do with him, nor him with me—at least not until now.

I immediately guessed why he was at my walkway. Mr. Seal walked slowly right up to our house and knocked. My face burning, I opened the door and let him in. My daddy, seated at the table with Irene, looked as surprised as I was.

Introductions seemed too complicated for me to manage, and I was calling Nana to interpret when Mr. Seal reached for my father's hand and shook it. To my surprise, the two men undertook to converse almost immediately. At first all was well, both of their faces stayed formal and pleasant. Except for repeated glances in my direction, they may not have even known I was there. Nana heard the conversation and came to my side.

My daddy was starting to look angry. Nana began to interpret for me, keeping her signs as small and unobtrusive as possible.

"They're talking about you going to Gallaudet," she said.

"I know," I said.

"All costs will be paid as part of vocational rehabilitation," Mr. Seal was saying. "Travel, tuition, room, and board."

My father shook his head. "Too far away," he said.

"Catherine deserves a chance to continue her education," said Mr. Seal.

"Washington, D.C.?!" my father almost spat the words.

"She can't continue her education in Louisiana," said Mr. Seal.

"It's not safe up there," said my father.

"Catherine will be safe," said Mr. Seal. "She'll be on a campus almost like the Louisiana School."

My father stopped talking. His face had grown even redder than mine. Irene left the table and poured herself another cup of coffee. Mr. Seal motioned to the papers that he had brought with him. My father jumped to his feet. His mouth moved violently and he pointed to the door.

"He's telling him to leave," Nana said.

Mr. Seal stood up, too. He was a little taller than Daddy, and his eyes and lips were steady.

"You must think about what's best for Kitty," signed Nana. "You must let her go!"

My father said something and Nana forgot to interpret.

". . . proud of her," was the next thing she said. I'm not sure if she was interpreting Daddy's words or Mr. Seal's.

Then her hands stopped completely. I glanced over at the two men. They were staring into each other's faces. Both were perfectly still.

Daddy called me over to him. *Do you want to go to this school?* he asked, his finger moving rapidly through the air, his eyes hard on my own.

I glanced at Nana to make sure I understood. Then I looked back up at my daddy and summoned every ounce of courage.

"Yes," I said.

Abruptly he sat down and signed the papers. Then he put down the pen and left the room.

Mr. Seal touched my arm and moved his mouth and his hands before he left. I've no idea what he said. I smiled nervously and nodded. In a trance, I walked him to the door. I've since replayed this scene in my head a million times, and each time I breathe an appreciative, "Thank you, thank you," to Mr. Seal. But in real life, I was too overwrought to thank him.

I was totally caught up in the events that swirl and coalesce during senior year. It is amazing that every year another junior class rises up to become the senior class. To me, the class of '66 exists as a ridge in time, unique and unduplicable. Of the fifteen students in my graduating class, most of us worked on the yearbook, which we printed as well as wrote and edited.

Mr. Corbett and Mrs. Gremillion were our advisors. Superintendent Funchess and principal Scouten included encouraging notes. The yearbook, which doubled as the May issue of *The Pelican,* was dedicated to Mr. Gremillion. He was devoted to his work, "like a father to us," we wrote.

Our class trip was to the magical state of Florida. While Daddy was getting married to Irene back at home, I was with my classmates visiting students at the Florida School for the Deaf before heading to Daytona Beach. We returned, sunburned and exhausted, the night before graduation.

The next day, I sat stiffly in my place of honor on the stage, looking for my own family among those gathered to watch the commencement ceremony. Finally I saw them: Daddy, Irene, Nana, Aunt Cecile, and her daughter Betsy were seated in a row toward the back of the room.

I was class secretary and salutatorian. The valedictorian was Charles Luther Green, who was also planning to go to Gallaudet in the fall. Charles Luther and I would both make a speech at graduation. Here is what I said as it was recorded in *The Pelican:*

> On behalf of the graduating class of 1966, I welcome you to this commencement program which is one of the most important and inspiring events in our lives.
>
> We realize it is the end of our schooling at the Louisiana State School for the Deaf and it is rather sad for us to leave our beloved school. However we hope the future holds for each of us happiness and success.
>
> Again we want you to know that we are very grateful to have each and every one of you attend this program. Thank you very much for coming and helping to make our last day at L.S.D. complete.

Charles Luther Green said almost same thing, but his presentation was longer than mine. He spoke for five weighty paragraphs. Of course, I use the term *speak,* but fingerspelling was required as always, and both of us fingerspelled every word throughout the public ceremony.

Years later, a student would beg for permission to sign her speech. Hearing parents were assured understanding of the proceedings because as the speech was fingerspelled, it was read in English. But this student's parents were deaf, and she knew that even if they were sitting in the front row, they would not be able to see the motions of her fingers clearly enough to decode the finger-spelling and understand what she was saying. Permission was denied. The student's parents understood nothing of their daughter's graduation address.

The deaf teachers didn't understand much of the graduation ceremonies either. They sat politely watching as the students they had taught and cared for received diplomas and moved their fingers up on stage. Afterward, they hugged each of us in turn, shook our hands, and read our speeches. As I say, it is something of a miracle to me that teachers in schools can do this every year, in our case nursing along a group from infancy to adulthood, watching them laugh, fuss, learn, and, above all, grow. It must be like constantly being pregnant and constantly having a baby.

Still, in the face of all of this, the biggest honor for me was my selection as homecoming queen. Rose White Barbin said that her mother, Geneva Caldarera had founded the tradition of homecoming queen at the Louisiana School in 1937. Geneva spotted the ritual at a public school and asked the faculty if such an event could happen at the Louisiana School. She received permission, the football team voted, and she herself was elected the first queen. In 1960, Rose, her daughter, was also elected queen, and in 1989, Rose's daughter Juliet Barbin was elected, making queenship at the Louisiana School homecoming a three-generation tradition in that family. Pat and Jeanette had been in the homecoming court the year before, and Thelma, the year before that. Now it was my turn.

It may seem weird that being a homecoming queen could feel more important to me than being secretary or salutatorian of my class, or even passing the Gallaudet test. But there it is. Football is the pinnacle of success for boys; popularity for girls. I wasn't alone in perhaps overvaluing this honor. Unlike all my other achievements, this one achieved mention in my hometown newspaper.

Daddy was gruff when he showed me the article, but I knew he was pleased. Nana said he showed it to everyone. I wished Mama were there to see it.

12

Gallaudet: McDonald's In Thailand

Heard melodies are sweet, but those unheard
are sweeter; therefore, ye soft pipes, play on . . .

—JOHN KEATS, "ODE ON A GRECIAN URN"

When it came time to leave home for college, Daddy and Irene took me to the bus station. I would take the bus to New Orleans, and in New Orleans catch the train for Washington, D.C. Nana, off I knew not where, didn't come. I was so excited, I was hardly even afraid. I hugged Daddy and even Irene and climbed aboard the bus.

Once inside I made my way to the window. Poor Daddy. He was trying not to cry, and Irene was looking mighty disgusted with him. I could see her urging him to leave the station, but of course he paid no attention. He stood there with his red nose and threatening-to-fill eyes and waited for the bus to pull out.

"I'll be okay," I mouthed through the glass. It seemed like forever before the bus finally lurched forward and I was on my way. In New Orleans, I still felt more excited and curious than scared. I saw another deaf person following the conductor's exaggerated hand and mouth gestures. When he took a seat near my own, I was ecstatic.

"Are you going to Gallaudet?" I signed.

He looked at me a moment quizzically.

". . . *Gallaudet!*" Amid a string of words that sprang from his lips, I caught only that one.

Oral, I thought, disheartened. He was deaf, like me, but he knew no sign language. So much for conversation.

Communication was impossible, so we didn't bother to try. We sat next to each other in our totally separate worlds. He seemed like a nice enough person, a little weird, but nice. As I watched the swamps and farmland rush past, I thought about Daddy and Irene and Nana. I half laughed to myself thinking about my daddy's lecture. Before he dissolved into a puddle of mush in the bus station, my daddy had been all strength and purpose. He stood in the doorway of our home, slid my suitcase out to the stoop, pulled the door closed so the neighbors wouldn't see, and scratched the air with his finger.

"*You get pregnant,*" said Daddy, pausing to draw a big stomach on himself with his hand to make sure I understood, "*you don't come home.*"

I nodded. Pregnant was not what I planned to be.

In Mississippi, two deaf brothers, graduates of the Mississippi School for the Deaf, boarded the train. They were also bound for Gallaudet. Through some kind of telepathy, we found each other. It took about three minutes. One was a prep, but the other had a whole year of college experience behind him. I was curious, but careful to restrain my questions. No sense in looking too eager. That most decidedly wouldn't be cool. In any case, I was thrilled to have someone to talk to. They were witty and friendly, and time began to roll as fast as the passing countryside.

In Alabama and Georgia, more deaf students got on. By the time the train turned up the coast, there was a little group of us sitting together and excited to be going North. I don't know if Gallaudet administrators had arranged this gathering with our parents. Ron Nomeland, a former school administrator who came to Gallaudet from Minnesota, said the same phenomenon occurred on his train, bound to Gallaudet through Chicago.

The oral boy sat alone among us, left out of the conviviality. Raised and educated without sign language, he moved his mouth like he was chewing a great big plug of tobacco that kept getting stuck against the roof of his mouth. It was downright ugly. It was unsuccessful, too. Hearing people drew away from him and stole glances from a distance.

I felt intermittent sympathy for him. It probably wasn't his fault that he was oral. It's not anyone's fault how they get raised. There are some deaf people who take pride in the fact that they don't use sign language. They "don't need signs," they tell people. For these deaf people, daily use of speech and lipreading is an important measure of their own success. "I don't use signs," the rationale goes, "therefore I must be superior to those deaf people who do." Of course this attitude builds on a tenet still evident in deaf school culture, especially in programs where sign language is forbidden, as well as the larger hearing community. The tenet goes like this: Hearing is superior to deaf; therefore speech is superior to sign; therefore, it is immeasurably better to talk like a handicapped hearing person than to sign like a normal deaf person.

The irony is that the decision to live on their speech and lipreading skills bears no relationship to how well an individual actually speaks and reads lips. Some are good, some are not. More than a few are sad creatures whose voices are abrasive and whose lipreading skills are nonexistent. They are cut off from hearing people by their inability to participate in normal sound-based conversation and avoided by deaf people because they resist the Deaf community. Locked in an isolation partly of their own making, they develop behaviors that result in being shunned by both groups. They exude this air of superiority among deaf people, because though they may just be dirt under hearing people's feet, we, the signing deaf people, are not even that.

This boy didn't seem like that at all. It was late in his life for him to learn signs. A deaf adult who signed would have little patience to teach him, and his ability to learn language and execute fine motor skills was reduced from what it would have been when he was a child. Nevertheless, this boy had made a decision. He was off to Gallaudet, a place that ran on sign language. He was ready to grow into the deaf person that he was. He was ready to learn sign language.

And we were ready to teach him. Sort of.

"This means 'good morning,'" one of the Mississippi brothers told him and demonstrated a sign for him.

There is a slight but significant difference in handshape between the sign for morning and the most recognized of all gestural obscenities. Like the obscenity, the sign MORNING entails one hand ascending beneath the opposite arm. The hand however, is held open, and the outstretched palm rises up like the sun. Make the palm into a fist or extend the middle finger, and the sign takes on a totally different meaning.

Not just deaf teens, but hearing teens know that gesture—and not just in the United States, but in Europe, too. Anyone with any experience in the world beyond their parents' living room and their school desk would have just laughed. But our young oral student lacked experience as well as sign language. He watched the gesture with wide eyes and copied it eagerly.

"Good morning," said our student's lips, proudly.

"Fuck you," said his hands.

We collapsed in laughter around him. This boy was so isolated that he not only didn't know the significance of the gesture, but he also didn't pick up on the tone of our laughter. He executed the sign a few more times, while his mischievous teachers added a twist of emphasis in their rising hands, and the rest of us grew uncomfortable. A few of us shook our heads registering disapproval, however friendly, and the boys finally dropped the production. Conversation resumed, the oral boy fell still and watched, and the train made its way through South Carolina, North Carolina, and Virginia.

By the time we arrived at Union Station in Washington, D.C., there were six of us. The Mississippi brothers, old hands at the cross-country commute, hailed a cab, and I joined them, the oral boy, and another male student as they clamored aboard the taxi and headed for Gallaudet. Gallaudet is only ten minutes from the train station, and the taxi threaded us swiftly through a few blocks of run-down residences. I stared at the houses as if I were on a grand tour.

When we slipped through the gates, the campus embraced us. Suddenly I felt eerily comfortable. We had left the strange and entered the familiar. While the cab driver watched, we asked other students directions to the dorms. After our trip through the land of the hearing, we had arrived in the land of the deaf.

From the moment I entered Gallaudet, I felt a sense of belonging, even though I had never been there before. For deaf people, Gallaudet is familiarity tucked into strangeness. It is a bit like when a traveler discovers a familiar restaurant chain in a foreign country. We, Gallaudet's new deaf students, were like Americans at a McDonald's in Thailand. We knew what to expect, while our D.C. cab driver did not. The driver followed our gestures dumbly. He was the outsider; we were home.

I was the only girl in the cab, and I got out with the others in front of the boys' dorm. The other boys met friends and disappeared. The oral student had the misfortune to approach a nearby group of students alone.

"*Good morning,*" he said, signing the obscenity he had learned on the train.

I don't know how the other students responded. I looked away and pretended not to see.

But I got mine. Standing outside of the boys' dorm, in the midst of a whole series of unlabeled buildings, I stopped the first student who brushed by me.

"Where's Peet Hall?" I asked. Peet Hall was the girls' dorm.

"Way over there," he responded, pointing to a building at the far end of the campus.

"Thank you," I said wearily.

Picking up my two suitcases, I schlepped in the August heat to the other end of the campus. As I got closer, I thought the building he had pointed toward looked like some sort of student union. In fact, that's exactly what it was.

"Where's Peet Hall?" I asked the next student I saw.

He had seen me trek over from across campus. Now he looked at me like I had two heads.

"Way over there!" he said, pointing in the direction from which I had come.

Peet Hall was right next to the boys' dorm. I'd been trundled across campus by an upperclassman as a prank.

※

In 1966, Gallaudet was the center of intellectual life for the nation's deaf people. Most of us had been the stars of our schools. The bright kids. The smart ones. Here we were no different than anyone else. No longer stars. No longer smart. Just average students.

Of course, there were exceptions to this and one was my roommate. Like me, she was from the South. She was older than most of the students, and the first thing she unpacked were her medicine bottles. She lined them up six deep on her bureau.

"What's wrong?" I asked her.

"Many things," she said.

I should have cut out right there. I hung around in spite of myself while she explained the etiologies of her various illnesses. Not everyone was suited to college life, and my roommate was totally out of her element. *How did she ever pass the test?* I wondered. She took the Gallaudet test several times, someone told me. Perhaps the final time the administrator felt sorry for her. I didn't. I tried to help her with math and English. But she was in so far over her head, she threatened to drown *me*. I was relieved when, after a few weeks, she left for home. I spent the rest of the semester in a private suite.

As a prep, I could take no elective courses; all of our courses were assigned. The dean was George Detmold, who had come to Gallaudet several years earlier from Columbia University. He restructured the curriculum at Gallaudet and achieved our long-sought accreditation. Dr. Detmold was a remote figure, rarely seen by the students. Most of our information came from Richard Phillips, dean of men, and Elizabeth Benson, dean of women. Ms. Benson, the hearing daughter of two deaf teachers at the Maryland

School for the Deaf, began teaching in 1926 and become dean in 1950. A beautiful signer, she interpreted for presidents John F. Kennedy and Lyndon Johnson, and helped to found the Registry of Interpreters for the Deaf. She had a reputation for toughness, but the toughness was tempered by a heart that could prove unexpectedly soft. With her long hair pulled into a tight bun, Ms. Benson maintained an air of correct primness.

I knew less about Dr. Phillips. We signed his name as a *P* in a curly line that emanated from the ear and continued swirling halfway down the chest because he wore a very strong hearing aid that consisted of an earpiece connected by a wire to a box on his chest. Dr. Phillips was deaf and a graduate of Gallaudet. Like Ms. Benson, he had deaf parents and a reputation for being fair but stern.

The sternest was Frank Turk, dean of the prep boys. Mr. Turk, who later went on to administrate several schools for the deaf, called a meeting soon after we got there and emerged in front of us like a drill sergeant. We had gathered in the auditorium, eager and curious, wanting to learn more about our new college and each other. Mr. Turk quickly disabused us of any notion that he was eager to work with us.

"You are not babies!" he informed us in signs that looked like he was directing aircraft on a runway. "I don't want you behaving like babies. I don't want you running to your parents. I don't want to *see* your parents.

"Drinking," he intoned, "is forbidden."

We didn't need a picture, but he drew one anyway: a glass, representing an alcoholic drink, an equal sign borrowed from math class, and the word *home*.

"Drinking means getting kicked out," my roommate signed to me.

"Phrase it any way you want," I responded.

Back at the dorm, we exchanged looks with each other. The party was over and it had never quite begun. My biggest priority was finding a job. Fortunately, Mary Longlois, a graduate of the Louisiana School and now assistant to the head of the library at Gallaudet, was willing to help me. Within two weeks, I was stamping, cataloguing, and bringing home a whopping $3 an hour. I blessed Mary. I blessed the head of the library, Adele Krug. I blessed the students who opened the books they were borrowing for me to place the date due on the back flap, and I blessed the cash. The wolf hadn't quite left the door, but he'd stopped his incessant pacing and growling.

Across town was the White House, where President Johnson was committing hearing men to war after promising that he wouldn't. Opposition to the fighting was growing, and it flowed often and colorfully into the streets of Washington, D.C. We, the students of Gallaudet, were indifferent. We occasionally saw the news, the raucous demonstrations, the demands for equality. However, there were no captions on TV, much less any interpreters at the rallies. None of us equated the rights of black Americans with those of deaf Americans.

We had passionate debates, of course, but not on anything so remote as a war in Asia. Our heated discussions concerned deaf education and how to improve it. All of us were aware of the limitations our home schools had placed on us. While our hearing peers tackled literature and wrote term papers, many of us had tackled only worksheets and responded to fill-in-the-blank questions. We knew already we had been done a disservice. We copied the clothing of the hearing, but defining our anger and desire—equality— would not happen until later.

On campus, Bill Stokoe, a professor brought to Gallaudet by Dr. Detmold from Cornell, had recently published a landmark book with two deaf colleagues. *A Dictionary of American Sign Language on Linguistic Principles* was one of the first attempts to explain linguistically the signs we used. Dr. Stokoe had come to Gallaudet as an English teacher and become fascinated with sign language. He wasn't interested in classroom signing, which used signs to help with lipreading—but the signs that we students used after class and around it. These were real signs, Dr. Stokoe was the first to say, which were part of American Sign Language. If the truth be told, I knew as little about Stokoe's work as I knew about LBJ's.

For the new students at Gallaudet, 1966 mostly meant meeting each other. We were delighted to see so many other deaf people, and delighted to learn that we hailed from so many different places. Place of origin was the beginning of every conversation. A division manifested itself immediately between Northerners and Southerners. New Yorkers considered themselves at the top of the geographical and sophistication pyramid, and certainly no one contested their opinion. The girls wore earrings that matched their dresses. They had on stylish bell-bottoms while the rest of us were still in skirts. The New Yorkers did everything fast, including sign, and they were quick to mock the slow signs that flowed from those of us from the South. If we bumped into them in the hallways, we would turn to apologize, only to find they kept moving without slackening their pace. Their signs were a little different, too. Most of us fingerspelled the letters *M* and *N* by curling our first two or three fingers around our thumbs, but the New Yorkers straightened these fingers, extending them sharply downwards toward the ground.

This was only one of the regional variances that we discovered in the sign language that we all used. Southerners shared the tendency to sign *orange* with a *Y* handshape, *gray* with a G handshape sliding across the forehead, *birthday* by pulling on the ear, and *hospital* with an *H* at the wrist. We dropped all these signs. We picked up signs that I still use today—*orange* as *O* at the nose, *gray* as open hands where the tips of the fingers brush up against each other, and *hospital* with an *H* that forms a cross at the shoulder. As for *birthday*, we still have a hundred different signs for that.

Sign language battles ensued. New Yorkers took to signing Louisiana in a derogatory fashion, by fingerspelling the appropriate abbreviation, *LA*, but pulling the letters from the opposing hand in a gesture that looked exactly like *LA-shit*. I know a New Yorker who as a grown man still believed that this was the correct way to sign the name of my state. We Southerners banded together and retaliated, making the *Y* handshape for *New York* and using it to mime washing our armpits.

While Southerners found Washington, D.C. sophisticated, booming, and even exotic, New Yorkers found it provincial and boring.

"There's no transportation," they complained. "If you want to get someplace you have to walk or take a cab."

"Same as my hometown," I said. "Except much more expensive."

After years of residential life, where every step was precisely delineated, the boys found themselves with no rules at all. Most professors required showing up for class most of the time, but other than that, the boys were on their own. The girls contended with the regime and rigor of *in loco parentis* policies. We had curfews and lectures, and dorm rooms that were forever off-limits to the opposite sex. However, in comparison to the schools we had just left, the only thing we noticed about the structure was how there wasn't much.

At the Louisiana School, students slunk away to the hallway of the bowling alley to neck. We quickly learned that Gallaudet had a small wooded area on campus that was eminently suited to the purpose. There wasn't a lot of necking—at least not heavy necking—those first few weeks on campus. The girls were only too aware that the boys they would kiss at night would be there in the cafeteria in the morning. Anyway, like the Louisiana School, there was no need to rush. The boys weren't going anywhere.

❧

Campus parties started almost right away. A beatnik party, sponsored by the student body government, was among the first I attended. I walked over with a group of girls, and once we were through the door, the conversation and alcohol flowed easily. It wasn't long before we played one of those party games of the sixties that seemed real daring when it was played and real stupid only a few weeks later. In this game, we formed two teams. Each team lined up, alternating boy-girl-boy-girl. The object of the game was to pass a fruit-flavored Lifesaver candy from one team member to the next using a toothpick we each held in our mouths. While the Lifesaver wended its increasingly misshapen way down each line, boys tried to maximize and girls minimize lip contact. All of us tried to move fast, smooth, and without making fools of ourselves. The first team that managed to maneuver the Lifesaver to the end of the line won the game.

Soon afterward, I was perusing photographs from the party. One of the students had taken several. Now he displayed them for sale, part of an entrepreneurial effort to pay his way through school. A group of students gathered around.

"Nice party," said a student next to me.

"Nice party," I agreed.

Smirking, another student pointed to one of the photos in my hand. I turned away a little embarrassed because it was a picture of me and a boy. It had been snapped just as I passed the Lifesaver to him, and it looked like we were embracing.

"You kissed a black man," teased a third student.

I was at a loss for words when the first student interceded.

"Stupid joke," he said.

I turned to him and realized that he was the boy in the photograph. A shadow fell over his face in the photo, darkening his already tan skin. The jokester and his friend slunk away, and I clutched my books and turned to leave, too.

"Hey, what's your name?" the student from the photo asked.

I told him.

"I'm Lance Fischer," he said.

I nodded, still embarrassed, and hurried away to class.

Two nights later, it snowed. It was the first snow of the season in D.C. and the first snow ever for me. Entranced, I went outside to see it up close and touch it. Other students were coming outside too. I was conscious of a presence at my elbow.

"First snow?"

It was Lance, with snow in his hair and eyelashes.

I nodded. "The very first."

Lance scooped up a handful, sculpted it into a ball, and tossed it to me. I ducked and it disappeared into the softness at my feet.

"I'm sorry they called you a black person," I managed to say.

Lance looked at me, puzzled.

"Oh, I don't care about that," he said finally. "I just don't like racist jokes."

With that another snowball sailed overhead, launched by a boy on the other side of the quadrangle. I scooped up a wad of snow, molded it, and aimed for Lance, who dodged easily, grinning the whole time. More snow was in the air. It was girls against boys. I maneuvered to the center of the girls, where I felt somehow safer. Snow lit up the sky. To make and throw snowballs was one of the best things I learned at college.

When the battle ended and both sides of the gender divide proclaimed victory, Lance and I stumbled back to my dorm together. He wasn't allowed up to my room of course, but miraculous things used to happen in hallways, even when they were filled with florescent light.

Shortly afterwards, I heard a friend use the term, "typical Jewish New Yorker." I was startled to see someone sign the word *Jewish* so freely. Practically the only time I'd seen the sign for *Jewish* in Louisiana was when we talked about Jesus in religion class. When I arrived on campus, I was startled not only by the geographic mix of the students, but also by our ethnic and cultural mix. Unlike at the Louisiana School, I found myself among students from a variety of religions and cultures. Yet for the most part, we interacted with each other as if we had no other affiliation than "student," as if all that was important was how nice an individual was, if he or she could play sports, if he or she were smart.

Still, it was a little frightening that Lance was Jewish. Except for Max Ray, I didn't even know any Jewish people. There seemed to be lots of them here at Gallaudet, though. They were among those sophisticated New York people. They came from other places, too, and they seemed to blend in with everyone else.

I was pleased that Lance took an interest in being my friend. When the weather turned cooler, he was appalled to see the flimsy jacket that passed for a winter coat in Louisiana. He insisted that I use some of the precious money that I had earned in the library to buy a real coat. He even knew a place where a coat could be bought for very little money.

"Cheap, real cheap," he assured me.

He came with me, of course, and helped in the selection. When we got back, and I discovered a faulty button, he was furious.

"No problem," I told him. "I can sew it!"

"They should sew it for you," he said.

"It's no big deal," I said.

"It goes back!" said Lance.

So back it went. The two of us trooped back to the very same store to make the exchange.

The store was a small one in downtown Washington. The salespeople weren't mad at all when Lance showed them the problem. In fact, they were apologetic. The button was sewn into place in a matter of minutes.

"How old are you?" I asked Lance as we returned to the dorm.

I had hinted at the question before, but he had always refused to answer. He looked at me and smiled. I think I felt about him the same way Jeanette felt about David. He liked me, and I knew it— and I found I liked him.

"How old?" I asked again.

Again he dodged the question. I looked at him for a long while. Why wouldn't he talk about his age? I didn't date older men, my cut-off age was twenty-five. *But he couldn't be that old,* I told myself. I felt he must be somewhat older than me, but I was sure he wasn't twenty-five.

13

✤

The Race to Who We Are

two solids in (all

one it)

solution . . .

—E. E. CUMMINGS, "WELL, HERE'S LOOKING AT OURSELVES"

"Do you want to go downtown?"

I felt awkward and embarrassed as the signs fell off the hands before me. I tried to keep my face open, and not show any astonishment or fear. Even looking back, I am surprised by my own discomfort. I had been on campus for weeks already, one person among many going about my business in the nation's capital, one student among many studying at Gallaudet. I'd felt acclimated, even sophisticated. Then this question was dropped on my unsuspecting plate.

It wasn't the question itself, of course. I was taken aback because the hands that asked it were dark hands; they belonged to Plumie Gainey, the only black girl in our class. Plumie, so gentle and quiet, seemed an unlikely person to approach me so directly. At home, no nice black person like Plumie would ever ask such a question. Not if they didn't want to be laughed at—and maybe tarred and feathered besides.

154

"This is Washington, D.C.," someone fussed at me when I mentioned it.

Okay. I lived in a big city now. Of course, I had noticed that black and white people mixed freely here, at least compared to my home in Louisiana. Downtown there were even interracial couples, black and white young people holding hands right in front of everyone, as if the whole world could take a collective leap off the nearest bridge. No one seemed to notice anything askew when different colored bodies walked or kissed or coupled up.

Two years before I arrived, people—mostly black, but white, too—converged on Washington, demanding racial equality. Blacks and whites physically mingled here. I didn't quarrel with this principle, though I couldn't quite embrace it. It was just another trauma to be borne, not like the heavy traffic and smog, which were evil things. More like the signs of the New Yorkers, which were neither better nor worse than our own, but fast and strange, and still sometimes forced me, rattled, to make conscious mental translations in order to comprehend a classmate. They were like all the demonstrations that filled the capitol—people walking around, hollering, carrying signs. They had a point, sure. I agreed with it, though it made me uncomfortable. Aware that the racial prejudice I'd brought with me from Louisiana was totally uncool, I stared back at Plumie, embarrassed, and at a loss about what to say.

My stillness didn't matter, though, because around me all was commotion.

"I'll go!" cried one girl.

"Me too!" said another.

"Let me get my jacket," said a third.

And the inevitable: "First, the bathroom!"

To my flat-out astonishment, my white classmates were hurrying to go downtown with Plumie. As they prepared, I was left standing alone. Plumie looked at me expectantly.

"I have to work," I finally managed to lie.

She smiled and nodded, seemingly not too concerned one way or another.

"Can I borrow your lipstick?" someone asked.

I turned and grappled in my purse, but they were making the request of Plumie.

"Sure," she said.

A hallmate brushed me aside as she buttoned her jacket.

"Washington gets cold," she counseled from the wisdom of her Southern blood.

Shaken, I returned to my room. I couldn't resist walking to the window and watching them leave campus, a brightly-colored throng. From deep down in my head, my daddy's words throbbed.

If you get pregnant . . .

I'm not sure why that particular warning sprang to consciousness, why my memory chose to throw this particular snippet of interaction before me. Hearing people tell me sometimes songs lodge unwillingly in their memories to resurface and continually replay even though they try to think of other things.

If you get pregnant . . .

That was my song. It ricocheted around my head like some sort of spastic pinball.

I wouldn't tell anyone of course. I sat down and worked on my homework. I was feeling out of sorts. The afternoon dragged on. I finished some English assignments and returned to the window. The girls were returning, walking through the gates in an animated clump. They headed directly for the snack bar, barely even glancing in my direction.

They look no different, I thought. By that I meant the white girls. An afternoon spent socially with Plumie hadn't changed those girls one bit. It was a revelation.

❧

The Supreme Court's decree that schools should be racially integrated had been announced almost the same year that I entered the Louisiana School. But the decision did not affect the racial composition of my school in the slightest. There were two or three students with dark skin on the social sidelines, Jeanette reminds me, but I always believed their heritage was Spanish. They were exotic and, as exotics, in some sense off-limits to our friendship. African ancestry? Impossible. After all, we shared the same bathrooms, showers, and meal calls. That white people did stuff together and black people did stuff together, and that the white events remained somehow more desirable than those of the blacks, was just another physical feature of the land I lived in. I had never thought too much about it.

Once, Jeanette and I were riding back from school on the bus when Jeanette noticed a black man staring at us. She elbowed me. It was something of an affront for black people to stare at white people so openly, but when I looked over, something in the man's face intrigued me.

"Are you deaf?" I asked him bluntly in sign language.

A broad smile spread across his face.

"Yes," he signed back with a pleased nod.

Jeanette was curious then, too. "Deaf?" she repeated in disbelief.

"Deaf." He signed it as elegantly as anyone I've ever seen.

"Go to school?" I asked.

Again he nodded.

"Where?" It was Jeanette's question.

"The State School for the Deaf," he answered.

We looked at each other in confusion. Neither of us had ever heard of it.

"It's for Negroes," he said.

He signed *Negroes* with the handshape for *N*—the pointer finger and middle finger positioned tight together—pressed down against his nose. At least I think he signed *Negroes*. We said *niggers* when we made that sign; I really don't know what term the man used.

"State School? Where's that?" I asked finally.

"Baton Rouge," he smiled.

I looked at Jeanette startled.

"Our school's in Baton Rouge, too," I told him.

"Where in Baton Rouge?" asked Jeanette.

"Really, it's in Scotlandville," he fingerspelled swiftly. "About five miles north of Baton Rouge, on the campus of Southern University."

Jeanette looked at me and I looked at her. His school was within ten miles of our own.

We talked briefly before the inevitable stop in Rayne ended our conversation. When I returned to school after the holidays, I told my teachers of the encounter. They were not at all surprised. They had known of the nearby black school all along.

The State School for the Deaf was established in 1938, almost a hundred years after a school had opened for Louisiana's white deaf students. Forty-four students enrolled immediately. Students were admitted between the ages of six and twenty-one who were "of sound mind, free from epilepsy, skin eruptions or any contagious diseases and because of deafness cannot attend the public schools."

Teaching was done through lipreading and fingerspelling. The school seems to have offered both academic and vocational training. Among the courses listed in a 1957 booklet were beauty skills, cleaning, pressing and laundry, home ec, shoe repair, tailoring, upholstery, and woodworking. As students completed their training, jobs were sought, primarily through the state vocational rehabilitation office.

More than a decade after I graduated, more than twenty years after the Supreme Court declared that separate education was unequal education, Louisiana became the last state in the United States to desegregate its deaf residential schools. Officials gave the staff in the black school a few weeks' notice, and the State School for the Deaf and the Louisiana State School for the Deaf became the Louisiana School for the Deaf. It was 1978. One of the first acts of the administration was to have the students elect a new mascot. By student vote, the State School's Blue Wolves and the Louisiana School's Mustangs became today's War Eagles.

So much elapsed time made it no easier.

Geraldine Armstrong, a teacher for eleven years at the State School, who retired from the Louisiana School after a total of thirty years of teaching, remembers that it was wrenching. A born teacher who knew her life's vocation when she was in first grade, Mrs. Armstrong decided to teach at the State School because it was nearby and it had an opening. When she showed up for the interview, she learned that the students were profoundly deaf.

"Of course you have to go back to school," the principal told her, as he hired her on the spot. She would learn fingerspelling, he explained.

Our future principal at the Louisiana School would have been proud that years before he arrived at the white school, communication between teachers and students at the black school was exclusively in fingerspelling.

Overwhelmed at the thought, Mrs. Armstrong came home, put on the TV set, turned down the sound, and stared. The sight frightened her. *However do deaf people do it?* she wondered. She bought a book on fingerspelling and began to practice. Back by the TV set, she was again taken aback by the sheer speed at which conversation progressed. Everyone talked so fast. My God! She had never given a thought about the language around her before. Now her heart went out to deaf children.

She planned to stay at the State School for one year. But one year led to the next and the next. When she and the entire State School staff came to the Louisiana School, fingerspelling was all she knew. By this time the Louisiana School had already embraced and abandoned it as a method of instruction. The students had signed among themselves over at the State School, too, she remembered. With a determined sigh, Mrs. Armstrong took up sign language.

"Where there are deaf kids, there will be signs," she said.

The administration—superintendent Harvey Corson and his assistant Marvin Sallop, two educators from the northeastern United States—welcomed those from the State School, she felt. The kids did not. Nor did some of the teachers. She was surprised to feel racial prejudice from deaf people.

"I thought deaf people must have felt prejudice, too," she said once.

For a while, she remembered, the black teachers endured the slowest classes and the problem kids. As luck would have it, the arrival of the black teachers coincided with increased pride in sign language and deaf culture. Consequently, the reliance of the black teachers (every one of whom was hearing) on fingerspelling was cause for considerable head shaking and clucking on the part of the white staff.

"They can't sign," the white teachers said.

The phenomenon of deaf adult power was just developing at the Louisiana School, but it had been almost nonexistent at the State School.

So integration brought a prolonged collision of rights. Both groups—black and deaf—struggled for self-respect, acceptance, and expression. And sometimes the priorities of their struggles conflicted. Even today at the Louisiana School, few teachers are deaf, and fewer still are deaf and black. Still, like its black staff, the Louisiana School kept on keeping on, and there have been black homecoming queens, cheerleaders, and student council representatives. Interracial dating, though it may not yet be as accepted as gumbo, occurs regularly.

"It's better now," says Mrs. Armstrong, though she is thinking of resource allocation as much as the way the children are met in the classroom. Integration meant an increased financial base behind education for black students.

A native of Mississippi, Mrs. Armstrong had never dealt with white people during her first years of teaching. She encountered them for the first time at the Louisiana School, then again when she attended Gallaudet University to pursue graduate studies in education. Equipped only with fingerspelling, she found the experience at Gallaudet unnerving.

"What are you doing here if you don't know sign language?" a black woman demanded of her as she tried to settle into the living quarters that were her dorm.

Her teacher, Francis Higgins, a deaf, white professor and fluent signer who was teaching chemistry to Mrs. Armstrong's summer school class, was more understanding.

"Don't worry," he told her, when she admitted how nervous she was about presenting a paper she had written for the class. "Signs are not a reflection of intelligence."

She appreciated this, and I'm glad one white person behaved respectably.

During my time, race aligned every facet of our existence. When white children faced the black community, we felt on edge, under siege. One wrong step and, like the crew of Columbus, we might fall off the edge of the planet. Daddy cautioned us to stay home after the sun went down. There were men out there at night. Men to be avoided at all cost. It was something that we understood and didn't question. There was evil in the Louisiana darkness.

Sometimes it spilled into the daylight. When my friends and I went to see the movie *Guess Who's Coming to Dinner*, we found the theater closed and pickets outside the locked door. We knew immediately why—the story line entailed interracial romance. Of all the violations a white girl could commit, none was less excusable than finding a black man sexually attractive, except maybe responding to the attraction.

Another time, our school bus was on the way to a sports match when white men in white robes forced the bus to the side of the road. They climbed on board as if their presence on our bus were their natural right. They were grim and purposeful. If they weren't so dangerous, they would have been comical—wearing bedsheets, carrying rifles, and sporting the strange little cone hats. When they finally filed out no one laughed. We just breathed one long sigh of relief.

For some reason, before I met the man on the bus, it had never occurred to me that there might be black people in Louisiana who were deaf like me or that they might need, as I did, some kind of education. In fact, for a long time, I was astonished to meet African American people who were deaf, as if maybe having dark skin immunized one from hearing loss. It still embarrasses me, this attitude I grew up with. It embarrasses all of us. One graduate from the Louisiana School, now a professor at Gallaudet and a leader in the deaf community, describes how she was at a meeting of regional representatives of the American Athletic Association of the Deaf and started talking with a black man from the Midwest. Their conversation deepened, and she asked where he was from. He was from Louisiana. The same as her. Class of 1969, the same as her. He was deaf, the same as her. She felt that wave of embarrassment. If it were not for racial segregation, they would have been classmates.

Plumie was the first black and deaf person I had any real acquaintance with. I couldn't deny the evidence of my eyes. I couldn't pretend something was wrong when so clearly it wasn't.

The next time Plumie suggested going downtown, I quickly agreed.

A group of us headed off campus together. We walked several blocks to Washington's old shopping district. I picked up stockings and Plumie bought some greeting cards. We browsed through one of the big department stores. Then we stopped and had a sundae. I felt just a little self-conscious. If people gave us any trouble, I promised myself I would give it right back to them. My fears were for nothing. People didn't even notice us.

Another time, the two of us lay in the grass outside of the dormitory in the warm spring sun, recounting tales of family and home. Plumie became deaf when she was six years old. It was sleeping sickness, the doctor told her mama. It was encephalitis, another doctor clarified for her later. It ravaged her body with fever for several days, then left her blind, deaf, and paralyzed for another several months. Slowly her eyesight returned, and a year of therapy in a school for crippled children restored her limbs. Her spirit grew strong from the experience.

"I just knew I was going to beat it," she said. "I was a fighter."

Nevertheless, the all-white college across the campus from Kendall School was intimidating.

"I was referred to as 'the colored girl,'" she remembered.

When the prep students at Gallaudet went on an outing to Milford Mill, a favorite swimming spot in Maryland where water fills an old quarry, she was left behind. No blacks were allowed.

"It was no excuse for my low esteem and shame," she wrote later.

Well, it sure seems like a stellar "excuse" to me. The following year a group of black students would enter Gallaudet, but that prep year, she was alone, a reluctant pioneer in the territory of expanding black rights.

"My father dropped out of college," she remembered. "He was adamant that someone in the family would get a college degree."

So she persevered. Unfortunately, Gallaudet, a university that seemed downright progressive to me, was about as mired in prejudice as any other small university in the South.

"Black deaf people felt Gallaudet was not for them," said Ernest Hairston, a 1961 graduate. He began his education in the West Virginia School for the Colored Deaf and Blind and would go on to earn his doctorate at Gallaudet University. Hairston, an administrator for the U.S. Department of Education, was more accurate than I ever dreamed. Racial prejudice seared and deformed education for America's deaf children just as it had everything else. In 1940, Gallaudet's president, Percival Hall, discouraged the application of a black student from New York. Hall wrote to the student's inquiring superintendent that there was "not a ghost of a chance" the young man would ever be employed as a teacher and suggested that local mechanical training be found for him. A 1913 article in the *American Annals of the Deaf* speculated that the "cranial nerves of the colored child knit together as a rule at an earlier age than those of the white child," thus precluding their ability to pursue advanced learning. Hume Le P. Battiste, a dark-skinned American Indian, according to the Gallaudet archives, became the first person of color to graduate from Gallaudet. Battiste's skin color had warranted his school superintendent writing an apologetic letter to Edward M. Gallaudet, then Gallaudet's president. The superintendent, A. C. Manning, cited Battiste's excellent character and academic achievement, and made the bold suggestion that this might entitle him to a place at the university.

Battiste went on to graduate, but Andrew Foster, admitted in 1952, is officially cited as Gallaudet's first black graduate. Foster was a minister by the time I arrived, in the midst of founding more schools for the deaf than anybody else has ever done either before or since. Foster, who graduated from Gallaudet in a speedy three years, was on a lonely crusade though, erecting schools in Ghana, Nigeria, and Togo, and spreading the teaching of deaf students through signs as far east as Kenya. All of his schools were Christian schools and all of them were in Africa. A few still flourish. But I wouldn't hear of his work until much later.

Plumie probably hadn't heard of him either. She stood before us, with her quiet eyes and her hair damaged by the chemicals she used to straighten it, the only black woman in a class of whites, half of whom were subtle racists while the other half were overt racists in what was still a Jim Crow South. In 1955, Gallaudet Student Council President Doug Burke, a white student who was head of the student body government, responded to a request from the United States National Student Association, with a scribbled hand-written note to Gallaudet's president:

> I have been aware of little or no prejudice at Gallaudet. What prevails here is the customary south, nothing else. . . . It passes through as a habit. Gradually, both [races] learn to assimilate each other's reflections as they would upon recognizing the difference between a black Angora cat and a white Angora cat.

So there it was. Black and white angora cats. Deaf black and white Angora cats. Deaf black and white Angora cats who could do anything.

Thank goodness for the transition, painful and awkward, to a discontented but at least more equal society. The Louisiana School and Gallaudet are different institutions today.

I say, "Go War Eagles!"

14

❧

Summer of '67

We all want to change the world.

—JOHN LENNON AND PAUL MCCARTNEY, "REVOLUTION"

They say the longest stretch for new college students is the time before Thanksgiving. I had no such stretch. Hours, days, weeks whizzed by. It was Thanksgiving and then it was Christmas. I'd looked forward to going home, but like so many college students, my arrival there quickly destroyed my expectations.

When I got off the bus in Rayne, Daddy took one look at me and exploded. My skirt was too short, he boomed. How dared I ride all the way from Washington, D.C. in such a skirt? What kind of shameful person had I become? I was to put on respectable clothing, immediately.

I climbed into the taxi next to him and he continued his tirade. *"Everyone wears skirts this short,"* I told him.

He was unmollified. His hand sliced at the air, his face gleamed red, and his lips worked so hard he spit. I stopped even trying to understand him. I rode most of the way home in tears.

Home was a different place. Nana was rarely there. Totally involved with Gerites, she was enjoying an increasingly happy junior year. She got along better than I did with Irene, who now ruled the house from her perch in the kitchen. Nana even called her Mom. Some part of me felt the thrill of a returning conqueror, but mostly I felt an awkwardness that I was at loss to explain.

Over in Branch, Lenora and Gerry provided relief. Alpha and Jimmy dropped by, but I was quickly disabused of any notion that I might fit into my former place, and I was happy when it was time to return to school.

The second semester passed even faster than the first. By spring, I noticed a new confidence, and I felt it was shared by most of the preps. By now we knew that we had made the grade, and we would be accepted into Gallaudet as full-fledged freshmen that fall. Some of my classes I relished; others I grumbled about. Just as at the Louisiana School, some of our teachers couldn't sign well enough to ask their way to the bathroom. Later, this would be cause for anger, but as a first-year student, I accepted it. No one ever said that God created the world—even the world at Gallaudet—to accommodate me and my deaf friends.

To my amazement, my former principal Mr. Scouten, who had worked at Gallaudet for so many years, was not disliked there. He had instituted his Visible English forcefully in the classroom, writing all over the blackboards, but apparently, outside of class, he had not fingerspelled with the students—he had signed, and signed skillfully. They liked him, the older boys said. He was a legend. A legend!

I heard that the legend left the Louisiana School soon after I did. Although the policy of fingerspelling would endure a wee bit longer, commitment to it as a communication system faded with Scouten's departure. Sign language came out from the closets and corners. Most of the students and deaf faculty rejoiced at the change.

It was spring of that first year when one of the audiologists noticed my place of birth on the form that held my audiogram.

"Are you Cajun?" she asked me, curious and cheerful.

"What?" I wasn't sure that I had seen the word correctly.

"C-A-J-U-N," her fingerspelling was clear and careful. "Are you Cajun?"

I couldn't answer. While I mulled over the term, she filled in for me.

"I love Cajun food," she said.

"I am Acadian." I remember spelling the word for her carefully. A-C-A-D-I-A-N.

She looked at me a moment, puzzled. "Isn't that the same thing?" she asked finally.

I stared at her uncomfortably. Without replying to her question, I made an excuse and fled. I was unnerved to see that word bandied so readily about. The "C-word." I had never seen it used quite that freely before. I had certainly never seen it used with regard to myself. And that woman had suggested that *Cajun* and *Acadian* were the same thing.

They were not the same thing. I had heard of Cajuns. They were the people who had no education, lived in the deep swamp, and ate wild animals. Their real name was Coon-ass. It was important not to mix up *Cajun* and *Acadian*. I should have explained it.

I am Acadian, I thought, puzzled and distressed.

Soon after that, classes broke for summer. I think my conversation with the audiologist prompted the dream I had as I rode the train back home. I didn't usually sleep on the train. Most trips, I spent almost every moment of daylight with my eyes glued to the passing scenery. Maybe it was the heat. Maybe it was the motion of the wheels. Maybe it was not wanting to face the summer that awaited me back in Rayne.

In any case, I fell asleep and dreamed. In the dream, I was back home with my family. We were having one of our cookouts on the Calcasieu Bayou, and Grady was showing me one of his bad snakebites. His arm was ugly, blue-red and swollen. It was bloody, too, where Uncle Frank had cut at it and tried to suck out the poison.

"A rattlesnake," Grady said.

"Good thing," said Uncle Frank just next to him. "A cottonmouth and you'd be dead."

Grady didn't answer. He'd been bitten before, twice. I hadn't known about it the first two times because I was deaf and no one told me. In the dream, I may not have been deaf because I understood everyone. Understanding was a natural thing. I took in the words of my family like I took in the colors of the day. Either I was a hearing person or I was understanding without noise.

We were ankle deep in the water, the boys using a net to catch crabs. Grady bent to adjust the net so that it would spread wide when they threw it. Nana and my cousin Velma stood together just out of our way. I wondered if Velma could hear and see now in some mysterious way and follow everything clearly, just as I was doing. Velma touched Nana's shoulder and pointed to something above my head. Thinking of the snake, I jumped back.

"It's a flower," said Nana, and she led Velma closer. The flower was small and pale yellow and growing right out of the tree.

"An orchid!" cried Velma.

Mama came over, then Aunt Happy. Grady and Uncle Frank, fiddling with the net, looked up for a minute, too. There was a lot of pointing.

"An orchid," Nana repeated.

Maybe I was still deaf in the dream because Nana fingerspelled as she said it, or maybe she was signing for Velma, or maybe she was signing because signs are so very beautiful. I don't know. I watched Nana talk and sign and fingerspell, and wondered at her.

"An orchid is an epiphyte," said Velma.

"E-P-I-P-H-Y-T-E." I spelled it back to her.

"There are many epiphytes in the marsh," said Velma. "But orchids are the most beautiful."

Grady yelled over and asked Mama if she wanted him to get the orchid for her.

Mama was shaking her head. "Let it be," she said.

"What's an epiphyte, anyway?" I asked.

Nana shook her head and looked at Velma, who paused as if considering how she could capture the wonder of an epiphyte in words—signed or spoken. Then she explained.

"Epiphytes are plants that live in the trees—up high in trees," she said. "They have special leaves to trap water. They drink right from the air."

"They drink from the air?" Nana was doubtful.

"Well, they can't nestle their roots in the ground," said Velma. "Sometimes they have a little cork-like stuff around their roots, but that's all. If you look close enough you might even find water in their leafy cups and tiny flowers hidden in those tall stalks."

Grady and the boys tossed the net, and it spread wide in the air before it drifted down into the bayou. They would let it set a minute more, and then pull in some crabs.

"Didn't you do some kind of book report on orchids or something?" I asked Velma.

Velma nodded and said, "There are six thousand kinds of orchids in the world."

Nana flashed Grady a grin. "Thousands and thousands of orchids—and you've never seen a one," she called over to our brother.

"And I wouldn't have seen that one if you hadn't shown it to me," Grady responded.

"This one's a Green Fly Orchid," Velma said, pointing to the spidery-looking flower. "It's not as flashy as some of the other orchids."

I tried to talk but the effort woke me up. My cheek was wet and sweaty from being propped against my hand. Outside of the dirty window, the landscape raced past. My head felt like it held something heavy. I stared without seeing.

Deaf people are just like orchids, I thought.

That's what I was going to tell them in the dream. If I hadn't awakened, that's what I would have said. Unable to establish roots the way most people do, deaf people bloom anyway. I had seen it at the Louisiana School, and I had seen it again at Gallaudet. Deaf people are like orchids in the swamp. There are lots of us around, but no one ever seems to know we are there.

Once home, I told my daddy I was going to go visit Pat and Bobby. Daddy had become reconciled to my being gone. Nana was probably relieved not to worry about taking me with her. Irene was probably relieved, too.

Pat and Bobby had been married for almost a year, and they were living next to Bobby's mother. Laura Trosclair, already known affectionately as Grandma Laura, was a former Louisiana School student. She was often in their house during my visit.

"He's a true Cajun man," Pat told me, gesturing towards her husband.

"True Cajun?" I asked. I was startled to see this word again.

"Yeah, two weeks after we were married, we were driving along the highway, when the car ahead of us hit a rabbit. You know what Bobby did?"

I didn't.

"He pulled over, picked up the carcass, and brought it home."

I was appalled.

"And *cooked* it!" said Pat.

"He cooked it?" I couldn't believe it.

"Skinned and cleaned the rabbit. Put a little water in the pan, and yeah, cooked it."

"Did you eat it?"

Pat hesitated a moment. "Yeah, I ate it," she said.

"How did it taste?"

She didn't hesitate this time. "Delicious," she said.

"I taught him everything he knows," said Bobby's mother. Pat and I glanced over at her. Mrs. Trosclair was almost seventy, and she used lots of home signs—signs she had invented in her own home—having dropped out of the Louisiana School when she was in third grade.

"She's a great cook," Bobby said smiling at her.

I really liked Bobby. Pat was right. He was hearing, but he signed just fine. After hesitating, I asked him what it meant to be a true Cajun.

"Cajuns are French people who settled in Nova Scotia, Canada. They didn't call it Nova Scotia though; they called it Acadia—and the Cajuns were Acadians. They were kicked out by the English," Bobby said.

"My daddy never liked the English," I said.

"I don't like the English," Bobby's mother agreed.

"Me neither," said Pat.

"Well, it was 1755, and I guess France and England had been at war." Bobby always was the most moderate of us. "So the English put thousands of French people on boats and sent them away. Ten years later, the ones that hadn't died made their way to Louisiana."

"My parents weren't Cajun," said Pat.

"Pat's parents spoke French," nodded Bobby, "but they weren't Cajun."

He wasn't pure Cajun either. His daddy was German.

"But that don't make no difference," he said, as his mother watched him. "Mama was Cajun, and Mama was the person who raised me."

Bobby was the second oldest of four brothers. His daddy was a trapper who died of a heart attack when the boys were still small. His mother took over, raising Bobby and his brothers so far up the Mississippi that their neighbors were mostly snakes and muskrats. Anyone who lived more than ten miles north of his family was considered a Yankee, Bobby laughed, never mind that the land might still be thousands of miles short of the Mason-Dixon line, and in fact still in Louisiana.

"We had a cow, a pig, and some chickens," Bobby remembered. "We planted vegetables in whatever space we could find in the yard—which was any land we used around our house and extended to the land that the neighbor used around his house. If a neighbor didn't use the space, we did."

The boys hunted and fished, and the family accepted help from their neighbors.

"Charity," Bobby didn't mince words. "The priest finally even stopped sending us a bill for school."

Somehow they got by.

"Except for what we could kill, catch, or grow, we lived on red beans, white beans, and rice," remembered Bobby. So a slaughtered rabbit was a treat.

"Do *Cajun* and *Acadian* mean the same thing?" I asked Bobby.

"Do *Injun* and *Indian* mean the same thing?" Bobby laughed. "*Acadian* was just too many syllables for the American tongue."

He saw my expression and laughed again.

"Actually they don't mean quite the same thing," he amended. "There were lots of Acadians kicked out of Canada. About half of them made it to Louisiana, but not all of them. Cajuns are what Acadians became in Louisiana."

"It was the sun," said his mother.

"The roadkill!" laughed Pat.

There were lots of good times to be had in Louisiana in the summer of '67—and I was out to have them all. I lived with Bobby and Pat for one week and then two weeks. Ben, a printer from New Orleans, began to visit regularly. He had graduated from the Louisiana School several years before me. Already he had amassed a car and what seemed like lots of money.

Ben and I went to see Grady one afternoon.

"Brother!" I cried when he opened the door.

But Grady wasn't happy to see me. As soon as he opened the door, his mouth dropped open, and he made frantic motions. He gestured and talked and gestured some more. I couldn't understand. Neither of us thought to get a pencil.

"Go home," Grady said.

"I plan to go to Rayne this very Sunday," I explained.

"No. No. No," Grady said. *"Now. Go home now. Now."*

"What's wrong?" I gasped.

Grady said something about Daddy, but I couldn't catch the other words.

"Something's wrong with Daddy?" I was frantic.

"Go home now!" said Grady.

Ben drove me. The drive from New Orleans to Baton Rouge is an hour, then it's another hour to my house. I spent every one of those 120 minutes praying. When we pulled up, there was a blackened structure where my house had been. Horrified, Ben and I got out of the car. Daddy and Nana emerged suddenly from a neighbor's house. Daddy wore a white bandage on his head.

"Are you okay?" I asked.

"Fine. Fine," Nana said.

I gestured toward the bandage on Daddy's head.

"It's nothing," said Daddy.

"The fire," said Nana, and she gestured toward the scorched and mutilated heap that had been our home, and burst into tears. I cried, too, partly at the sight of the ruined house, but partly because I was happy. The house was gone, but my daddy and Nana were alive and with me.

"What happened?" I asked Nana.

"Electrical," she said. "Three days ago."

We picked gingerly through the rubble.

"Look," said Nana.

She held up a photo of my mother, still in its frame and only slightly charred. We both wept over it. Irene looked away, and Daddy cried too. Nothing else seemed important. Which was a good thing because almost everything we owned was in that fire, and it was gone.

Later, Nana told me that it was because of our dead mama that she had survived. She was asleep and dreamed that Mama was saying to her, "Come, come," and beckoning her to wake up and follow. It was Mama's image that woke her, she said. Mama might be dead, but she was still looking out for us from heaven. I have to admit, I was skeptical. It made Nana feel better, though; I could see that. She believed that Mama had returned in a moment of peril and saved her life. She knew people would mock her for believing this, though, and she swore me to secrecy about the dream. Even when my daddy said that the firemen told him that Nana should have died, that the fire had advanced along the roof and the smoke from it should have suffocated her in her sleep, I didn't repeat Nana's story. I never told anyone about it to this day.

Grady helped Daddy contract to rebuild. They could find someone real cheap, he said. They would dismantle the little house in the backyard, charred but still standing, and use the wood to structure a new home. Daddy explained that my expectations of returning to school had gone up in smoke. The money they had doled out every week for insurance was nowhere near enough to pay for rebuilding our home. I would need to stay in Rayne and work. I couldn't go back to Gallaudet until the damage done by the fire was repaired.

I didn't argue. That's another part that Bobby could have mentioned about being Cajun. Family is always first. I might have preferred to hightail myself right back to college, but my daddy and my sister needed me. Daddy was pleased that I accepted the change in plans without complaining. He knew everyone in Rayne, and he already had found me a job. His good friend was president of the bank downtown, and Daddy was proud to say that he had already mentioned to his friend that I was in town from college and needed a job, and he had offered me work in the bank.

"I'll have to buy a dress," I said.

"Buy many dresses," said my daddy.

My spirits rose. Ben went back to New Orleans, but he promised to come back and visit the very next weekend. I selected the nicest, least expensive, and most conservative outfit I could find. I wanted Daddy to be proud of me. He was, too. I saw it on his face when I walked out in the dress two days later to go to the bank with him. Even Irene gave me a little pat on the shoulder. Daddy summoned the taxi and we rode to the bank together. He was almost happy. I could feel it. Maybe it wasn't so bad being home.

Once at the bank, we were led directly to the president's office. Daddy talked a little with the secretary. I tried to smile at her, but she only glanced at me and didn't bother to say anything at all. She nodded several times at my daddy, then disappeared into the president's office. After a few minutes, she came back out, sat down at her desk, and ignored us. Daddy took a magazine and pointed out one of the stories. Students were protesting in California and Washington, D.C. They were calling for peace in Vietnam. One of the photos was taken very near Gallaudet. I recognized the buildings and nodded. We each picked up a magazine and read. We picked up another magazine, then another. It began to seem like a long time.

Finally Daddy looked up and said something to the secretary. She jumped as his mouth moved and almost seemed to run into the president's office. Daddy's face was changing color, a sure sign that something was wrong.

I touched his arm. *"Let's go home,"* I urged.

There was clearly no reason to be sitting here like this.

Daddy acted like I was one of those little mosquitoes in the Louisiana swamp, except he didn't even swat in my direction. Abruptly he stood up and walked to the bank president's door. I saw his fist rap against it. The secretary opened it finally, her face whiter than I remembered, her mouth hanging limp and open. Daddy pushed past her and proceeded inside.

Through the open doorway, I saw the president of the bank rise from the chair behind his desk. The secretary froze in the doorway. I stood up to get a better view.

The bank president's mouth moved. All he said was one sentence, maybe two. Then he seemed to remember something and threw out his hand to my daddy as if to shake it. My daddy just ignored the outstretched hand. He talked now, his hands and lips flailing together. The bank president started to move his lips. Daddy's flailing hands and lips stopped him.

He was screaming, I realized. My daddy was screaming.

I was too scared to move. The bank president must have been scared, too.

Before he could call security, Daddy turned on his heel, returned to the waiting area, and grabbed my hand. To my horror, he proceeded to drag my unwilling self into the president's office. More words flew from Daddy's mouth, while I stood there determined to not cry. I stared at my daddy, then the bank president, then back to my daddy. The bank president kept starting to move his lips and stopping in mid flap. Daddy finished his speech and whisked me out the door.

With me at his side, he strode through the bank and out the door. We stood in the sunlight for a moment, he catching his breath, me still trying not to cry.

He hailed the first taxi he saw. Still breathing hard, he turned to me in the seat.

"He thought I meant Nana," he said.

I understood. The bank president wanted my little sister. He didn't want a deaf woman to work in his bank. He wouldn't hire me.

Daddy crossed his arms over his still-heaving chest.

"And I told him you were not mentally retarded," he added.

He didn't say anymore, and he didn't have to. The words sent a chill down my spine. It's a prejudice that deaf people fight every day, every hour, especially in small towns like Rayne. I hate it.

In anger and defeat we returned home. But Daddy got on the phone almost immediately. When he hung up, I had another job. I would work in a textile mill.

This is exactly where I don't want to be, I thought that first morning on the job. Chevys and Fords filled the asphalt parking lot, and a rusty-roofed building hefted itself upward in a weary configuration of wood and peeling paint. The woman who had given me a ride there, a fellow employee, smiled cheerfully, chatted merrily with the other women in the car, and said nothing at all to me, carting me on the twenty-minute drive like I was a sack of potatoes.

At least it didn't smell. In the book we had read about factories at school, the stench was said to be terrible. So it could have been worse, I guess. As I remember, I earned ninety-five cents an hour. We had scheduled breaks: fifteen minutes in the morning and afternoon, and thirty minutes at midday to eat. Otherwise I would sew.

An Asian woman bent over me as I filled out my application. When I checked one year of college education, her finger landed hard on the paper.

"No," her mouth said, when I looked up at her.

She went on for several minutes and her finger jabbed down on the paper next to "high school." She took my pencil right from my hand and made a mark in the box next to the words.

"No!" Now my lips moved back at her.

I took the pencil from her hand, erased her mark, and replaced the mark where I had originally put it.

She was the boss here, and I knew I had to explain. So I did my best. We wrote and gestured back and forth, and I tried to make her understand. I had spent last year in college up North, I told her, at Gallaudet College, a special college for deaf students. She left the mark where I had put it and didn't disturb me as I filled in the rest of the form. I don't know if she finally did understand or if she just gave up.

Four hundred people worked in the factory. They were mostly women. Men were present to take care of the machines if they broke down. It looked deadly boring. In the main room, they worked in rows, separated from each other by their machinery. One woman made sure that fabric was constantly on the table ready to be sewn. Then another woman sewed flat material. Another added a pocket, still another added a zipper. And a fourth carried the finished product away to be ironed. In another room, they cut the material. In still another they ironed what we had stitched together. Each of us had a small job that when combined with the jobs of everyone else produced a pair of pants. I suppose I was lucky to have a job. Nevertheless, looking around that floor, my heart sank.

I followed my supervisor into the training room. I would be the first person in the sewing line, she explained. I would make the initial transformation, stitching a cut of fabric into the first shape of a man's pants. I was a serger, she said, pausing to write the word on paper. I would use automated zigzag stitching that extended the life of the seam.

"Your job," she said, using words and gestures, and Lord knows what else. *"You take the material."* She held up material already cut into the shape of a pant leg. *"You stitch here, here, here, like this."*

Up, down, around, and up, she went, sewing a seam along the leg, around the hem and back up the other side of the leg.

"Your training will take two weeks," she added.

I nodded. She'd already told me that at least twice.

I had done a little sewing at school. It didn't look hard, but if she said two weeks, so be it. I put my foot on the pedal and the machine whirred to life. Smoothly, I slid the cloth under the needle, and the stitches began their bold march down the pant leg. *This isn't so hard,* I thought. I tried to turn the material around to begin stitching along the cuff. Suddenly the material rolled into a mass beneath the needle and bunched crazily at the point of contact. I wondered if there were some kind of horrible noise that ensued, too, because as the pedal lost its rhythmic feel, everyone turned to stare at me. I pulled apart the material, threw away the training sample, and began again. This time I sewed more slowly, but at the hem the whole process snarled again, though not so badly as before. The Asian woman appeared as if by magic, shook her finger and her mouth, and made some motions in the air. She threw away the sample this time.

I waited until she left before I tried again. No longer fooled by the firm march of thread down the leg, I was aware of the disaster that impended at the hem. I needed a technique. With a sigh, I glanced toward some of the more experienced workers. These women had no problem turning the material 90 degrees. Their material slid through the machine easily, up one side, around the crotch, down the next side, around the hem. I watched and realized that while they stitched the leg seam quickly, they slowed down before they reached the hem, controlling the speed by releasing the foot pedal slightly in advance of the turn. This gave them and the cloth plenty of time to complete a 90-degree rotation before they resumed their full-speed ascent up the other side of the pant leg.

I copied them. It was awkward and slow, but the pant leg made it through. The second time was easier. By the third time, I was slow but I had it right. I worked on. The pile of pants grew. At the end of the day, the Asian woman was at my side again. Saying nothing, she inspected each pair of pants.

Finally she looked at me. *"Tomorrow, report to the floor,"* she said.

"I'm out of training," I told Ben when he picked me up that Friday.

He looked at me, saw I was serious, and laughed.

"So much for the two-week training period," he said.

❧

So much was going on that I hardly had time to miss Gallaudet and the people I had left up North. I didn't talk much about Gallaudet to my friends. Somehow, talking about it made me feel guilty. Whatever I said about Gallaudet, it sounded like I was bragging or complaining. There was no in-between. My friends had never been there. It was sort of like describing a dress for a grand ball when your best friend had just purchased a cheerleading outfit.

My college experiences just didn't fit into the conversation.

My life was here, and here I would be.

When letters from Lance arrived, I could think of no other way to talk about them except by representing Lance as a nuisance. Lance wanted me back at Gallaudet, I told Jeanette. That was a nuisance, wasn't it? She looked at me and shook her head. She was more interested in Saturday night than a letter from Washington, D.C.

"You coming with us to the dance?" she asked.

I folded Lance's letter and put it in my pocket.

"If Ben can get off," I said.

Many students home from college feel a distance from their old friends. Not me. I adored being with them. Still, I felt restless sometimes, and I missed my friends up North.

15

❧

*A*n End to All That

oh you can't
unring a bell

—Mary Ellen Carew, "Can't Unring a Bell"

Louisiana has three seasons: hot, very hot, and the few weeks after the winter solstice when the heat lifts. It's almost chilly enough to wear a light jacket during the day, and natives turn on the heat, if they have it, at night. The days are shorter, too, if not appreciably cold.

Except for weekends with my friends, my life took on a colorless pattern. I rode to work in a carpool with five women who ignored me. I took my place in the sewing row at eight o'clock and, except for specified and regimented breaks, stitched steadily until five o'clock. My life was devoted to creating cotton pants.

By now, I knew a little about some of the women around me. The old white woman on my right was fifty-three years old, hard faced, and already wrinkled. She had spent the last twenty-one years of her life working at the same place in the sewing line, and the decade before that working in another place in another line in another factory. A skinny white teenager worked next to her, well on her way to forging a similar career. The young woman kept the older woman chuckling throughout the day. They both ignored me. I didn't care. I got chills just looking at them.

The woman who made sure I had a steady pile of material in front of me, ready to be sewn into shape, was Lucy. Lucy was black and about my age with soft curls about her face, her body already a little bit fat. I took a chance and wrote her a short note a few days after I began work. She looked astonished, then pleased, and scribbled a short reply. We didn't do this too much. Note swapping was considered subversive. If Bonnie, our supervisor, or the Asian woman who had given me such a hard time on my day of application, saw us, it was cause for scolding. We mostly contented ourselves with exasperated glances.

"Hot," her mouth would say.

"Very," my mouth would answer back as I continued to sit and sweat and stitch.

Every Monday, we stopped work for a few minutes while the manager's voice crackled at us over the loudspeaker. It was part pep talk, part information, and eventually, dire warnings about what would happen if we joined a union. I know because Lucy began to write down the words the manager said and then pass them to me. For ten minutes, he reviewed our quotas, offered encouragement, and exhorted us to work faster.

Lucy scribbled dutifully.

"Best stitches for company equal best fabric for our lives," she wrote.

He continued speaking and she reached again for the paper.

After a moment's hesitation, she scrawled: "and so forth and so forth."

I laughed and nodded.

After a few minutes, she took the paper again.

"A union is no good," Lucy paraphrased our peerless leader. "Workers are better off when they work with management with NO intermediary."

"Lord knows our wages are piddling enough without giving some away every week to a union," she added, mouthing what was clearly an ad lib.

I touched her shoulder and shook my head. Don't make me laugh, I was saying.

The boss offered up information during these talks, too. But whether her script concerned restrooms or unions or the froth of weekly polemic, I appreciated Lucy's writing for me. I appreciated the information, and I appreciated feeling included. It was worth suffering through the propaganda. I felt like Lucy was my friend.

"I'm getting out of here and going back to Houston," she told me one day.

Houston, I knew, was where she'd been born and grown up. I gave her the thumbs-up sign.

If I could contrive to do so without getting caught, it was good to talk to Lucy. It pulled up my spirits. There was another benefit, too: The furtive conversation took my hands away from sewing and slowed me down. This was a good thing. The women in the next row and even the women who followed me in my own row had become irritated by my speed. They had noticed that my pile of sewn-up pant legs grew faster and higher and quicker than anyone else's, and they didn't like that.

A note appeared on my chair one day. It bore three words: "Slow down. Anonymous."

I threw it out.

"You work too fast," Lucy told me bluntly.

"We're supposed to work fast," I reminded her.

"Ah, but you make those other women look bad," she said, and gave me a conspirator's smile.

For every twelve pairs of pants I sewed over the forty-five-a-day quota, I was paid an extra ten cents. The result was that I never stopped sewing. Even as the clock ticked down at the end of each shift, I kept working. Also, I never turned in the extras if I had less than twelve of them. Instead I would put the extra work aside, and it would become the basis for the next day's work. Perhaps if there'd been other deaf people there, I would have worked slower. But as it was, I was alone on that crowded floor most of the time, as isolated from the other workers as I had been from my family.

"It's a really stupid place," I told Ben that evening as we talked at dinner. "They treat us like we're dumb."

It didn't take Ben long to cheer me up, and soon I was laughing at his jokes. He had seemed happy and excited since the moment he picked me up. He even insisted on taking me to dinner, even though it was another four days until payday.

"I hate that place," I told him. I couldn't help it. The words came out by themselves.

"Just get the paycheck," he counseled in the wisdom of his twenty-five years.

He was still smiling as he said it.

"You're sure in a good mood," I teased. "Did you get a raise or something?"

"No," he said, smiling even wider, if that was possible. "I got something else."

With that he pulled out a diamond ring.

I felt something like awe flood through me. We had talked about marriage, but always abstractly, as if it only happened to other people. On the one hand, it seemed inevitable. Thelma had just married Luther Green. David and Jeanette had married while I was at Gallaudet, and were expecting their first child. Even my little sister, Nana, had a serious relationship. Pat and Bobby already had their first child. On the other hand, I thought it would never happen to me. I looked at Ben and smiled back, delighted. Marriage seemed our next logical step.

We set the date for June 15. At Gallaudet, my friends were taking courses about women and women's rights. In Rayne, I practiced writing Ben's last name.

"Soon it will be mine," I told Nana.

☙

At work, the talk about a union escalated. The woman who carted me back and forth had said nothing to me about it, but she had told my father. Daddy told me he favored unions.

"You get more money and get more respect," he told me through Nana's hands.

"That's not what my boss says," I told him.

Daddy laughed ruefully. He was eating breakfast and getting ready to go to work. Nana stood by the refrigerator pouring orange juice, and Irene sat at the table, the ubiquitous coffee cup at her elbow. Having cooked up the biscuits and gravy for my father, she could relax a moment.

Weekday mornings were the best time for our family. Daddy still nipped on the sly, but he was fine in the mornings and he never missed a day of work. For the most part, we had stopped complaining. We still threw out the bottles when we found them, but he hid them better now, and there was a marked reduction of fury in our tossing. Even Irene accepted it. If we had something to discuss, we approached Daddy in the morning during the week. It was a way of life.

"If the union comes up, you vote for it," he said.

Irene said something, and I looked at Nana to find out what.

Nana put down her juice. "She says they've got a union in the mill over in Lafayette," she said.

I raised my eyebrows to show interest and surprise. Nana looked over at Irene again.

"Maybe it's over in St. Martinsville," signed Nana, watching Irene's mouth. "She can't remember."

"It's about respect," said my daddy. *"That's what it's about."*

The words zoomed out of his mouth, with no warning or supporting motions from his finger, and I missed them. My eyes swept to Nana. She interpreted what he said, then she gulped her juice and was up and gone. Outside, Gerites waited in his car. She was lucky to have a boyfriend to drive her to school.

At work, Lucy had a note written for me as soon as I got there. I had arrived a bit early, as always, and I didn't think of myself as on company time. So I didn't hide the note. I just unfolded and read.

"Meeting on Tuesday," it said.

The union! I looked up in astonishment—right into the face of my supervisor. Caught.

A grimace on her lips, my supervisor held her hand out, and I placed the crumpled note in it. When she saw the message, she snapped her head back up and looked at me.

"You follow," she said, with a sharp gesture of her finger.

I stumbled to get up. With her arm on my elbow, she half led, half pushed me into the coolness of the boss's office. It was the only place in the mill with air conditioning, and I shivered as we waited for him to look up. He sat behind his desk, a thin man with salt-and-pepper hair and eyes as sharp and hard as the machinery. My supervisor handed him the note, and their conversation leapt back and forth across the space between them. The boss's mouth twisted every which way. Even the best lipreader couldn't decipher that mouth. When I looked at my supervisor's mouth, I thought I could catch the word *union,* but not much more.

The boss leaned toward me. *"Who passed you that note?"* he asked.

I looked back at him scared and defiant. No way would I tell him.

"What do you know about a union?" he continued, his face all blotchy red.

Feeling cornered, I considered flight. Then I had a brainstorm. Nervously, I gestured for a piece of paper.

Feigning all the earnestness and cooperation I could muster, I wrote: "Union? What does *union* mean?"

When I finished I looked up, letting the fear, which I really felt, dominate any other emotion on my face. I partly handed him the paper, and he partly snatched it from my hand. His brows knit tight together as he read. It seemed to take him a moment to understand. Then his eyes narrowed and his hand slapped at the wind.

"Get her out of here!" he snarled at my supervisor, and I was sent back to my pants.

❧

On April 4, Martin Luther King Jr. was shot. The family TV, blurry and black-and-white, stayed on all the time now, and I watched a few of the pictures speed by.

"What does it say?" I begged Nana.

As always, Nana was on her way out the door. She paused and her fingers flew.

"He was shot in Memphis," she said. "They caught the guy."

"Who?" I asked.

"MLK—Martin Luther King," she said, the initials and then the letters passing in a rush on her fingers.

"I know MLK, but who *shot* him?" I asked.

She didn't answer. Her eyes returned to the car outside. She could see it through the window.

"Now they'll make a hero of him," she said, and she dashed away.

At first, I thought she meant her boyfriend. Then I realized she was talking about the black people and Martin Luther King. I wondered what Ben thought. Probably the same thing Nana did, but stiffer and uglier.

In some ways, the hopes that King had mustered had only aggravated the prejudice that was part of my home. Why couldn't the black people be happy, the white people muttered, they were getting their way on everything now. Of course, the white people couldn't quite bring themselves to say "black people." Sometimes they said "colored people"; mostly they said "niggers."

I wondered what Lance thought, too. We exchanged friendly letters from time to time, but I hadn't heard from him for months now, even though I was thinking more and more about going back to school. I turned away from the TV. I had been fifteen when President Kennedy was shot. There had been this steady coverage on TV then, too. They had brought us together to watch it at school. Now another leader had fallen. What's happening in this country? I wondered. I was dismayed that King was shot in Memphis, another Southern city. I could just imagine Lance and the New Yorkers snickering about rednecks.

The next morning when I arrived at my slot at work, Lucy was already there. She looked over at me, her eyes swollen and red. I shook my head, trying to convey as much sorrow as I could. Lucy had brought some black material and was clipping it into ribbons. I watched as she pinned one on her blouse.

With a sigh, I picked up my pile of material and slapped the first piece on the machine. When I turned the material to finish the hem, I happened to glance over at Lucy. She was watching me steadily, waiting for me to notice her. As our eyes met, she offered me a scrap of the black material. I could have my own ribbon. Lucy was giving me a chance to honor this dead man.

I didn't really want to put on that ribbon. This wasn't up North, and I couldn't help but notice that not one other white person was wearing a ribbon. Still, knowledge won't be denied, and I knew as surely as I knew that the Louisiana grasses are green and crawfish are sweet, that the prejudice that had endured in our land for such a long time was evil. And I knew that this man had died because he chose to fight that evil. And I couldn't pretend not to know. Further, in the whole place, there had not been any other person who had been nice to me. I couldn't deny Lucy. She was my only friend there. I didn't want her to think I was racist.

I pinned the black ribbon to my blouse.

We didn't talk after that. We sewed in a stillness deeper than usual. My pile was a little higher than normal when 10:15 arrived, and I stood up for my scheduled break. As I began to walk down the aisle to the restroom, I felt something soft brush against the back of my neck. Before I could react, hands were at my shoulders, pulling at my shirt. I whirled around just as my blouse dissolved into two pieces. Outraged and humiliated—feeling nothing but air against the skin on my back, and clutching the remaining shred of blouse against my bra—I stared at my tormentors. The old white woman and her young white henchwoman who worked next to me, flanked by two other women I hardly knew, stood together in a clump, their faces contorted and ugly, their mouths and hands working furiously, and a piece of my blouse at their feet.

I don't know what would have happened if my supervisor hadn't intervened. She ran over to us immediately, and the women retreated. Expecting to be scolded, I was astonished when my supervisor put her arm around me for a moment, almost protectively. Then she took off the blue smock she wore over her own blouse and folded it gently around my shoulders. Her mouth worked in the direction of the other women, and she led me to her office. By this time, I was crying.

"Stay here," she said, helping me into a wooden chair.

She left to restore order in the sewing room. I sat alone and cried. She popped in after a while and looked at me, but even though my tears had stopped, she made no effort to get me back on the floor. The effort to get back to work came from me. I fought the heaviness in my body, stood up, stuck my nose as high as I could, and returned to my station. I didn't look at anyone except Lucy.

"I'm sorry," her mouth said.

I shook my head. This wasn't her fault.

I clasped the blue smock tightly around me, and took up where I had left off. I sewed all day.

The repercussions continued. When work was finished, my carpool refused to take me home. Those women left me standing in the parking lot. Dumbfounded, I returned to the supervisor's office, where a helpless Lucy apologized again for an incident she wrongly believed was her fault, and the supervisor called my daddy.

When he showed up, Daddy was furious. Not at the people who were so mean, but at me. Why had I ever accepted a black ribbon from a black woman to honor a black man? Didn't I know anything?

I was unrepentant. *"Lucy writes for me,"* I told my father. *"She helps me!"*

At loss what to do, Daddy called everyone he knew to see if a ride could be found for his daughter.

Finally an old white woman agreed to be my chauffeur. Part of my wages would go to pay her. She made it clear from the start that the chore was almost unbearable. Not only did she not talk to me, she didn't even look at me. I tried hard not to care.

Soon afterward, I told to Lucy I was going back to school.

"College?" Lucy was pleased.

"Gallaudet," I said, nodding.

188

I was sure of it now. A new house stood where our old one had been, and it was a better house, too. A little smaller, maybe, but you couldn't see the ground through the cracks in the floorboards, and it had a new tin roof. I had accumulated a little money, and I would have more by the end of the summer. Further, vocational rehabilitation would pay tuition, room, board, and transportation. There was no point in staying here.

"What does your boyfriend say?" Lucy asked.

That was a lot to lipread, and she repeated it for me.

I showed her my finger. The diamond wasn't there. *"We broke up,"* I told her.

It had happened several weeks before. I don't know what prompted it exactly, except that I wanted to go back to school, and I hadn't figured out how to do so and still marry Ben. I didn't actually tell Ben the marriage was off when I handed back his ring.

"I just think we should do it later," I told him. "Maybe after I finish my education."

Ben nodded without expression. He knew that education had always been important to me.

"Keep the ring anyway," he said.

"No," I shook my head. "That wouldn't be right."

Other stuff didn't feel right either. Daddy had Irene. Nana had Gerites. Jeanette had David. Pat had Bobby. Grady was far away. Everyone's lives went on. My life had become rooted in a job I despised and in outings with my friends. I loved my friends, but jobs take up a lot of a person's being. I wanted something better. I wanted more.

Further, Lance had finally written to me again. After the King assassination, riots had broken out in Washington, D.C., he wrote, and the Gallaudet campus was surrounded by the National Guard. His letter filled me with longing. I wanted to be back on the college campus. I wanted to be with other deaf undergraduates. I felt a similar sensation every time Lance wrote. I felt like Gallaudet was where real life happened, and Rayne was where I watched real life on captionless TV.

I continued to complain about Lance's letters to my friends.

"He won't leave me alone!" I told them.

Not until much later did I admit that I cared about those letters. I had his most recent one in my pocket even as Lucy questioned me about breaking off my engagement to Ben. I had to resist the urge to touch it. If my supervisor saw me, confiscation was assured. If she read that letter, I'd never hear the end of it.

"What about your daddy?" Lucy asked.

"He doesn't know yet," I confessed.

Lucy just looked at me. Her eyes said everything. I had made my decision but I still had a lot of explaining to do. When she finally mouthed back something, it was to change the subject.

"I'm leaving too," she said.

Now it was my turn to look at her.

"I'm sick of this place," said Lucy.

I gave her an enthusiastic thumbs-up on that.

At the end of summer, I drafted my resignation letter.

"It has been a pleasure to work here," I wrote.

I was not embarrassed at all to be lying. I felt I was following some proper and mysterious protocol and that this is what a resignation should say.

"I am sorry to go, but I want to go back and finish my college education."

It sounded good to me, but perhaps the letter was a mistake. I submitted it in the morning, offering to work the next two weeks, and I almost didn't finish the day. My boss burst out of his office. My letter was in his hand and he was shaking it back and forth, like a baby with one of those little toy rattles.

For once, I read his lips clearly.

"So you don't know what a union is?" said his lips sarcastically.

I stared at him, feeling embarrassed and exposed.

Lucy left less ceremoniously. She was gone before I was. I never saw her again. I always hoped she made it back to Texas and made lots of money. As for me, never did I feel so free as the day I walked out that door.

Of course, I still had to tell my daddy.

Ben was easy to tell compared to Daddy. Telling Daddy was a bit like falling into a time warp. Suddenly I was a little girl again, and he had completely reverted to the man that he had been before I ever started school.

"No!" he said adamantly when I broached the subject.

"Daddy, I've made up my mind," I told him with all the firmness I could muster.

"No," he said again, more forcefully this time. "I forbid your going!"

"I'm going." I was trying to stay calm in the face of his wrath.

"How?" he demanded. "You'll get no money from me!"

I told him I didn't want his money. I didn't need it either. I opened my purse and showed him my ticket and tuition bill. I had applied for vocational rehabilitation money, my application was accepted, and the bill was paid. I even had a ticket for the train.

Grady happened to be there, and I really feel it was my brother's intervention that convinced Daddy to let me go. "Let her go," Grady said.

Nana supported my going, too. "It's good for Kitty to go," she told Daddy.

Finally he relented. Later, Nana approached me in the room alone.

"Can we use the chapel reservation?" she asked.

"What?" I had no idea what she meant.

"June 15 . . . the chapel . . . Gerites and me," she said.

It turned out that my sister had tried to schedule a June wedding for herself, only to find that the chapel was completely booked. Now there would be an opening—the time I had scheduled to marry Ben.

"Of course you can have the chapel," I said. It was meant to be.

"This time I'm going to stay in college until I graduate," I told her.

"And I'm going to get married," she smiled back.

16

☙

*T*he Reentry of a Coed

And all I ask is a tall ship and a star to steer her by.

—JOHN MASEFIELD, *SEA FEVER*

Back at Gallaudet for two weeks, I felt like I had never been gone. I was a freshman taking the prescribed curriculum—English, biology, and for a short time, three foreign languages. I dropped Russian after the first semester, and Latin after the first year, but I kept pursuing French, feeling through it a connection to my Acadian home.

"What the hell's this?" my father demanded when he received a portion of a letter written in the language I was learning. I don't know if I failed in my attempt to apply my first-year French because I'd used the formal *vous* instead of *tu,* and *tutoyer*ed when I should have *vous voy*ed, or whether my father was just disconcerted because he had never learned to read his native tongue. In any case, when Nana wrote to me about his perplexed ire, I immediately gave up writing French to communicate with him.

My favorite subject was art history, taught by Debbie Sonnenstrahl. When Debbie was finished teaching me, my lifelong understanding that a picture was a picture had been replaced by a kind of confusion that I think is more accurately called appreciation. Scale, purpose, color, history, culture, spirit—all captured and transformed by human art.

"Another reason to visit Europe," I told Lance.

My life on campus had already become comfortable, and my year in Rayne slipped over into a nodule of memory. Mary Langlois was happy to see me, and even our boss, Adele Krug, seemed pleased when I reclaimed my job in the library. I was relieved and happy to be there. Plumie was still there, even quieter than I remembered. I learned later that I'd been wrong in imagining that my white friends in the North had looked at the King assassination with horror and sympathy. Violence had exploded in the neighborhood around Gallaudet, and the mostly white students were enraged and undiscriminating in their anger toward the black rioters and black people in general. Plumie, finally developing a sense of belonging when a cohort of black students appeared the year that I was in Louisiana, was stung by it. She remembers notices that appeared around campus, warning about "robbery and rape . . . and nigger things." An accusation of rape was raised by one of the students, and until a white construction worker was charged, the students took for granted that the perpetrator had been black.

Plumie was now a year ahead of me, and we didn't talk much anymore. I didn't know until later that she had found the environment so hostile she considered quitting. Her mother wouldn't hear of it.

"You want to give up because of those white people?" she demanded of her daughter. "That's not a good enough reason."

Plumie, showing the same quiet courage that had helped her heal from a crippling disease, stayed in school.

My bad luck with roommates continued. My new roommate passionately pursued self-destruction. Every Friday she was drunk and throwing up, and almost always doing both these things in our room. I had little patience and less stomach for living like this.

Kathy Meyer, a quiet student who had taken the previous year off to work as I had, had been granted a room to herself when her roommate decided to live off campus. Kathy grew up in St. Paul,

Minnesota, where she was among the deaf and hard of hearing students who were placed in resource rooms of public schools, in a venture that predated officially mandated mainstreaming. Kathy was among the brightest inside and outside the resource room, she remembered, and schoolwork was more a pleasure than a challenge. She was hard of hearing with a voice that hearing people easily understood, an attribute that offered the dubious plus of academic acceptance and the small hope of social acceptance, but no hope at all of assistance in the way of interpreters, note-takers, or even sign language instruction.

After graduating from high school, Kathy spent a year in business school and then left to work as a typist in an insurance office. For fun, she joined a deaf bowling team and learned her first signs. At the same time, Bob Lauritsen, the son of deaf parents and a counselor in the vocational rehabilitation office a block away from her office, learned about the deaf woman working nearby and paid her a visit. Lauritsen told Kathy about Gallaudet University and asked if she were interested in taking the entry exam. She and five other young deaf people took the test that March, and Kathy passed it with the same ease that she had passed so many tests in public school.

"If not for Bob Lauritsen, I would not be here," Kathy once said, referring not to her college dorm or classroom, but to the life and career that would develop in Washington, D.C. "I should thank him for changing my life."

But the life required hard cash, and after a year at Gallaudet, she had gone back to work. She spent two years doing word processing, before she was able to return to classes. We, who had been preps together, were two years later freshmen together.

"Would you mind if someone joined you in your room?" I asked and explained about my roommate.

Kathy paused. "Do you drink?" she asked.

"No," I answered.

"Do you smoke?" she asked.

"No," I said again.

"Fine," she nodded. "Come on."

Her room was on the first floor, an excellent location for circumventing the rules still in place for the female portion of the campus. While the men were on their own, the women were supposed to return to the dorm by eleven o'clock. Lights had to be turned off in every room by midnight. Just to make sure we complied, a supervisor checked each room every night, just like at the Louisiana School. So our ground-floor window became a point of exit and entry for many a female student.

At Gallaudet, the antics among the students resumed. *No Parking* signs removed by gracious students looking out for the citizens of Washington, D.C. rested in the dorm lobby. As soon as the nights grew cold, someone pulled the fire alarm, forcing early morning evacuation of the dorm. While we stood and shivered, Dean Elizabeth Benson would try to lull us into confessing by promising us that as soon as she knew who had done the dirty deed, we could go back inside. Of course, no one ever told who it was.

Several of the deaf students at Gallaudet were from other countries and they provided out-of-classroom learning experiences. Once, a boy from Norway joined a group of students in a foray to the Potomac River where it runs through Rock Creek Park, the expanse of greenery in northwest Washington. Overjoyed to see water, the Norwegian decided to swim and removed his clothes. Apparently this is normal behavior in Norway, but it caused a chuckle here.

Another student who had been born and raised in India established himself in the student lounge one morning, ready to read the newspaper, still wearing his pajamas. The boys saw him and informed him that in the United States one could not recline in a lounge or appear anywhere in public in one's pajamas. Having seen coeds parading around campus in bikinis, he puzzled for a while about the customs of dress in this strange country.

This was Madan Vasishta, who later became Dr. Vasishta and superintendent of the New Mexico School for the Deaf. Madan underwent several learning experiences, beginning the moment he set foot on the Gallaudet campus. Arriving with several languages under his belt, including English, which he used with fine grace and authority, Madan had encountered sign language only through a book of handshapes for fingerspelling. These he practiced diligently in his own country, and he was pretty swift by the time he arrived here. Still his first conversation was a comical disaster. It turns out the illustrations that Madan had studied were drawn from the perspective of the person observing, not making, the finger letters. Thus, when he had his first conversation with deaf persons in American, he made his letters facing the wrong direction. His conversational partners found themselves watching the back of his hand. After they stopped laughing, they unceremoniously turned it around.

Lance remembers encountering Madan at dinner, midway through a hamburger, in a break from the vegetarian customs of his homeland.

"Why don't people in India eat beef?" Lance asked him.

"There's a belief in reincarnation," explained Madan. "If life recycles and we are born again in different forms, it isn't good to eat any meat, so I don't eat meat in India."

"You could be eating your ancestors," Lance pointed out.

Madan smiled. "We could be eating our ancestors," he agreed mildly.

Lance pointed to the half-eaten burger in his hand. "But it's okay for you to come here and eat *our* ancestors!"

Madan saw he was teasing, and they both laughed.

The teachers who could sign well were tougher and had full classes. Those who could not sign had easy classes. Almost a week after I got back, I noticed a group of girls talking outside of my room.

"This place is hearing!" a new girl was saying to others in the hallway. From the tone of her signs, one would have thought hearing was not a good way to be. I watched as she continued.

"I went to the business office and bookstore, and all the employees are hearing people. At the registrar's office, they are hearing. At the bank they are hearing. And no one understood me! Not only are they hearing—they can't sign!"

I'd never thought that the term *hearing* could be derogatory, but it sure looked that way flashing off that girl's fingers. I felt nervous with her talking like that right there in the hallway. The other girls around her must have felt nervous too. They nodded in agreement, but it was clear they didn't want the houseparent—here they called them residential advisors—to see us talking about this. Down the hall, a young woman, recently graduated from Gallaudet's education program, entered her office and closed the door.

"She's hearing, too," said the new girl, shaking her head in exasperation. "In North Carolina, at least all of the people who worked in the middle school and high school dorms were deaf."

"She signs," one of the other girls said.

"Not skillfully," said the new girl, to muffled laughter.

I joined the group and fell in step next to the girl who had been talking.

"What's wrong with hearing?" I asked her.

She turned to me, surprised. "Nothing," she said. "But I'd prefer deaf people."

"Why?" I asked.

"Communication!" she responded. Ms. Benson was the exception. Most of the hearing people on campus might as well have grown up in a different country for all they knew of sign language. Then came an afterthought. "Also, deaf people are cool," said the new girl.

No one had ever told me that before.

I glanced at her, startled. She was smiling, looking as if what she said was perfectly obvious.

"What's your name?" I asked her after a moment.

"Rachel Stone," she answered. She fingerspelled it and then showed me her name sign, *R* at the chin.

I tried to tell her I was Kitty, but she had already heard my name was Cathy and she fingerspelled it precisely. As usual, I didn't have the heart to insist I be called Kitty. I had tried several times to get people to call me Kitty, but it didn't work. They didn't use my Louisiana name sign; they just fingerspelled C-A-T-H-Y.

If any of us knew what we wanted from life and conveyed it in a way that was friendly and authoritative, it was Rachel Stone. While Kathy Meyer and I arrived at Gallaudet partly through the encouragement of others and partly through fortuitous circumstance, Rachel decided all by herself, while she was still a little girl, to come to Gallaudet.

"I knew what I wanted," she said. "My dad was a printer. My mom worked for a box factory for two years before she got married. My deaf uncle and deaf aunt worked in a textile mill for many years, and my other deaf uncle and deaf aunt worked on a farm.

"I wanted more than that."

Her parents, both deaf, had sent her to the North Carolina School for the Deaf in Morganton, the school that they had attended and where they had met each other. The program was oral, Rachel remembered, with signs used only in the dorm. She understood nothing of what the teachers said and they understood nothing of what she said. Partly she relied on her hard of hearing classmates to interpret, but mostly she read books and educated herself. She became known as a nonconformist.

"I was never interested in doing something just because everyone else did it," Rachel told me once.

Despite her determination to do it her own way, she managed to be extremely successful. When she took the Gallaudet test, she not only passed it, she passed it so decisively that she could enter the college-level program immediately. No preparatory year for her. Despite the lack of communication in her oral classrooms, Rachel Stone started Gallaudet as a full-fledged freshman.

She was smart, and pretty too, but what attracted me most was her outspokenness and pride. From the beginning, I admired her and felt intrigued by her attitude. While the rest of us tried to keep up with the hearing people, Rachel had it looped around. The hearing should keep up with us, she believed. She wasn't only unashamed to be deaf, she was proud of it.

"Deaf people can do anything," she told me flat out.

In 1969, this was a novel idea.

Seeing I had so little clothing, Rachel returned from Christmas vacation with cotton shifts for me. She had sewed them herself. Flowers, prints, and plaids in a gentle A-line shape, perfect for a '69 coed.

"How much do I owe you?" I asked aghast.

"Nothing!" she said.

There were textile mills in her hometown, she explained, and she had procured the material cheap.

"But I want to pay you!" I was serious. It might take the whole semester, but I would do it.

"Don't be silly," she laughed.

"How much?" I asked again.

"It was only about five dollars," she said finally.

"Each?" I asked. That wasn't so bad. I was doing the math in my head. It was lots cheaper than any of the dresses in D.C.

"Total!" she said. "And I'm not taking a cent." And she didn't.

I was too busy with work in the library to join a sorority. I had lots of friends though, and Rachel and Kathy were among the closest.

Lance and I began dating again. We stayed cheerful and busy, and both of us dated other people as well as each other. I adored Lance. Still, I couldn't help feeling that our relationship was unreal, like some kind of dalliance that could only occur in the unreal world of a college campus. True, everything was fine at Gallaudet. With a life centered on academics, we shared a lot by definition. Outside of the campus, a relationship seemed more problematic.

"We're just so different!" I told him.

He nodded. He knew what I meant.

Lance was born deaf into a hearing family just like me, but his family came from Brooklyn.

"Not New York," he corrected me time and time again, "Brooklyn—the best of the five boroughs of New York."

While my family and then school encased me in what they believed was a safety net of rules and fears, Lance's mother had encouraged him to explore. He spent the night in friends' homes, walked all over the city, and went to the deaf club by subway. Not that communication was any easier for him than for me. Like most deaf people with hearing parents, his folks wanted so much for him be able to speak and read lips—to be as hearing as possible for a deaf boy—that they didn't learn sign language. They sent him to a public day school known for its zeal in educating deaf children through speech.

Lance hated the school. Every morning he cried and fussed and begged not to go. His mother, instead of ignoring his tears, decided to pay a surprise visit to his classroom. Lance was about nine years old when she arrived at the school unannounced. The principal tried to persuade her to postpone her visit, but she was adamant. She wanted to see her son's class, and she wanted to see it immediately. Accompanied by the principal, she walked to Lance's room and opened the door.

Inside, a half dozen children sat in a semicircle around a teacher. The teacher was working with a single child, rehearsing sounds and portions of sounds that make up the English language. The rest of the children had their heads on their desks. Some, including Lance, were sleeping. As Lance's mother tells the story, the teacher was startled and embarrassed by her sudden appearance. The teacher's first act? She gave the desks before her a solid thump and roused the dozing children.

Outraged, Lance's mother asked for an explanation.

The teacher responded that the children had been doing exactly as they were told. She could only work with one child at a time, and they were instructed to put their heads down and nap in between their individual lessons. It seemed to be a method of control—if the kids kept their unoccupied heads on their desks and their eyes closed, they couldn't distract each other from their lessons, and there was no possibility of conversations escalating into mischief.

This was not Lance's mother's idea of an effective education.

At his desk, Lance found his mother standing next to him with her hand extended. When he took it, the two of them walked out. Lance would never return. Instead he went to the residential school for the deaf in White Plains. It was almost an hour away, nothing by Louisiana standards, but a hike for a boy used to getting where he needed to go with public transportation. Although his mother often said she missed her son dreadfully, she never had any doubts about her decision. Lance thrived at the residential school where signs were used for classes and conversation, and there was no need to ask whole classes of students to put their heads down.

Another big difference between Lance and I was religion. While I was raised Catholic and had become more deeply involved with my religion when my mother died, Lance was a Jew. I wasn't exactly sure what that meant yet. But it seemed an enormous difference.

Something else I worried about was his age, because he seemed so much older than me. Finally, one night when we were getting ready to go out to dinner, I took a prolonged peek at his ID. At that time, in Washington, D.C., it was legal to drink wine and beer at eighteen, and few of us ever left campus without some sort of identification that proved we were legally of age to drink. I had looked at Lance's card a million times and had never really seen it. That night, for the first time I realized that the birth date was altered. At first, I thought it was some kind of ridiculous bureaucratic mistake.

"Look," I told Lance. "This card was typed wrong."

A glance at his face told me the mistake wasn't a bureaucratic one.

"You've been using a fake ID?" I asked. It seemed so out of character.

His color deepened. "Lots of people in New York have fake IDs," he huffed.

He tried to snatch away the card, but I held it tight.

"How old are you?" I demanded.

He was intent on taking the card.

"Lance, this is silly," I was prepared for him to be older. Maybe a lot older. I was sure he wasn't twenty-five though. That would truly change things if he were twenty-five. Or maybe it wouldn't. The thought of our having such an age difference was as confusing as everything else.

Finally he told me. "I'm eighteen," he said.

I was shocked. He was two years younger than me.

"I was sixteen when I came here," he added.

So that's why the fake ID. And that's why he had refused to tell anyone his age.

A few weeks later, the two of us went to an ice cream shop near campus. Lance made a joking apology about having to make the excursion on foot. He was ready to buy a car, but his parents wouldn't allow it.

"I have the money saved," he said, "and I should be able to make my own decision on how to spend it. I need a car. I'm a sophomore now."

It was true. Now that I had spent a year at home, Lance the Younger was one year ahead of me in school.

On the way back to campus, four young men appeared out of nowhere and encircled us.

"Give us your money," one of them told Lance.

Lance angled to get between me and them.

"Go back to campus," he signed swiftly.

I felt I shouldn't leave Lance, but I broke from the group and ran through the campus gates, hollering all the while for help.

Outside, the boys around Lance began to hit him. Lance didn't try to defend himself—that would have been silly when it was four against one. But he wouldn't give them any money either. Lord knows what would have happened if a security guard hadn't heard my cries and come running. The boys around Lance were gone as soon as the guard appeared, leaving Lance bruised and angry, but basically unharmed.

"You're lucky you weren't killed," I told him.

At the library, they made Lance out to be a hero. He had protected me, they said. He had held onto his money, saved me, and enabled truth and justice to prevail. Maybe so. I remained shaken up for months. The incident did have a silver lining: Lance's parents finally agreed to let him have a car.

I didn't want to go back to Rayne that summer. I asked Mary if I could keep my job in the library. She talked to Mrs. Krug, and they found some grant money to let me work full-time. Lance had a summer job lined up at the First National City Bank in New York.

"When I come back, I'll have a car," he reminded me.

I laughed at the thought. "That will be fun," I said.

With three months of summer separation ahead of us, Lance wanted to make promises. He was ready to make what we used to call a commitment.

And I wouldn't do it.

"We should date other people this summer," I told him.

He didn't answer, but he looked hurt.

"It makes sense," I insisted, and of course, he agreed.

Religion. Culture. Geography. Age.

It was a lot to overcome.

17

❧

Kitty and Lance: An Item

And then I asked him with my eyes to ask again yes
and then he asked me would I yes . . . and his heart was
going like mad and yes I said yes I will Yes.

—JAMES JOYCE, *ULYSSES*

When Lance left, I was startled to find that the sense I had of my own completeness evaporated. I walked around feeling like someone had taken away half of my person. I had no idea such a feeling would strike me on his departure. When it did, I thought it would pass. It didn't. I lived missing Lance. When I went to work, my feet whisked his name, again and again, on the sidewalk. I kept thinking I saw his face in the library. Even a dandelion, its cheerful yellow cap mocked and isolated by the surrounding green, reminded me of him.

All this obsession was especially acute because I thought I had lost him. I was so stupid to have bid good-bye like that. So dumb to have been straightforward and rational. So idiotic to suggest that we each continue our lives through summer as if neither had existed during spring, winter, and fall. I was insane to have let that man go, to actually have encouraged him to be free.

Now he was in New York, a Mecca for deaf people because so many deaf individuals lived within the reach of public transportation. He was working downtown, too, in that busy city full of females. I would stay on our small campus, face books in the daytime and dorm walls at night, while he gallivanted around the nation's largest city. And partied.

While New York had a ton of distractions, there were precious few at Gallaudet. The graduate program was most active in the summer, and most of its students were hearing. I felt fortunate to be able to stay and work with Mary and Mrs. Krug. Mrs. Krug's strictness, passed on by Mary, didn't bother me at all. I enjoyed working in the library. And I was living in the dorm for practically nothing. It felt good to be working and saving for the coming semester. I could save up a lot of money in those three empty months.

I could also stew. I stewed deep and I stewed often. Lance was clearly the best man I had ever known. He was smart, honest, and kind. He had a great smile, and he could be funny. He cared about me, too. What more could a woman possibly want? What was Jewish anyway? And what was Catholic? These words were fine for conversation, but they were without application in the real world in which I lived. We had studied *Romeo and Juliet* in our freshman English class, and the words that stayed with me were those of Juliet. "I'll no longer be a Capulet," Juliet said. We had discussed that line at length. What in the heck was a Capulet anyway? Did *Capulet* have any more substance than *Catholic* or *Jew?*

On the basis of foolish abstraction, I had given Lance his freedom. What was wrong with me? The TTY—the device based on Baudot technology that transmitted type over telephone lines—had been invented, but its use was not widespread. Neither Lance nor myself nor anyone we knew had one. Further, I probably wouldn't have called him even if I could. The thought was frighteningly forward. Two years on my big-city campus hadn't sufficed to disabuse me of that notion that girls didn't seek out boys, even and especially if they cared about them. We didn't even write. Committing thoughts to paper seemed more daring even than calling.

So I waited. And waited. It was the slowest three months of my life.

When it was time for the upperclassmen to return and I caught sight of Lance across campus, my heart jumped. It was August. The football team was practicing. The preps were getting used to the campus, the freshmen were playing pranks on the preps, and Lance, a knapsack in his hand, was heading from the parking lot toward the men's dorm.

He must have his new car, I realized. He had probably unloaded all of his luggage except the backpack and parked the car before returning to his room. I eyed him warily across the quadrangle, feeling too timid to run over and say hi. He had probably found someone else by now anyway. I was sure of it.

I thought again of all the deaf clubs in New York. Even if Lance didn't go to them, he had lots of friends. New York women were nowhere near so shy as Southern women. In fact, New York women were forward. As I watched, Lance ambled into the dorm, unaware of my existence.

He'll probably go to the registrar's office, I thought, trying to anticipate his natural course of action. Then the bookstore and, if the past were any predictor, the library. My work shift was over, but if I walked back to the library, I could wait there for him. It would be easy to talk in the library. People would leave us alone. We could catch up.

Yes, my mind decided, the library was the place to be.

Nope, my feet disagreed, and walked me to bookstore.

I sat outside and waited. He would come here first, I was sure.

He arrived just before it closed.

"Hi!" he said as he gave me a quick hug.

"Hi!" I hugged him, too. It was no different than all the hugs that I gave and received during the first week of each school year. I was trying to look surprised to see him.

"You're not working in the library?" he was cool and pleasant.

"I'm finished for the day," I said.

He nodded.

"How's New York?" I asked, not wanting him to disappear into the bookstore just yet.

"Fine," he said, still nodding.

I was feeling it already. Lance hadn't forgotten me. I could see it in his eyes, in his smile, in the eagerness of his expression. I felt relief all over. He still liked me.

"Better hurry," he noted, gesturing toward the bookstore. "It's getting ready to close."

"Looks like you already have books," I said, pointing to his full hands.

"Yeah, I stopped in the library," he nodded.

Did he blush? Maybe. As I glanced over the titles he held, he answered my unasked question.

"I thought you'd be there," he said.

And that was that. After our first encounter, we became, in the parlance of the campus, an item. We were a couple again. A real couple this time. We were serious, which meant in some way considering eventual engagement and marriage. We were always together. He was mine, and I was his, and it felt great.

Around me, my friends found themselves headed down serious roads, too. Rachel was dating a Gallaudet graduate, Ray Harris, who was as handsome as she was pretty. Rachel met him after a captioned movie, when he showed up to visit a friend on campus. While her friend talked interminably with Ray, Rachel waited. As they got ready to part, Ray hugged her friend and then turned to embrace her. Hugging and touching are much more a part of deaf culture than hearing culture, but Rachel still felt that the embrace was a wee bit sudden. As she and her friend turned to walk to the dorm, Ray followed. Uncomfortably aware of his continued presence, Rachel turned suddenly.

"What do you want?" she asked with her characteristic directness.

"I want another hug," he responded. "And a kiss."

With that Rachel fled. She practically jumped into the dorm and slammed the door behind her, while her friend dissolved in laughter.

"He's a tease," the friend told her later, still chuckling, but Rachel didn't think it was funny.

Ray persevered. After a while, Rachel consented to a date. Then another date. Slowly, like Lance and I, she and Ray came to be seen as a campus couple. Some people tried to warn her away from him. Ray likes women, they said, and women like Ray. Plus he was twelve years older than she was, which seemed like an enormous difference. I didn't say anything. Clearly this older man made her happy, and maybe being older, he would give up the other women and finally settle down.

Plus, who was I to preach? I still hadn't gotten used to the fact that Lance was younger than I was. I've no idea why a two-year difference seemed like nothing at all when the man was older than I was and seemed some kind of irreversible chasm when I was older than the man. Lance was virtually the only male I had dated who was younger than I was. After all this time, it still felt strange.

❧

"Buy a dress," Kathy Meyer told me one day. "I'm getting married!"

"Terrific," I said, though she looked more harried than cheerful.

"The campus altar," she explained. "Two weeks from now!"

"So fast!" I exclaimed.

The reason, she explained, was logistics. We chose new roommates every year, and this year the student she had planned to room with had become an officer in one of the sororities, and sorority rules specified that its officers room only with other sorority members. When she requested a new room assignment, the new dean had sent her to fill a vacancy on the fourth floor. Kathy was appalled. It felt like banishment. All of the other seniors roomed on the first floor. Worse, the room already had an occupant—a freshman.

Kathy's boyfriend was Bob Jones, a hearing man she had met during her year at work. They had been engaged for three years and planned to marry after Kathy graduated. When she explained the situation to him, Bob noted how much easier it would be to live together. His family was religious; therefore, living together necessitated marriage.

"Why not get married now?" Bob suggested.

"It made a lot of sense," Kathy said later. "And it was better than living on the fourth floor with a freshman!"

Thus the hasty wedding was arranged. It was a nice wedding, in a small chapel on the Gallaudet campus that has since been torn down. Kathy and Bob have remained married all these years. Bob never learned sign language. Like many women who take responsibility for almost everything that doesn't go right in a relationship, Kathy blames this on herself.

"I wasn't aggressive enough in asking him to learn," she said.

I could barely communicate with Bob, of course. When we were together, Kathy interpreted. But it made including him in our group a bit difficult, and double-dating something like impossible.

That fall, for the first time, Lance asked me to go home with him. I would meet his family, stay overnight, and attend a cousin's wedding. It meant buying another dress. Thank goodness I had some extra money from my summer work. Lance came with me to the department store. I headed for the rack with cotton smocks, and he grabbed my arm and steered me toward the formal wear.

"That's not me," I said shaking my head at the fancy clothing.

"You have to." He was adamant.

He picked out something with spaghetti straps and sequins. I'd never worn such a thing in my life.

"It's not me," I said again.

"It's perfect," Lance assured me.

My whole soul was protesting.

I looked again through the rack and pulled out a simpler dress. It was black velvet with white beads around the collar and an empire waist. Lance looked it over like it was some kind of contract.

"Okay," he said finally.

A week later, we took the train to New York. When we got off in Penn Station, Lance moved nimbly through the hordes of people, guiding me in front of him like I was some kind of grocery cart.

We made our way to an interior corridor of the station, where a draft caught us as we headed down, across another ramp, and then down another escalator. Finally we were deep inside the earth, running for the open doors of another train, only this train was called a subway. I gripped Lance's arm, walked as fast as I could to remain abreast of him, and steeled my soul against the throngs of hurrying people executing similar maneuvers all around us. One false move and I would have been just one more battered tile under that rushing throng. The whole time, I tried to see everything, the corridors and their colorless rooftops, the people who hurried past. Just like my first visit to Washington, D.C., I couldn't stop staring.

The subway shot forth into the darkness, and I looked at this man that I loved.

"Almost home," he said.

When we got off the subway, I found a street exactly like the one he had described to me. It was in Brighton Beach, the southernmost part of Brooklyn, where the Atlantic Ocean meets New York. The houses were small, like in Rayne, but they clung together, side by side, making a solid row of cement and brick, doors, porches, windows, and front walks. We saw fewer people about, but Lance's step remained quick on the pavement.

I was nervous. Traveling is an adventure, but arriving can be a chore. Lance had hesitated to tell his mother about me. He hadn't wanted to fall in love with a Louisiana Catholic any more than I had wanted to fall in love with a New York Jew. When he finally told her, she had reacted with the open-mindedness and trust that had characterized her relationship with him since he was a small boy. She was simply glad her son had found someone he cared about. At least that's what she said. At least that's what he said she said.

Lance turned onto a concrete walk and mounted the steps, pushing me ahead of him again. My fear mounted. His mother was at the door. She embraced him—and then me—immediately. She was warm and welcoming. My fears began to evaporate. We sat down in the dining room for sandwiches. So far, so good.

Is it especially awkward for deaf people to meet the hearing parents of the people they love? I don't know. We smiled, gestured, and wrote. Lance's sister, Gail, was still in high school. Unlike Nana, she couldn't sign. But she was friendly and eager to try to communicate with me. Lance and his family groped for expression and repeated for each other just like Daddy and I did. Lance caught more of what they said than I could, of course, and helped interpret.

After lunch, I was pleased to help clean up. His mother allowed me to clear the table and carry the dishes into the kitchen. Their refrigerator, split down the center with a special ice bucket on one side, was unlike any I had ever seen. Back home, the split was between the top and bottom, and ice coated the inside of the top section where we chipped and fought to wedge stuff in and out of the freezer. This had no ice coating. It was shiny and clean throughout.

All proceeded smoothly until suppertime. Lance's father would arrive home late that evening, and his mother went into the kitchen to prepare the dinner for just the four of us.

Gail was talking when Lance's mother came back into the living room. We were puzzled by her worried expression. Her lips moved and Lance interpreted.

"Where's the lettuce?" Lance asked.

"Oh, in the ref!" I remembered. Both hearing and deaf people dispense with the multisyllabic word *refrigerator* in conversation, I've seen, but where hearing people abbreviate to *fridge*, deaf people abbreviate to *ref*. I jumped up to show her.

Together we returned to the kitchen and I opened the door to the refrigerator—and there was the lettuce just as I had left it. As I pulled it out, the look on her face and the rock hard texture in my hand told me what I had done.

"I'm so sorry," I said, my face scarlet.

Lance's mother was laughing and calling in the rest of the family. Lance and Gail gathered around the refrigerator for a look at the lettuce, now a sculpture of pale green ice.

"You could knock out a robber with that thing," said Lance.

Even I had to chuckle.

I had worried that I would be overdressed for the wedding, but Lance was right. I had never been to an event where everyone dressed so extravagantly. With my pearls and velvet, I fit right in. The family seemed to approve of me in some kind of way. I saw their glances. I felt their warm handshakes and hugs. Still, I was nervous.

"They don't like me, do they?" I asked Lance as we returned to Gallaudet.

"They like you," he beamed.

When I returned to campus, I felt as settled as I'd ever been in my life.

But the real test of our relationship came later, when I took Lance to Louisiana with me. With my library job extended through summers, I only saw my family during the Christmas holidays. I wrote and asked my daddy if Lance could come home with me. Then, with trepidation, I wrote, "He's Jewish." I didn't want Daddy to make the discovery later. "Lance has left the decision to me, and I decided that our children will be raised in the Jewish faith. I hope that's okay."

I sent off four letters with the news, to Aunt Happy, Nana, Grady, and Daddy. Only Nana and Aunt Happy wrote back.

"It doesn't matter what religion he is," Nana wrote. "What is important is your happiness."

Aunt Happy said almost the same thing.

"So what?" she wrote, in handwriting that I noticed was exceptionally large. "I married a Baptist!"

It was a revelation.

No response came from Daddy. But sometimes no news is good news, and even when it's not, there's nothing wrong with hoping. I told Lance that he could sleep on the sofa in the living room.

"If my daddy didn't want you there, he would have said so," I assured him.

Together we took the train from D.C. to New Orleans. In the bleakness of mid-December, my state looked even more poor and ramshackle than I remembered. We stopped in New Orleans to say hello to Grady, and Lance loved it.

"Reminds me of Europe," he told me.

"You've never been to Europe!" I reminded him.

"Pictures!" he exclaimed, and we both laughed.

"We'll go to Europe some day," he promised.

I watched Grady's face as he shook Lance's hand. It seemed to be going okay, I thought. The next day, we boarded a bus for Rayne. My misgivings deepened.

Daddy was gracious though. He greeted Lance with a handshake and a beer. Lance didn't drink, even then. He was polite, of course. He accepted the beer, and it sat there on the table, growing flatter and flatter. Our rebuilt house was nowhere near as bad as it had been before. The floorboards joined to each other now, and you couldn't see through the floor at all. Still, in a few places, the walls didn't meet the floors at exactly 90 degrees, and the toilet needed a little assist to complete its flush.

Lance was appalled. "It's like a hunting camp," he said. "A place where people might spend a weekend—not even a whole week."

"Not a lifetime," I amended.

He realized he had said too much and looked embarrassed. My home was okay by him, he said.

What upset him most was the food. The first night was catfish, which I ate happily. Not Lance. He had never seen a real catfish, but he had seen pictures, just like he'd seen pictures of Europe, and he was amazed that people really ate such a thing. He couldn't refuse a small portion, and it lay dead on his plate before it was transmitted without fanfare to his lap. I ended up taking some from him and transporting it to the trash can, in a kind of assembly line of subterfuge. Daddy didn't notice and neither did Irene.

Eggs were the fare for the following morning. Lance, who was sleeping in the living room, had a clear view of the kitchen. As he watched, Irene scrambled the eggs with the same grease that she had used for the fish the night before. This time he couldn't even fake politeness. He shook his head.

"I don't eat eggs in the morning," he apologized.

He had to adjust that explanation a bit the following morning when, desperate to eat, he got up early and scrambled eggs for the entire family. He used the butter that we had bought at the store and cooked up quite a repast. The whole family agreed that eggs cooked in butter were quite tasty, if needlessly expensive. Grease was not so expensive. We kept it in a jar in the kitchen. After cooking, whatever grease was left in the pan, we dumped back in the jar. Lance looked at that jar like it festered with copulating salmonella.

For the rest of the week, he had to figure out new ways not to eat.

In frustration, he turned on the television. He didn't expect captions, of course, but he was flummoxed by the meager offerings. We had two channels. On one channel, a man espoused the benefits of taking Jesus as a savior. On the other, a man took apart his tractor and, with excruciating slowness, explained each of its parts.

Poor Lance. His travails continued. He couldn't understand my father or Irene. He stared at me in wonder when Daddy did his air spelling.

"You have to read it backwards," Lance noted, "like Hebrew."

One day, while Gerites was at work, Nana drove us to make the rounds of relatives. We saw JoJo and Aunt Happy. Each brought us small cups of coffee and caught me up on the news.

"You okay?" I asked Aunt Happy. I could see she walked around her home with extra care.

"Tunnel vision," she said.

I thought of Velma. "I'm so sorry," I said. But she would hear none of it. We sipped our coffee and talked of other things.

❧

The ten-day visit was interminable for Lance. When Alpha stopped by, Lance was pleased to be meeting someone with whom he could communicate easily. But Lance's pleasure soon evaporated and he became frustrated. The conversation began pleasantly enough.

"Where are you from?" asked Alpha.

"Brooklyn," said Lance.

"New York," I elaborated.

"Where's New York?" Alpha asked.

Lance hesitated.

"Far away," I said.

"Past New Orleans?"

"Past New Orleans."

"What do you grow there?" Alpha asked.

"Grow there?" Lance was confused.

"Yes, what kind of crops?"

"No crops," said Lance. "It's a city."

Now it was Alpha's turn to look confused. After all, Rayne was a city, too.

"You must grow something!" he said.

"Apples," I said, remembering having seen some orchards from the train.

"Apples," Lance agreed, feeling like he had come to another planet.

Lance did enjoy the visit with Lenora and Charles Heinen. They came and picked us up and took us to their farm. Charles gave Lance the tour. He showed him how to plant rice and explained why rice had to grow in water, and how the water then provided a perfect habitat for crawfish, which are a crop themselves. Lance was fascinated.

Only as we were preparing to go back to Gallaudet did Nana tell me about Daddy's reaction to my letter. She came over by herself to Daddy's house to say good-bye to us. I got up my nerve and asked her about it.

"Did Daddy say anything about Lance being Jewish?" I asked her.

Her eyes widened. "Oh, my gosh, he was furious!" she told me.

"Furious?" I was surprised in spite of myself.

"I was over at Aunt Happy's when your letter arrived, and he didn't even wait for me to get back home," she said. "He called me up on the telephone and started screaming."

"He did?" He had shown me none of this.

"Oh, he was so upset!" said Nana. "He didn't even give me a chance to say anything. Practically hung up on me!"

"Oh no," my heart sank.

"Then he went to see Dr. Cann," Nana was smiling.

"What?!" Dr. Cann was our family doctor and the only Jewish man in Rayne.

"Barged right into his office without an appointment," said Nana. "His secretary had to calm Daddy down. When Dr. Cann finally let him into his office, Daddy sat himself down on that little chair of his. Dr. Cann asked him what was wrong, and Daddy goes, 'What does Jewish mean?'"

Nana burst out laughing as she told the tale. I, on the other hand, was mortified.

"So he told Dr. Cann about me and Lance?"

"Oh, you know he did!" she said still smiling at the thought. "You know he told him the whole story. And he asked him if Jews believed in God."

I shook my head.

"Daddy told me so himself," she said. "He asked Dr. Cann if he believed in God."

Only when he was satisfied that I hadn't broken away from monotheism did Daddy leave the poor doctor's office. I looked at Nana and sighed.

"That's our father," I said.

"Nothing you can do with him! So what are you going to do?" laughed Nana.

The following summer, we were engaged. I was home with Lance in Brighton Beach, and he suggested that we take a walk on the boardwalk. After a few minutes of admiring the stars, I looked down and Lance had pulled out a small box with a big diamond. The diamond glistened in the darkness, and he asked me with touching nervousness if I would marry him.

I guess I'm lucky that a moment that was meant to be so perfect, actually was.

I did ask him one thing before we set the wedding date. "Will you love me if I go blind?"

He was taken aback. "Of course!" he replied finally. "Whether you can see or not has nothing to do with my love for you."

We looked at each other a few minutes. I guess I was as startled by the question as he was. I didn't plan to ask it. It just popped out, seemingly of its own accord.

18

❧

$\mathcal{W}$hy Me?

Doth God exact day-labor, light denied?

—John Milton, "On His Blindness"

"You're a snob." The student was smiling and waving books at my face.

I knew that he was teasing. And I knew what else he was going to say before he said it.

"I tried to get your attention, but you wouldn't look up!" He placed the two books before me. "Are you familiar with these? Do you know which one is better?"

I looked at the science fiction in front of me. "It depends on what you like," I told him.

He settled on *Dune,* by Frank Herbert. I grabbed the date-due stamp.

"Next month," I told him.

He nodded and disappeared, leaving the library empty. My final years at Gallaudet had passed with remarkable calm. Graduation came and went quickly. Lance's family was there, though my own family didn't come. Neither Daddy nor Aunt Happy were feeling up to it. Nana was pregnant, and Grady stayed busy with his job and wife. I made the transition from coed to working woman and wife, knitting the two experiences together into a single fabric during my senior year. After graduation, a library position opened up in the new secondary school on the Gallaudet campus, and I got it. It was already my second year of full-time work. Called by its acronym MSSD, the Model Secondary School for the Deaf was a product of President Johnson's Great Society, funded by the federal government to develop curricula for deaf students around the nation to prepare them for college.

This was an exciting time. Three years after graduation, Jason, our son, was born. I dropped him off at the day care center every day on my way to work. Like many deaf parents, Lance and I were determined to make sure our son was comfortable and at ease in a world that was hearing. At home we all used sign language, but Jason, who is hearing, needed exposure to the language of our society and to be able to speak and use it freely. It was a tool he was entitled to. It was part of the reason we sought out day care.

I looked at the clock again. Almost 4:30. Time for me to go home. I didn't go home though. I went to the infirmary, connected through a hallway to the high school where I was working. The nurse greeted me, and I told her why I was there. It was actually a visit I had long postponed.

"People wave to get my attention, but I don't see them," I had to write it for her. It didn't surprise me that she would work in the infirmary of our signing school and be utterly ignorant of sign language. It had been that way since I was a student.

The nurse read my note and looked at me closely. Then she led me into a side room.

"I'm going to call Art Roehrig," she said.

She wrote down the name and now I studied it. Who was Art Roehrig? A doctor, maybe? No, she would have said if he were a doctor. She would have called him Dr. Roehrig. I looked at my watch and settled down to wait. Having postponed this visit for so long, I wanted to get it over with.

The problem was my eyes. Since college, my friends had been complaining that they couldn't get my attention. I always thought I was just too engrossed to notice them. There was so much on my mind—the new job, Lance. Then Jason was born, and I experienced a striking loss of sight. My visual field contracted dramatically inward. It was instantaneous, as if a telescope closed down a notch.

I looked at my watch. Why was it necessary to call in someone from another building when clearly there was a doctor right there? Why couldn't that man see me and save us both a little bit of time?

When Art finally appeared, my impatience turned to horror. A former football player, now robust and handsome in his early thirties, Art made his way toward me without seeing me. He moved agilely, one foot in front of the other, while his hand slid along the wall. I was more upset than ever. Why had the nurse thought I needed to see this man? His condition did not relate at all to my own. I had a small problem with peripheral vision; this man was almost blind. Clearly our cases were very different. The two of us had nothing in common.

By coincidence I was wearing a beige dress, an unfortunate color that blended with my skin and the walls of the infirmary, and totally destroyed any chance that Art might have had to discern my outline. All he could see was my dark hair and the expanse beneath it that he knew must divide into segments—face, arms, dress, neck, torso. He explained the problem, then took one of my hands and raised it so that it was directly before his eyes.

"I can understand what you say now," he said.

I tried to stifle my discomfort.

Art Roehrig was the director of deaf-blind services at Gallaudet. He himself had had limited vision since he was a small child. Like me, at first he took his narrow visual field and limited night vision for granted, assuming that everyone's vision was the same as his. His first inkling that he might be different from others occurred when he was a ten-year-old student at St. John's School for the Deaf in Milwaukee, Wisconsin. He was playing hide-and-seek one night with his friends and joined the other boys, crashing through bushes and trees and tripping over rocks and inclines as he looked for good hiding places. He didn't suspect anything was amiss until the boys returned to the lighted dorm. There, a look in the mirror revealed that he was covered in dirt, scratches, and bruises—and the other boys looked no different than before they played the game.

For a long time, Art thought the other boys had simply memorized where everything was and it was memory, not eyesight, that kept them free of scrapes. Two months later, he joined the boys sledding. Again it was night, and Art relied on his memory. He made several runs, avoiding the trees and the barn below. But on the final run, in an area that had been clear, he bumped into something that toppled over and landed on top of him. As they both got up, Art was embarrassed to realize that he had collided with his teacher, a nun. Art tried to apologize, but the teacher would have none of it.

There was no reason to apologize, she told him, she knew that Art couldn't see at night like the other boys. Art was struck equally by her kindness and her assertion. From that single sentence he knew that the other boys could see and he could not. He remembered the bruises and scrapes he had earned playing hide-and-seek and realized suddenly that the boys' memories were no better than his—it was their eyesight that kept them safe at night.

Art's vision continued to deteriorate. Like me, he could still see during the day when he entered Gallaudet, and he maintained a small tunnel of vision through college. After he graduated and began teaching, the tunnel began to collapse. By the second year of teaching, his field of vision was so small that he couldn't read the board or see his students sign.

He quit his job and set out on a personal quest to find out what was wrong. He visited many doctors without receiving an accurate diagnosis. In effect, he was left to diagnose himself. This happened when he returned to Gallaudet as a graduate student and McCay Vernon came to speak to his class.

Dr. Vernon, a noted psychologist and professor from Western Maryland College, described a condition called Usher syndrome. Art was rigid in his seat as he watched the presentation. Everything Dr. Vernon said applied him. After class, he approached Dr. Vernon to check it out.

"Were you born deaf?" asked Dr. Vernon.

"Yes," responded Art.

"Do you have balance problems?" he continued

"Yes."

"Are you experiencing progressive tunnel vision?" he asked.

Again, Art responded that he was.

"That sounds like Usher syndrome," said Dr. Vernon.

Art, relieved to have a name for the situation he had endured for so long, asked where he could find more information, and Dr. Vernon told him to go to the National Institutes of Health (NIH), just outside of Washington, D.C. in Montgomery County, Maryland.

That was four years before we met.

In that first conversation, Art talked to me like the counselor he had become. There were many causes of eye disease, he said almost gently. Each disease produced a different outcome and each required different treatment. Some were highly curable. We couldn't yet tell what kind of disease I had; perhaps my situation was very different. I had no reason to despair.

"There are four terms I never use when I talk to people the first time," he explained later. "*Blind, cane, braille,* and *Usher syndrome.* People are just not ready to hear those words."

I wasn't ready either, but I did manage to elicit one set of the forbidden words from him.

"What do you have?" I asked him bluntly.

"Usher syndrome," he replied. He signed a *U* at the brow and an *S* at the mouth.

I had never seen the term before.

"U-S-H-E-R S-Y-N-D-R-O-M-E," he fingerspelled slowly.

Then, using both hands, he mimicked touching a four-sided box, directly in front of his eyes. His hands were first perpendicular to the ground to indicate two vertical planes, then parallel to the ground to indicate two horizontal planes. I knew that sign immediately: *tunnel vision.* That's what Velma and so many other deaf people in Louisiana had. They saw in a steadily narrowing tunnel until they tunneled out into total blindness.

My heart swelled with pity for Art.

"You should go to NIH," he said. "They have a good program there."

The proximity of NIH is fortunate for the people in Washington who require sophisticated medical care. I agreed with him, more out of politeness than conviction, nodding my dark hair emphatically in an effort to make the motion clear so he would understand. I just wanted to leave, but the nurse stood in the way of my escape.

"I'll call," she gestured.

I was imprisoned between the two of them. Art wrote down the telephone number and she called immediately. When I left the infirmary, I had an appointment. I didn't necessarily want an appointment. But there it was. I didn't have the energy to protest.

I told Lance about it when I got home. He was surprised. While everyone else was complaining and teasing me about the difficulty in getting my attention and I was defending my unique capacity to ignore the world when focused on something else, Lance had noticed nothing strange, accepting my behavior as a characteristic peculiar to his wife.

"I want to get it checked," I told him, hating the words even as I said them. "I want to find out what's wrong with me."

He sighed. A complete exam was called for. He would take me.

On the day we were scheduled to go for testing, his mother appeared. I greeted her stiffly, torn by strong and mixed emotions. Lance was privy to my most interior being. But no one else was, certainly not my mother-in-law. She had supported me in the same unselfish way she supported her son, and by this time I loved her. Still, she was a guest in my home and I didn't feel like dealing with guests, even—maybe especially—guests who were close family members. I would have preferred privacy.

Nevertheless, I needed an interpreter. My mother-in-law could fingerspell a little and she used her fingers to support the words on her lips. Now I realize what an unfair imposition such a procedure was on all of us. After the passage of the Americans with Disabilities Act in 1990, expecting a relative to interpret for a deaf individual under such circumstances was illegal and unthinkable. In 1976, it was a normal part of being deaf. Mothers-in-law, sisters, aunts, even children explained intimate physical details of medical exams to their deaf family members. Children interpreted for their teachers. Sisters and brothers showed up in courtrooms and hospital emergency rooms. Often, doctors used these hearing people not only as interpreters, but also as decision-makers in treatment. Involving other human beings so inappropriately increased the pain to those closest to us, greatly increasing the pain we felt ourselves.

The testing lasted three days. I remember only pieces of it. I was led into a dark room and told to find the white chair. I was given a headset with goggles and told to push a button when white lights assaulted me, one after another, from every direction. In another test, lights slid out from the periphery, and I was told to press a button once I saw them.

The last day, the four of us—Lance, myself, Lance's mother, and the doctor—gathered in the doctor's office to learn the results. I've been told that hearing people often have a personal reaction to their doctors. Either they like them or they don't. The doctor is good or bad, and occasionally the doctor is wonderful. Unable to communicate with him directly, I felt little human connection to the man who was my doctor. I didn't have occasion to like or dislike him. I had little more feeling for him than I did for the white chair in the darkened room.

Instead I focused intently on my mother-in-law. Lipreading is difficult under the best of circumstances, and now I just tried to catch whatever words I could. I saw "Usher syndrome." The words flowed off her lips not once but several times. Once she tried to fingerspell the words, awkwardly, slowly, beginning several times before she made each letter. I watched her complete the word in horror, trying not to think of Art with his football body and his crippled eyes. I repeated the words back to make sure. She nodded. There could be no mistake.

I tried to ask questions. I tried to force the doctor to tell me that I was different than most people with Usher syndrome. I *was* different, he said, at least I seemed to be different.

It emerged that it was unusual for a twenty-eight-year-old with Usher syndrome to have lost so much peripheral vision, yet be able to see well enough in the dark to find a chair. This indicated that I still had more night vision than might be expected, the doctor said. But he quickly clouded up this temporarily shining point. My night vision would probably fade soon, he said. With that my mother-in-law fingerspelled two more enormous words: R-E-T-I-N-I-T-I-S P-I-G-M-E-N-T-O-S-A. I knew the words, the clinical term for tunnel vision, and showed her the sign, *R* at the eye and *P* at the lips. RP, the slow and progressive degeneration of the retina, is the reason that people with Usher syndrome become blind.

"What's the time frame?" I managed to ask.

"Unpredictable," said the doctor through my mother-in-law. *"We just don't know. Some individuals lose their sight rapidly; a few people seem to hold on to increasingly small tunnels of vision into old age."*

Lance's mother asked a question then, and I didn't catch it. I let the two hearing people talk to each other, grateful not to have to think anymore, which in any case I couldn't do. I hardly paid attention. The more they talked, the more the single thought obsessed me.

I would be blind. I was on my way to blind.

I was no stranger to blindness. At the Louisiana School, not only Velma but several students had vision problems so profound that they walked from class to class with a wide-legged gait to compensate for walking on a floor they couldn't see. Others slid a hand along the walls of the hallways. They groped for chairs before they sat, unsure exactly where to lower their body. They moved hesitantly, using all the feedback that their hands and feet could provide.

I had deaf and blind neighbors at home, too. Alpha's family for example. Alpha—like his five brothers and sisters who were deaf—lost his vision rapidly as an adult. He was deaf at birth and blind by thirty-five.

Why Me?

At the deaf club in Lafayette, a special light bulb glared without shade day and night in a corner so that deaf-blind people would always have a place to converse. Many of these people, like Velma and Alpha, had a narrow circle of vision directly in front of their eyes. With some, we could communicate by restricting our signing to this small space. With others, we would either fingerspell into their hands or sign slowly as they placed their hands lightly around our hands and arms.

So much familiarity with blindness made my own loss of vision no easier.

Another thought materialized from the mist of fear: *How would Lance adjust to a blind wife? Would he still love me?*

On the drive home I was completely occupied with my own thoughts. Lance drove, and his mother reached toward me periodically and patted my shoulder. They were in a different world from me now, I thought, the world of people who would probably always be able to see, the beautiful world of sight and vision, the world that I was about to leave. When we picked up Jason, he ran to me and I gave him a hug, but even my little son seemed somehow remote, as if I couldn't really reach him from my new place of the soon-to-be-blind. Lance and his mother continued to be gentle with me, asking no questions, just touching me, stroking me, and glancing my way to include me in their conversation.

On arriving home I abandoned my frozen exterior and fled up the steps to the bedroom, convulsed in rage and grief.

Why me? I was already deaf. Wasn't that enough? Why did this have to happen to me?

I closed the door hard behind me and collapsed on the bed. I couldn't stop crying.

"Why me?" I demanded of my pillow. "Why me?"

I'd been a good person—not perfect, maybe, but good.

I try to be good. I want to be good, and by and large I have been good. And I'm already deaf, for God's sake. God! "Why me?"

There was so much fear. Fear of being left. Fear of being alone. Fear of being helpless. Fear of darkness.

After what seemed like a long time, the door opened a crack and Lance's mother poked her head in through the sliver of light.

"Can I come in?" she asked.

"No." I tried to stop crying, but I couldn't.

She came in anyway. She sat on the bed and she stroked my arm and hand.

"I know how you feel," she said finally. She was exaggerating her lip movements and speaking in short sentences. Even in the darkened room, I could understand her easily.

"No, you don't," I told her bluntly.

She reminded me of her battle with cancer.

I looked away. She had been diagnosed with cancer three years before. She had gone through treatments. She was okay now, but we knew it wouldn't last.

She waited for my eyes to return to her again.

"You're lucky," she said. *"You will live. Me? Who knows?"*

I just looked at her. What she said was true. Usher syndrome was devastating, but it was not fatal. I would not die from it.

"You have a beautiful family," said my mother-in-law.

I couldn't argue with that.

"You have a lot to live for," she added.

I couldn't argue with that, either.

After a while she suggested that I come down to dinner.

"Come on," she urged gently. *"Eat something."*

I got up, washed my face in cold water, and followed her downstairs.

We did what adults often do when stress strains our hearts and destroys our worlds. We watched sweet Jason in his high chair, perky and quite delighted to be served his meal. I picked at the food on my plate and oohed and ahhed over my beautiful son. Impossible to forget, the diagnosis was like a knife buried deep inside me, hurting each time I took a breath.

When Lance and I made our way to the bedroom, I burst into tears again.

"You are going to have a blind wife," I sobbed. I felt I had somehow let him down.

Lance hugged me and hugged me. "What are you talking about?!" he demanded.

I don't know if I told him I was afraid that he wouldn't love me anymore. I do know that he kept reassuring me.

"Of course I still love you," he kept saying. "I'll always love you. Vision has nothing to do with it. You are the same person whether you see or not."

He had said it before, and he would say it again.

All the testing, all the pain, and I could see not one pixel more than when I had shown up at NIH. My eyesight was falling away in chunks. Driving, once a skill I had taken for granted, was becoming problematic. My balance, never a sure thing, was disappearing, too. A few days before, when Lance suggested taking a bike ride, I had looked at the bike that I had managed so easily as a child, and had known I didn't have enough sense of balance to keep the two-wheeler erect. I couldn't always see the road underneath anyway. Underlying everything was the fear of being isolated and helpless.

Lance's face was surrounded by the void that encroached from all directions.

"I don't want to be blind!" I said.

"I don't care if you arc blind," said Lance.

In Lance and in my family, I was so lucky.

19

❧

"Yes, I have Usher Syndrome"

Anatomy is destiny.

—OLD MEDICAL SCHOOL SAYING

More than half the individuals who are deaf and blind in the United States have Usher syndrome. This is about ten thousand people, three percent of those who are born deaf. Fortunately, RP usually descends slowly and spares children. Even at my old school, those students who groped for the walls of hallways and felt for the table under their books usually had enough sight to learn through vision.

Art Roehrig says that I accepted my diagnosis quickly. Acceptance didn't feel quick. Painful, yes. Many layered, yes. Intermittent and reversible, yes. Quick? No way. For a long time, I couldn't even talk about it. There is an ancient story about a Spartan boy who found a mountain lion, hid it under his shirt, and went about his tasks, even as the lion, restless and hungry, clawed at his stomach. That was me and my diagnosis. I helped students in the library, consulted with teachers on appropriate readings for their classes, took care of Jason, and went out most weekends with Lance to visit friends. I laughed and gossiped. And all the while there was this little lion of a diagnosis clawing at me under my shirt.

Rachel Stone, now married to Ray Harris, was teaching at Kendall, the elementary school on the Gallaudet campus, just down the hill from the high school where I worked. Rachel and I had remained friends since our Gallaudet days. We were both part of a group of couples that got together once a month in each other's homes to watched captioned movies, available then through the federal government. Rachel would later write *Let's Learn about Deafness,* a book for teachers of deaf students that included historical information about deaf people and deaf education, and activities for the classroom. She was taking graduate courses in counseling and pregnant with her second child—her first had been a deaf girl.

"I feel great," she said, smiling and touching her stomach.

I was pleased that she had found time to stroll into the library and talk.

"You look good," I smiled.

She had just switched to maternity clothes, and she was as lively and effervescent as ever.

"I hope it's another girl," she said, "and I hope she's deaf."

I laughed. In those days, no one had a clue about a child's sex until he or she was born, and it didn't surprise me one bit that Rachel wanted another deaf baby.

"Did you save the baby clothes?" I asked.

"Oh, yes," she said. "They were hardly worn."

I thought about Jason. He was starting to walk now, a miniature man toddling about the room.

"They grow so fast," I said, shaking my head.

She nodded, still smiling as a student arrived with a book in his hand.

"Just a second," I told Rachel and turned to quickly stamp the boy's book. I reinforced the date that the book was due by pointing to it and meeting the boy's eyes. We always hoped that this would get our books back on shelves before the advent of summer, though it rarely did. The boy nodded and left. I turned back to Rachel.

"Why don't you admit you have Usher syndrome?" she asked suddenly.

"What?!"

Her question took me completely by surprise. I studied her face, looking for a smirk or an expression of fear. I saw only friendly concern. She had used the correct sign for Usher syndrome. She may have studied it in her master's program at Gallaudet, I realized.

"I don't have Usher syndrome!" I said my heart pounding.

Rachel shook her head. "You don't see us," she said.

She pointed at the boy disappearing around the corner, and I realized that he must have tried to get my attention before I saw him.

"We wave for your attention, and you just ignore us," Rachel was positively gentle.

"I'm busy!" I exclaimed, gesturing frantically at the papers before me.

Rachel's face softened even further, but it held a trace of exasperation, too. I tried to think of a way to change the subject and couldn't. Helplessly, my eyes returned to Rachel's.

"Are you afraid that you will lose friends?" she asked.

It was another question I wasn't ready to answer. I looked away. My frustration was fading. So were my defenses. I couldn't stay mad. Being mad took too much unpleasant energy. I glanced back at her.

"Everyone knows!" she was blunt without being unkind. "Everyone knows and no one cares. You are still the same person."

I looked away again. What purpose was served in pretense anyway? Who did I think I was kidding?

"It's best to just say it," said Rachel.

"Yes, okay," I burst out finally. "I have Usher syndrome."

I looked back at the floor after I said it. It felt good and bad at the same time, another kind of box was falling away.

When I lifted my eyes back to Rachel, I felt suddenly like crying. She hugged me.

"I've had it a long time. A long time," I told her.

She nodded. She looked like she might cry, too.

"It must be hard," she said.

I nodded. "I remember at my old school we would all go running for the dorm and I would always trip on the step. No one else tripped. Just me." I paused and laughed a little in my tears. "It never dawned on me that everyone one else could see the damn thing!"

And that was that.

They say news travels through the deaf community faster than through the hearing community. This may be true. Once any of us finds out information of any sort, we feel obliged to immediately inform our friends. After I told Rachel, I felt that everyone knew, and that helped me to be able to talk about it more easily. Somehow that made me feel better.

❧

From the beginning, Lance and I had wanted two children, but the dramatic loss of vision during my first pregnancy scared me. My mother-in-law came with me to the doctor's again. Again, I watched her hands and lips as the doctor spoke. The doctor said that no one knew why pregnant women reported accelerated vision loss and he agreed that a second pregnancy was dangerous; it might destroy more of my remaining vision.

"Do you think the child would have Usher syndrome?" I asked. It was the most important question of all.

He and my mother-in-law talked for a while before she turned to me.

"There's little chance that the child would have Usher syndrome," she said. *"Lance's deafness was a total surprise, and nobody in our family has ever been blind."*

"Our children would probably be safe?" I asked.

She nodded.

I glanced from my mother-in-law to the doctor. His face was impassive.

When I was pregnant, doctors couldn't test unborn children for genetic problems other than Down syndrome. A few years later, we could test for a number of the really outrageous recessive genetic mischief-makers—cystic fibrosis, sickle-cell anemia, Huntington's chorea, Tay-Sachs disease, some forms of breast cancer, and Usher syndrome—but most people didn't. Even when it was available, testing was no easy matter. Chromosomal material put through its paces to check for Huntington's chorea, for example, would yield no information about Tay-Sachs or Usher. Each test had to be performed separately, each cost a bundle, and most were not covered by insurance. No wonder testing was rarely even considered until one was in terror for oneself or one's children, and then it was almost always too late.

Still, our dream was for two children. We both felt Jason should have a brother or sister, just as Lance and I did.

"It's up to you," Lance told me.

That's all it took. As had happened before, I became pregnant the moment I considered pregnancy.

Lance suggested that if the child were a girl, we name her Rebecca, after his grandmother.

"Such a hard word to say!" I told him. Our lips went through the shapes of the sounds, three of them in percussive succession.

"I don't like it," I admitted. With Jason, we had chosen a name that was similar to his grandfather's without being exactly like it.

"How about Rachel?" I asked finally.

"You want to name her after Rachel Stone?" he asked.

"Partly," I said. "But partly I really like the sound of the name."

"It's a good Jewish name," Lance said.

Rachel Sara Fischer, six pounds, twelve ounces, was born nine months later. Like her brother, she was perfect. Her birth was easy, too.

"I'm a baby machine," I told my husband.

He shook his head. I knew what he was thinking. My visual field had swooped inward again with Rachel's birth; unremitting black closed in another pronounced notch.

"Well . . . at least from the nose down," I tried to laugh.

Like most deaf people, vision more than anything else defined my world. It was through vision that I had language and learning, vision that was sharpened by use and the need to survive. I didn't mind being deaf. Although deafness took away hearing, it gave me community—and that community was based on sight. No matter how I tried to look at it, blindness was terrifying. It was right up there with death.

Rachel was only a baby when I drove to an evening appointment and bumped over an unseen median strip. It had been painted the same color as the road, and I didn't see it even after I drove over it. Frightened, afraid of hurting other people as much as myself, I stopped driving at night altogether.

It is amazing how we can compensate for such loss. Even now, able to see only one-sixth of the range of normal human sight—under the best conditions—I sometimes forget how limited my eyesight is. I am surprised when I bump into things. I forget that everyone else doesn't have to look down just to be able to see the floor.

20

℘

*C*atherine: Acadian and Cajun

The force that through the green fuse drives the flower
Drives my green age; that blasts the roots of trees
Is my destroyer.

—DYLAN THOMAS, "THE FORCE THAT THROUGH THE
GREEN FUSE DRIVES THE FLOWER"

As my vision dissolved into the darkness that closed in from all around, I went through a period of introspection. The irksome recessive genes that caused Usher syndrome made me look at my parents with new eyes. Who were these people? And who were the people who had borne them? And why was this disorder encapsulated in the genes that had become me?

I couldn't help but feel that the key to my inheritance lay in the mysterious word *Cajun*. Now, as an adult, I undertook to learn about the heritage that was my birthright and slowly managed to overcome some of the ignorance that can occur when one is cut off from one's hearing family by being deaf.

The first thing I gleaned was that my ethnicity was prized. *Cajun* may have meant "illiteracy, ignorance, poverty, superstition, and an indecipherable tongue" in the early part of the century. But by the century's end, it meant fresh food intriguingly spiced and familiarity with French, a language that still seemed to carry some of its nineteenth-century cache. I had initially balked at the term *Cajun,* replacing it with the more palatable *Acadian;* now I embraced *Cajun.* I used it freely, even proudly.

The deaf community was changing its focus as well; instead of asking for services, we were demanding our rights. By 1980, Stokoe's research had led to a new linguistic understanding of sign language, closed captions were on prime-time television, and deaf culture was seen as offering something of value for hearing and deaf alike. The hearing people who came to work in our school were eager to learn signs; I taught those who arrived in the library, sometimes using stories of my Cajun homeland.

Deaf and Cajun. They were identities that made me proud.

Although chromosomes, not culture, had betrayed me, human bodies (and their genes) are products of human cultures. To find answers to the question, "Why me?" I had to look at people, and I had to look at history. I had to explore the precise human beings from whom I had sprung and peer into the leavings of my own genealogy.

As I look back through the people who begat the people who begat me, their numbers increase exponentially, by a factor of two every generation. Two parents, four grandparents, eight great-grandparents, sixteen great-great-grandparents, thirty-two great-great-great-grandparents. In 1628, approximately 4,000 of my ancestors were running around on this earth. If they had gotten together, they would have made a small town. One of these ancestors was Toussaint Hunault dit Deschamps ("Hunault of the fields"). Hunault was born in France and baptized in St. Pierre-aux-Champs in Normandy. When he turned twenty-six years old, he was advanced 120 livres, recruited to go to the New World, given money for his passage, and promised a salary of 75 livres per year. One hundred fifty-two other men signed up to make the journey. They were millers, carpenters, stone-carvers, and land-clearers; one was a brewer. Maison de Neuve and the other aristocrats who planned the colony were explicit in soliciting only the hardy—men, and sometimes their wives and children, who could face and eventually vanquish the unforgiving North American wilderness. Hunault was number eighty-nine. He would work as a land-clearer.

I don't know why he signed up, or why any of them signed up. Why would they have boarded a ship and faced an unknown ocean to make their lives in a wild, lonely land they had never seen? The people had revolted in Normandy that year, so perhaps my ancestor Hunault was among them. Perhaps he was desperate.

In any case, the French colony across the Atlantic was desperate to receive him and the other colonists. Public prayers had been offered to hasten their arrival. Montreal, founded only ten years before, was scarcely more than a hospital, a fort, and fifty people. In Quebec City, life was equally harsh. When the boat carrying Hunault arrived, officials initially refused to provide transportation for the final lap of their journey up the St. Lawrence to Montreal.

Of those who had signed up, several never boarded the ship and a few died. About ninety-five men arrived, setting foot in Montreal for the first time in November. With their wives and children, the newcomers tripled the population just in time for winter. Only half of the new colonists would live long enough to produce progeny. Hunault was one of them. Within a year, he was able to purchase a concession and work the land almost as if it were his own. Soon afterward, he married sixteen-year-old Marie Lorgueil, also from Normandy, who had traveled from France on the same ship that he did. Like most of the French settlers, Marie gave birth to several children in rapid succession—six or ten, depending on which source is believed or how many survived.

Already the Europeans had devastated the original American people. The Jesuits who came to convert, the trappers who came to hunt, the traders who came to make money, and the children who only wanted to play had sparked epidemics of smallpox, measles, and chicken pox that had been unknown on this continent. Most of the Indians—the Hurons and Micmacs—were already dead.

My ancestors prevailed. By the time he was fifty-six years old, Hunault had four guns, four cows, and nineteen arpents of land. As part of the Great Recruitment of 1653, Hunault was hailed as a hero and patriot. Thanks to him and his fellow pioneers, the tiny French presence in North America was strengthened. Hunault sold some land in 1689, but the occasion was not a happy one, the record notes, for he was forced to seek some kind of assistance from his daughter Jeanne, and to renew his obligation to the signore of Couagne. Apparently Hunault was a pioneer, but not quite a free-standing one.

The record is silent on much that I am curious about, even as it narrates Hunault's undoing. My ancestor was murdered—"cowardly assassinated"—when a navy lieutenant sent a "mortal thrust of the sword through his body" and took flight.

Jeanne, Hunault's daughter and my ancestor, married Adrien Quevillon, who had arrived from France in 1656. Frontier people, they lived with their seven children north of Montreal near the village of La Chenais, farming, fishing, hunting, and clinging to each other and their neighbors in the serious struggle to survive. In 1689, England declared war against France, and the Iroquois allied with the English. In 1693, they attacked La Chenais. The Quevillon daughters, Catherine, age seven, and Francoise Angelique, thirteen, were taken captive. The Iroquois were famous for the subtlety and intensity of their torture; but they respected bravery, and perhaps they spared Catherine because she was brave. Perhaps they simply considered Angelique too old for adoption. Perhaps like so much in life, an arbitrary occurrence around a blazing fire in the terror of a dark night determined the uncertain future. In any case, Catherine was adopted into the tribe, and Angelique was burned before her eyes.

Fearsome and deadly warriors, the Iroquois, like the armies of King Louis, attacked not only to garner glory and cause a fuss, but to annihilate. Attempts to make peace failed and the attacks persisted. So it was that Catherine lived with the Iroquois for three years. Finally, in 1700, a peace treaty made her return possible. What a reunion that must have been, an Indian-enculturated girl and her white family.

Three years later, at the age of thirteen, Catherine married Guillaume Lacombe. He wasn't my ancestor though. Lacombe died only a year later. Catherine remarried my many-greats-back-grandfather when she was twenty. He was Samuel Papineau, a soldier sent over to protect the settlers. No longer children of France, the Papineaus carved out their lives in the relentless North American wilderness. Much of the family would go on to achieve renown in Canada. Papineau fighters continued to bedevil the English long after there was any possibility for French return to the colony, and a Papineau nephew built the original altar at the church of Notre Dame in Montreal. Even today, the remnants of a trail that traversed their property is called Chemin Papineau. Catherine and Samuel had nine children and she named one, the next in a direct line to me, Catherine.

Catherine's granddaughter, Marie Charlotte Perrillard, traveled down the Mississippi River through French forts and settlements with members of her extended family. Her niece and sister married along the way. In New Orleans, Marie Charlotte met Thomas Hoffpauir, and she got married, too.

Thomas Hoffpauir, the man whose name passed to me through my father, doesn't appear in the record until 1778. He was about forty years old. My daddy says that he arrived in New Orleans with two brothers who turned around and went back home. Thomas gave his place of origin as Alsace-Lorraine and had social and business dealings with the German colonists who had been arriving in New Orleans since 1720. He fought as a member of the Fourth Company, Artillery, under Don Bernando de Galvez, who harassed the British along the coast of Florida. For once, one of my ancestors was on the winning side of a conflict. De Galvez and Thomas were fighting what turned out to be the Revolutionary War. When Thomas returned, he met and married Marie Charlotte, and together they began the family that would spread progeny throughout the American South, West, and Midwest.

A man of his culture and times, Thomas traveled with his wife to St. Landry Parish, where he bought some land and a slave, Josine, whose husband gave permission for the sale.

My father, Alexandre, was one of his many descendants.

❧

Daddy would never have countenanced that his founding ancestor on the American continent, the man whose surname he bore, was anything less than Acadian French. However, America's first Hoffpauir seems to have been French by adoption. My daddy, who served in the Pacific during World War II and referred to Japan's allies as "Kraut bastards," would have had a fit to learn that Thomas himself was probably German. My daddy spoke the same French as my mother when no one was around. He was as Cajun as anyone, despite the blue eyes he passed on to me.

But neither Thomas Hoffpauir nor his French-Canadian wife were Acadian—at least not if *Acadian* is defined as a person who came from Acadia. The name *Acadia,* which describes a political entity that existed for only about one hundred years, probably came from the fortunate convergence of *Arkadia,* a picturesque region of Greece, and *acade,* the Micmac word for "plentiful." Different countries tell different lies about its formation, boundaries, and history, but all agree on one thing: In 1713, France ceded portions of Acadia to England, and the region began its transition to what is today largely the Canadian province of Nova Scotia.

I traced my mother's ancestors—the Grangers—back to this land. Our many-greats-back-grandmother was Euphrosine Gauterot, a granddaughter of Anne LeBlanc and Jacques Landry, part of the great Landry family that had been among the first Europeans to set foot in the New World. Euphrosine married Pierre Granger and they lived in Grand Pré, just up the coast from Port Royal, the earliest French settlement in America, which predated the English settlements at Plymouth Rock.

Pierce was the grandson of the founding ancestor of the Granger family in Acadia, Laurent Granger, who married Marie Landry, daughter of Rene Landry. While his wife's family had been in Acadia for several generations, Laurent probably arrived about

1657. He may have come to trade, or he may have come to conquer. Not much is known about his life before he married my many-greats-back-grandmother. What is known is that he was born in 1637—in Plymouth, England. Laurent Granger, founder of the exiled Granger Acadians, was English.

***

Scholars believe that the Acadian French were different from the French Canadians of Montreal and Quebec. The isolation of these settlers—twelve days by the St. Johns River and four major portages to Quebec, longer to Montreal and to the English colonies of the south—enforced what may have been a natural self-sufficiency and independence. The Acadians produced large families, endured the indifference of their mother country, and coaxed a living from the land and sea. Dike building, necessary for draining their marshy lands, enforced a communal spirit. Most of the settlers had been farmers in France, and they were an independent and egalitarian people. They didn't shun the local Indians, but learned from them and as a result were able to supplement the food they raised with hunting, gathering shellfish, fishing, and trapping. They avoided paying rents, acting as if they had legal title to the land they tilled. In North America, they found themselves transformed from French peasants into New World pioneers.

Surely even after the treaty, they did not believe the English presence would endure in their land. When the British asked them to take an oath of allegiance to the British crown, they refused. After years of occupation, they finally agreed to consider it provided certain conditions were addressed. These conditions included recognition of certain aspects of political existence that the British in the colonies to the south would later call "rights" and go to war over. The Acadians wanted civil and religious freedom. They wanted the freedom to practice their Catholic religion. They wanted to be able to remain neutral in the event of war between France and Britain; and they wanted to be recognized as a distinct people.

The British were unwilling to support these extravagant notions, but they were willing, at least for a while, to negotiate with the settlers. In 1729, Richard Philipps, Britain's provincial governor, injected a note of either diplomacy or duplicity into the protracted negotiations, and assured the Acadians that their conditions had been approved; they would have the religious and civil freedom that they had tenaciously demanded. The Acadians accepted Philipps's assurances and signed the oath. Philipps, however, never informed his superiors of these assurances. Both the governed and the governors were deceived—and life returned to normal.

It may not have mattered. When fighting between the European powers intensified, demands grew for another set of Acadian signatures on another oath of loyalty. In the 1740s, Jean Melançon and Claude LeBlanc were among those who interfaced between the British government and the Acadian people. They responded to new demands for an unconditional loyalty oath by garnering thousands of signatures—affixed to a document that cited the previous oath, with its presumed assurances of civil protection and the Acadians' good behavior.

Indeed, my ancestors had generally behaved peaceably under British rule. Several times, when French Canadians from Quebec attacked British strongholds in Acadia, many of the local French Acadians refused to join them.

My ancestors may have been ahead of their time, pressing for civil rights and refusing to rise violently against civil authority. They may have been naive, refusing to accommodate Britain, the strongest power in the world and the civil authority in their land. They may have been stubborn—they had no army with which to hold their moral ground. And they may simply have been more concerned with their families and farms than with politics.

In any case, they were doomed.

In 1755, Charles Lawrence, governor of Nova Scotia, launched a plan to rid the land of its French inhabitants and fill it instead with English people. The French would call it the *Grand Dérangement;* the Americans called it the Expulsion. It was a plan for Acadian eradication.

On September 5, an order was posted in Grand Pré for Acadian men to come to the churches to negotiate with the British. When the men arrived, the church doors were bolted and British soldiers, most of them from New England, arrested them. Five days later, the soldiers forced the men and their weeping wives and children to the beach, where small boats rowed them to the ships that waited in the harbor.

A few people escaped, congregated in small bands, and even launched attacks before they were driven back by the overwhelming English force. Members of the Landry family dispersed to New Brunswick. Joseph Broussard formed a guerilla army in the wilderness. But most of the Acadians—10,000 people by some estimates—were forced onto those waiting ships. When the ships headed into the Atlantic Ocean, the British torched Grand Pré.

Pierre Granger, my many-greats-back-grandfather was on one of the vessels, along with nineteen other Granger families. At least my ancestors were able to be together. In the march to the ships, many children were separated from parents, wives from husbands. The plan was to send the Acadians south and dump them into the English colonies along the Atlantic seaboard.

Boston accepted 735 people; New York, 344; Georgia, 400; and South Carolina, 940. In Virginia, an estimated 1,500 were kept ship-bound through the winter before they were officially refused entry and sent across the ocean to France. Maryland accepted 913, including Pierre Granger, his brother who had amended the spelling of his surname to match its French pronunciation, Jean Baptiste Grangé, and their families.

It was a particularly inauspicious time to arrive, as Thomas Sharf would note in his *History of Maryland*. Originally founded by Catholics, Maryland was going through a bout of virulent anti-Catholicism. Even more harrowing, the first battles of what Americans would call the French and Indian War had begun, and the Indians, allied with the French, were raiding the settlements on the fringes of the colonies—fringes that seemed to be drawing ever nearer to the colonial city centers.

Into this terrified and intolerant cauldron arrived my ancestors—Catholic and French, destitute and starving. In November, their boats sailed up the Chesapeake Bay, the body of water that cleaves the state into its western and eastern shores. When they sailed into Annapolis, they were only an hour from where I now make my home.

The ships were dispersed to separate harbors so that the support of the Acadians could be shared equally among the Marylanders. Passengers disembarked in Baltimore, Annapolis, Fredericktown, Oxford, and other towns throughout the state. A few Marylanders distinguished themselves in compassion.

"Our aversion to their principles must not be allowed to destroy the seeds of humanity," wrote Henry Calister, a merchant at Oxford. But the seeds of humanity withered quickly, particularly because the winter was a cold one.

A 1763 census found Pierre Granger, his wife, Euphrosine, and six of their children among the sixty-eight Acadian inhabitants of Snow Hill. The Heberts and the family of Jean Baptiste Grangé were in northern Maryland, in the small towns of Fredericktown and Georgetown. In Lower Marlboro, there was a small colony of 26 Acadians. Several members of the Broussard family were in Port Tobacco. A contingent of Landrys and more Broussards were in Upper Marlboro, and still more Landrys were in Baltimore and Oxford.

Also in Oxford was Joseph "Le Sourd" Landry. No other family members lived with him, and no occupation is listed. *Sourd* is French for "deaf," so I seem to have had a long-ago deaf cousin, a cousin of culture as well as genes, who lived among my family members in their exile. Joseph the Deaf is one of the very few people who seems to have lived alone. The sight of his name with its single digit marking the solitary resident in his household is wrenching. There is no other notation, no record of occupation, of land owned, or of family attachment.

His neighbors and family would never have forgotten him, of that I am certain. When it was time to harvest, a group of children would have run over to his house, and roused him from chores or slumber. They would have had a jolly laugh if he didn't see them immediately, or if he looked at them befuddled, and they would have herded him off, like gentle soldiers, to whatever celebration or community undertaking was under way. They might have admired him, too—the way he used his tools, the size of his squash. But there were no schools and little understanding. He would have been blind to most of his experience because he was deaf. I can't help but wish, two hundred years after the fact, that there hadn't at least been a Mrs. Joseph the Deaf, that he had not been so entirely alone.

In the summer of 1765, the *Virgin* and perhaps the *Jane* pulled out of the harbor in Annapolis, bound for the Mississippi River and the French culture that blossomed on its shores. The Acadians' travail was not over, however, for one of the vessels went astray. Its passengers landed in Texas, not Louisiana, and the travelers were taken prisoner by the Spanish whose representatives would have welcomed them had they landed on target several hundred miles to the east. They were marched to New Mexico, where only the kindliness of a priest kept them alive until they were able to get to their kinfolk along the Mississippi. Some records say they made the last leg of this journey, hundreds of miles of it, on foot. How my ancestors traveled, I don't know, but they ended up in Opelousas, with those who had unwillingly detoured through Texas and New Mexico. The Granger families reestablished themselves in this burgeoning town upriver from New Orleans. Their neighbors were the Trahans, the Heberts, the LeBlancs, the Broussards, the Savoies, and the Legers, just as in Grand Pré.

The French pronunciation may be heard in most of these names to this day—but often not when referring to my mother's family. *Granger* is often not pronounced as the French would say it, "Gran-jay"; rather, it's pronounced just as it would be throughout most of the United States, rhyming with *ranger*. This may be because the tongues of some of the Cajun people remember in their speech what took me months of hunting to find out—that the male founder of the Granger family in the New World was English.

21

❧

*O*n with the Party

Although, I admit, I desire,
Occasionally, some backtalk
From the mute sky, I can't honestly complain . . .

—SYLVIA PLATH, "BLACK ROOK IN RAINY WEATHER"

I grew up in the land of my many fathers and mothers. Grangers, Trahans, Landrys, Savoies, LeBlancs. All of them are the descendants of
the Expulsion, that painful odyssey that ended in Louisiana.

MJ Bienvenu, several years behind me at the Louisiana School
and later a professor at Gallaudet University, says that her father
dragged her regularly to the statue that serves as a monument to the
Acadian experience. The statue sits demurely in the tiny courtyard
behind the church in St. Martinsville, managing to combine the sad
and pensive features of a Virgin Mary with those of a legendary
Acadian woman. MJ's father was deaf, so communication was no
problem in her family, and he passed on to her our story of exodus,
exile, and resettlement, through the tale of the legendary Emmeline
Labiche and her star-crossed lover, Louis Arceneaux.

In Cajun legend, Louis and Emmeline were engaged to be married when they were separated during the Expulsion. Louis arrived

first in Louisiana, and despairing of seeing Emmeline again, married another woman. Under a giant live oak, Louis caught sight of Emmeline as she arrived in St. Martinsville. Under another live oak, he told her that he had already married another woman. Louis moved; Emmeline died. Now both are long dead, and their ghosts meet under the Gabriel Oak on the grounds of the Acadian House museum. Certain nights, hearing people listen to them whispering and laughing, enjoying each other at last. Most Americans who know the story learned of it through Henry Wadsworth Longfellow's *Evangeline*, a melodrama of verse, recorded in seventy-seven pages.

Historians believe that about three thousand Acadians eventually made it to Louisiana, about half of those expelled. Most of them arrived between 1765 and 1785. Isolated by the surrounding swamps, shunned by the French Creoles of the cities and the English planters of the countryside, they turned, as they had in Canada, to each other. They sought out members of their extended families for mates and marriage, a behavior shared by the French communities in Canada and Maine. Carl Brasseaux, a scholar who is himself of Acadian descent, has theorized that these familial marriage patterns may have begun originally to minimize the conflicting land claims resulting from faraway and indifferent governing agencies, and that my ancestors may have practiced it more extremely than other French Canadians. Isolation—geographic, linguistic, and economic—surely contributed to this inclination, which is reflected in my own family tree. My distant great-grandmother, Euphrosine, was the granddaughter of a Landry. When her husband, Pierre, died during exile in Maryland, she remarried a Landry. Twenty-six years later and four thousand miles to the south, the Landrys and Grangers would still be neighbors, and a son, Joseph Landry, would marry Marie Ann Granger, the daughter of his half-brother.

Railroads and then highways ended the geographic isolation, and compulsory education, military service, and finally TV ended the linguistic isolation. By the 1960s, marriages between cousins were avoided, but by that time the family lines had been so crossed that sometimes it occurred without anyone knowing. For example, I didn't know my classmate, Dale Breaux, was a cousin until I was researching my own genealogy. Nana married a Cormier, unaware that Cormiers were already part of our family tree. This phenomenon—marriage among individuals whose families unknowingly share common ancestors—results in what researchers call a "high random inbreeding coefficient." It is probably the reason so many Acadians have so many recessive genetic disorders, and probably why I have Usher syndrome. Everyone has naughty recessive genes, of course, but when family members marry, the chance that mates will share the same genetic troublemakers multiplies.

Anyone can be slammed with Usher syndrome, but the twenty-two parish section of Louisiana known as Acadiana or Cajun country has one of the highest rates of Usher syndrome in the world. A few researchers believe the rate at the Louisiana School may be as high as ten percent. Of these children, one survey showed eighty-six percent began to lose their sight by the time they were nineteen or twenty years old, and almost half at less than ten years old. In recent years, these young students with Usher syndrome have formed their own self-help organization. They call it Brave Hearts.

Could I still be me, Catherine Hoffpauir Fischer, had I not been born of a mix that codes for Usher syndrome? I'm not sure that the screwy genes that caused deafness and progressive blindness are the most important of the thousands that make up me, but they certainly determine a lot about my life and how I live it. Certainly they affect me as much as Mama's early death and Daddy's drinking, and almost as much as the years at the deaf school and my time at Gallaudet. To some extent, the history of my people explains the constitution of my genes and the way my life has unfolded.

🙢

Our lives—most of them—continue. Nana smoked, just like Mama, and just like Mama, she got lung cancer. Just like Mama, she didn't even tell me she was sick.

Until she got sick, I thought that we were close. We called each other by TTY, and I visited her home almost every Christmas. In

1993, I noticed that she didn't look well. But when I asked her what was wrong, she assured me she was fine. The following January, she didn't come to the TTY when I called; her daughter-in-law typed at the keyboard instead.

"Nana is tired," she typed. "She's resting."

But I demanded to talk to her, and after a while Nana's own words appeared on the TTY screen. She still wouldn't say what was wrong.

That April, I flew down to see her, and the sight of her broke my heart. She was thin and weak and very pale. She had a tube attached to her breast so she could be fed intravenously. A friendly lady came to check on her, and I learned that she was from a local hospice.

Finally, Nana broke down and told me she had lung cancer.

When I returned home, I called Grady. He was horrified. He hadn't known either. That summer, Grady and I flew down together to see Nana for what turned out to be the last time. She died a few weeks shy of her forty-fourth birthday. Nana's sons—Bozo, Chris, and Quentin—have since grown up. Nana would be pleased to know she has five grandchildren.

My friends and I have watched our children grow up. Jeanette and David are grandparents. David had won me over—rascal though he was, he was Jeanette's rascal, and he had been a good husband and father. He teaches at the Louisiana School, and Jeanette works for a printer. Pat and Bobby have grandchildren, too. Thelma, now Thelma Scanlan Covello, went through some scrapes, and now she is busy with her teenage twins. Rachel is now Dr. Rachel Stone, and after teaching in the deaf education program at a private college in Maryland, she has become superintendent of the California School for the Deaf. She had two deaf daughters and then gave birth to a third little girl who could hear. She was careful to make sure her hearing daughter had radios, records, and telephones—all that she needed to be a complete hearing kid—and she clasped the hearing child into the family and loved her every bit as firmly as her two deaf children. Kathy Meyer, now Kathy Meyer Jones, became an accountant with the Library of Congress, in

Washington, D.C. She and her husband Bob—like Rachel and Ray, Jeannette and David, Pat and Bobby, and Lance and me—are still married after all these years. Jim Hynes, who works at the MSSD, married Maureen O'Grady, the deaf daughter of deaf parents, and they are raising two children.

Jimmy Guidry has married and is raising a family. Lenora Heinen and our neighbor Mrs. Richard lost their husbands recently, but they are both active and blessed with grandchildren. Mr. Scouten, who left the Louisiana School to work at the Florida School for the Deaf, went on to teach at the National Technical Institute for the Deaf in Rochester, New York. He and his wife, Eleanor, have retired in Frederick, Maryland, where they sponsor an annual writing contest for deaf teens. I still have never seen him sign.

Jason, our son, is married. He has a proclivity to fish and hunt and, as I finish this, is opening his own fast food franchise. I laugh and tell my Jewish husband that his son is a true Cajun man. Rachel, our daughter, takes after her father. She graduated from college last year with honors and is pursuing a master's degree in business administration. Velma Savoy, the cousin who escorted me back and forth to school when I was very young and who, like me, has the genetic combination that results in Usher syndrome, was one of the few people I couldn't contact for this book. The family says that Velma married, has five children, and has lost her vision completely.

The Louisiana School and Gallaudet have changed, too. During my junior year, Gallaudet elected its first black homecoming queen: Plumie Gainey. Plumie was so surprised, she didn't even recognize her own name when it sped from the fingers of the football team captain during the pep rally before the game. The coach had to go out into the audience, personally fetch her, and escort her to the stage, where she was cheered by all of us. Now she has one son who is an attorney and another just getting ready for college. She works for the federal government in Washington, D.C.

In 1988, after considerable protest and heartening national support, I. King Jordan, a Gallaudet graduate, became the university's first deaf president. More hearing people on campus have mastered sign language, and skilled signing is supposed to be a condition for them to keep their employment. Signs have become more accepted by people off campus, too. Although mostly people look embarrassed and explain they "took it and can't remember a thing," occasionally a waitress or a bank teller will sign a clear "thank you," or try to fingerspell an offering on the menu.

At the Louisiana School, Visual English died a dirty and public death. This happened in 1973, fifteen years before the uprising at Gallaudet that resulted in Dr. Jordan's selection as president. According to articles in the Baton Rouge newspapers, the students refused to attend class and demanded the right to communicate with sign language. The remaining administrator who supported the Visual English system asserted that the students didn't really understand what was happening, and the superintendent—who had maintained a hands-off policy on communication to judge from the newspaper articles—denied that he had ever supported flagrant signing. In the end, the superintendent was forced to resign. In the midst of the emotional controversy, the state planned a new building in a new location for its residential school for deaf children.

The idea that deaf people had rights and that use of sign language might be among them was growing in Louisiana. The new facility on Brightside Lane opened in 1977, and a year later, Harvey J. Corson became its superintendent. Corson, the son of deaf parents, was not only the Louisiana School's first deaf superintendent, he was one of the few deaf superintendents in the country. One of Corson's first tasks was overseeing the merging and racial integration of Louisiana's two deaf schools.

The process of integration was painful but it seems to have been something of a success. The current superintendent, Luther B. Prickett, feels that skin color has taken its place in the dustbin of what is important to most teenagers. The Louisiana School has had black homecoming queens and black presidents of the student body government. In a replay of the past, the new school turned out to be larger than the student body it was supposed to accommodate, and today other state agencies are located in some of its buildings. As the philosophy of including children in local public schools spreads, the enrollment has declined somewhat. Yet with 329 students at last count, the Louisiana School survives.

Like deaf people, Cajun people have a newfound pride. In 1968, the Council for the Development of French in Louisiana was founded to foster linguistic and cultural links with French-speaking nations and to bring the language of modern France into Louisiana schools. Since that time, it has become an official state agency with a mission to preserve and promote Louisiana's French language and heritage. Thousands of people in southern Louisiana have learned to speak French; thousands more still use the Cajun French of their grandparents. In 1980, the U.S. Supreme Court designated America's 500,000 Cajuns a national minority.

At Gallaudet, greater acceptance of sign language has meant a redefinition of the university's role as students explore education in a variety of program structures and as community colleges and state universities set up plans to make programming accessible for deaf students. The venerable institution finds itself at once competing with Ivy League and community colleges.

I retired from Gallaudet in 1999. I was fortunate to have a few good supervisors, including Dr. Ben Schowe Jr., who encouraged me as I got a master's degree in educational technology and became supervisor of the high school library. In the early 1980s, I wrote and lectured about Usher syndrome, an undertaking that brought me deep personal satisfaction. During a reorganization of Gallaudet's precollege programs, where I worked, I was diagnosed with epilepsy. While doctors measured and evaluated my new medications, I was downsized out of my job. I had to ask my boss to repeat himself as he used misshapen signs to tell me that my absence was necessary to advance the program's mission. By the time I got the official letter, I was almost relieved. So be it.

At the same time, good news arrived from NIH. Inroads are being made against Usher syndrome. This condition, which has flummoxed professionals for over a hundred years and devastated those who have had it for much longer, has recently been giving ground. Large daily doses of vitamin A appear to slow the progression of blindness in people who have the type of Usher syndrome labeled 1-B. No one can pinpoint exactly why this should be the case, but if vitamin A helps those people, my doctors believe it may help me as well. I admit I resist the enormous tablets. In fact, I don't swallow them as regularly as I should. Diltiazem, originally used for heart disease, has been shown to slow blindness from retinitis pigmentosa in mice, and researchers are planning to try the drug on humans. This isn't much in the face of advancing blindness, but definitely something.

The genetic programming at the heart of Usher syndrome is yielding, too. Every day advances are made and the entire genome has already been mapped. However, the advance has been slower than anticipated, and identifying the location and codes for Usher syndrome doesn't guarantee their elimination in the near future.

What seems to not change at all is the prospective fate of minority peoples. In my ancestors' time it was the Micmacs, the French, the English—each group decimated by the next in bloody succession. Today it is the Bosnians and Serbs, the Hutus and Tutsis, the Indonesians and the people of East Timor. One group decides it wants the land and property of another group and evicts them, or worse. It's happening in Europe, Africa, the Middle East, and the Far East; we call it ethnic cleansing and genocide.

Even those who are lucky enough to establish cultural claims—Cajun people, deaf people—say our cultures are as doomed as those of the long-ago people who walked at bayonet point onto those overloaded ships. While some aspects of our cultures, like Cajun food or the I LOVE YOU sign are prized, few people know or care very much about the other aspects of the cultures. Like orchids with big, showy flowers, our roots and our history are often overlooked.

Technology—some of it real, some of it rooted only in the inflated dreams of parents who want their children to hear and companies that are happy to sell products—is making inroads in the deaf community. Most deaf kids don't go to deaf schools anymore. At the Louisiana School, Superintendent Prickett notes that for many parents, acceptance and understanding of what it means to have deaf children continues to be difficult and delayed. He believes that plays a role in why enrollment has not increased at the Louisiana School. Too many deaf students struggle alone in the isolation of mainstream public school programs with only assistive devices and, too often, inadequate interpreters.

When people ask me about educating deaf kids, I admit I am biased in favor of residential schools where kids can get together for support and socialization, especially as they go through their teenage years. But when they ask me what deaf kids really need, I don't talk about schools at all. They need each other, I say, and enough "each others" to make a group of peers. They also need to know some deaf adults. Even the best hearing people can't help deaf people become successfully Deaf; only other deaf people can do that.

❧

Like me, Grady prefers celebration to reflection. He divorced that woman I couldn't stand. He is married to Dana now, a sweet woman who I am happy to have as my sister-in-law. Dana sells real estate, and Grady trains dogs and writes for a variety of publications. My brother and I are more in touch now. We are all we have left of our immediate family. I praise E-mail and tease Grady about coming East to celebrate. Lance will only turn fifty once, I tell him.

Nana once told me I was lucky. "You have a lot of nice friends. Your husband is wonderful and your children are beautiful inside and out," she said. "Who could ask for anything more?"

I think she was right. After looking at some of those people whose genes flowed into mine, I am proud to pass on the baton. My children and my husband. Cajun culture. Deaf culture. Jewish culture, too.

On with the party!